Hiking New York

Hiking New York

A Guide to the State's Best Hiking Adventures

Third Edition

Rhonda and George Ostertag

GUILFORD, CONNECTICUT
HELENA, MONTANA

AN IMPRINT OF THE GLOBE PEQUOT PRESS

To buy books in quantity for corporate use
or incentives, call **(800) 962–0973**
or e-mail **premiums@GlobePequot.com.**

FALCONGUIDES®

All interior photos by George Ostertag

Text design by Nancy Freeborn

Maps by George Ostertag and updated by Ryan Mitchell
© Morris Book Publishing, LLC

Library of Congress Cataloging-in-Publication Data
Ostertag, Rhonda, 1957-   Hiking New York : a guide to the state's best hiking adventures / Rhonda and George Ostertag. – 3rd ed.
     p. cm.
  ISBN 978-0-7627-4460-2
  1. Hiking–New York (State)–Guidebooks. 2. Trails–New York (State)–Guidebooks. 3. New York (State)–Guidebooks. I. Ostertag, George, 1957- II. Title.
  GV199.42.N65088 2009
  796.5109747–dc22
                                        2009002497

Printed in the United States of America

Contents

The Hikes

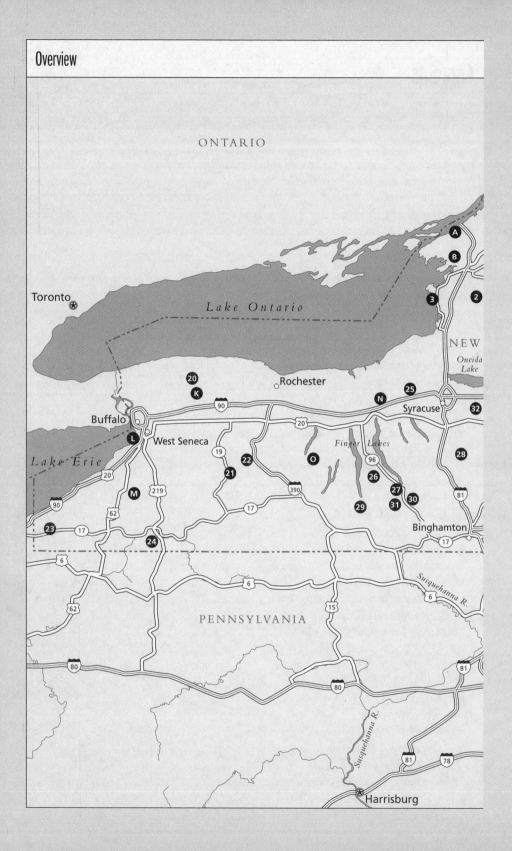

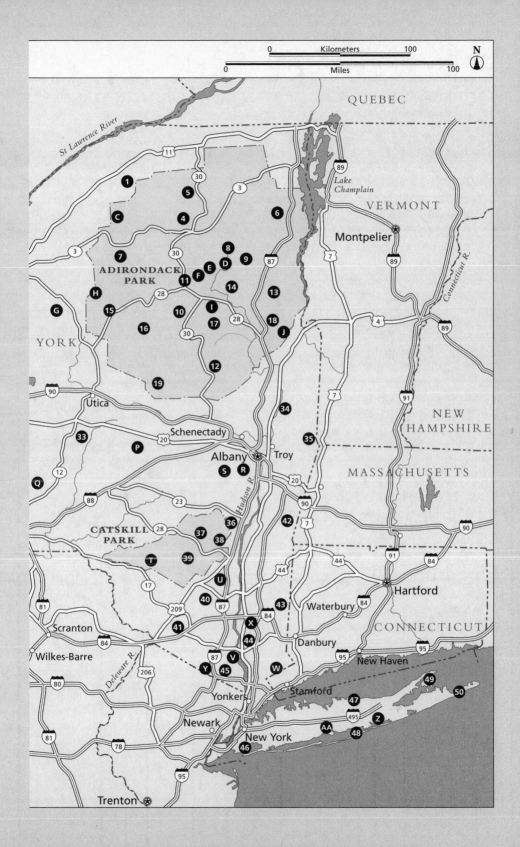

Acknowledgments

We would like to acknowledge the trail associations and individual volunteers who blaze and maintain the trails, the preservationists who work to save New York State's prized natural and cultural areas, and the many landowners who have allowed the state trail system to grow and endure. Many trails would slip from existence without their cooperation. We would like to thank the individuals who helped with our research and volunteered their ideas or faces to this book, and we would like to thank our East and West Coast base camps for freeing us to do our work.

Introduction

Despite bringing western expectations, and likely prejudices, to this project, we were dazzled by the hiking opportunities and offerings of the Empire State. There are not many places to warrant a 3,000-mile drive to the trailhead, but New York State just might be the exception. And over the years, we've done it multiple times and for months at a time.

To get your heart pumping with some of the best hiking the Empire State has to offer, give this book a look. It will take you from the Adirondack lakes and peaks to the gulfs and falling waters of the Finger Lakes Region, from the heritage of the Erie Canal to the lore of the Catskills. The selected trails explore premier parks, forests, mountains, gorges, flatlands, swamps, beaches, and private reserves. You will travel past sparkling waterfalls and daunting cliffs, bag summits, and tag valley floors, but mostly you will get to know New York. Although some of this treasury is well known, great expanses remain little tapped.

The advance and retreat of four glacial masses over a period of two million years sculpted the face of New York State, gouging out north-south lakes, scouring valleys, and depositing rock debris. This excavation of the ages coupled with nature's softening caress has left us all with a first-rate playground. The state boasts thousands of miles of trails ranging from short nature walks to lengthy canal and rail trails to outstanding rugged wilderness hikes. In this book we attempt to bring you a representative sampling of some of the best. But we did leave some for you to find. After all, discovery is the joy of hiking.

Through these pages, you will inhale mountain air from atop the flat ridges of the Allegany Hills, the blinding white quartzite ledges of the "Gunks" (the Shawangunks), and the chiseled peaks of the Adirondacks. You will admire the jeweled waters of the Great Lakes, the Finger Lakes, and the Saint Lawrence River Country, and you will enfold yourself in wilderness solitude.

Outcrop vistas, clear-coursing streams, beaver ponds, marshes, pine barrens, rolling hardwood forests, alpine stands of fir and spruce, meadows, and even desert plains will spice the journey. You will encounter the paths of past presidents and literary giants, soldiers and farmers. The sparks of independence and the tide of the Industrial Revolution brush the terrain. Yes, indeed, New York extends a remarkable open space where you can escape the ties of civilization and forge closer connections to nature, land, and self.

A fine and willing volunteer corps keeps the trails passable for all of us and protects the state's hiking resource. Established hiking organizations, such as the New York–New Jersey Trail Conference, the Adirondack Mountain Club (ADK), the Appalachian Mountain Club (AMC), the Finger Lakes Trail Conference (FLTC), and the Long Island Greenbelt Trail Conference, to name a few, not only advocate, maintain, and improve trails but also produce maps. As beneficiaries of their fine work, we

Canoeing on Fish Creek, St. Regis Canoe Area, Adirondack Park

should support these groups through membership and through the purchase of their maps, which typically hold the most current information on the lay of the trail, land ownership, shelters, facilities, and obstacles.

If the New York trail system has one failing, it would be the design of its peak trails. Many charge straight at the summit, creating runoff channels and broad erosion scars. Some of these were trampled into place long before trail design came into practice. As hikers, we need to take a role at the forefront of conservation and support, rather than thwart, land management agencies and trail crews in their efforts to reroute and improve trails. Switchbacks, contours, and other design features help retain the integrity of the land. Our adventure should not come at the price of the land or the enjoyment of future generations.

Weather

For the most part, hiking in New York is a three-season pursuit, with many trails doubling as winter cross-country ski routes and snowshoe trails. Spring and fall offer a preferred mix of mild temperatures and low humidity. Summer can bring extremes in both categories, as well as dramatic afternoon thunder and lightning storms.

Generally speaking, the climate for New York falls in the humid continental zone. Within that broad classification, the state has three weather regions: the milder and more humid southeastern lowlands, the chillier mountain uplands (Adirondack and

Catskill Mountains), and the Great Lake Plains of the northwestern state, where lake-effect weather can mean heavy winter snowfalls and increased wind year-round.

Like much of the East, New York endures a tormenting mosquito and blackfly season. Less troublesome in dry years, the insects can be unbearable in wet years. June through much of July, insects may keep you at bay, especially in the Adirondacks and in New York's lowlands and swamp country. Wildflower devotees learn to wear netting and a smelly armor of insect repellent.

For hiking and preparing to hike, it's a good idea to seek out current weather forecasts specific to the area of your chosen trail. This is especially true for long hikes and overnight outings. The Internet has become an indispensable tool for trip planning. Forecast sources such as weather.gov (the National Oceanic and Atmospheric Administration [NOAA] National Weather Service) or weather.com (the Weather Channel) are good places to start.

Seeking out the Web pages for newspapers and television and radio stations within the trail area can give you more detailed weather information for trip planning. A few minutes spent with an Internet search engine should help you round up the names. If you are not wired to the Internet, phoning trail area chambers of commerce and visitor centers can provide at least basic weather information. You can also purchase weather radios for when you are in the area. These radios pick up NOAA weather reporting stations that are in range for up-to-date weather reports. We've had hit-and-miss success with these because mountainous and canyon terrain and forest conditions can block signals, but they are another planning tool. Whatever your information source, though, it's always good to keep an eye to the sky.

Having a weather forecast to prepare and travel by is helpful, but do not discount the unexpected. These are, after all, only forecasts. Pack on the side of caution and know what to do in case the weather turns bad.

Flora and Fauna

With its variations in elevation and terrain, New York rolls out a rich floral tapestry. More than half of the state is covered in forest, with an outstanding representation of 150 tree species. Hardwood forests predominate, but the canopy will vary. Lower elevations and southern reaches have transition hardwood compositions of beech, birch, basswood, sweet gum, magnolia, hickory, maple, and oak. Red maples, which can like it wet or dry, claim northern swamps and decorate much of the Adirondack region. Sugar maples are common in the northern state, giving rise to the maple sugaring industry. The state's higher reaches support a rare-to-this-latitude boreal spruce and balsam fir complex filled out by mountain ash, white pine, and paper birch. Above timberline only the most stubborn species thrive.

Wild rose, the state flower, is a common adornment of the New York landscape. Meadow plains parade out such species as goldenrod, black-eyed Susan, milkweed, and joe-pye weed. Viburnum, sarsaparilla, bunchberry, baneberry, Solomon's seal, azalea, rhododendron, and mixed ferns shower the forest floor and midstory. Wetlands bring together cattail reeds, rushes, purple phragmites (a nonnative species), sweet pepper, high-bush blueberry, and sheep laurel. Altogether, this glorious tapestry of shape, shade, and texture fashions a sensory-rich frame for the state's pathways.

Populating the state's niches and habitats are some 600 species of mammals, birds, reptiles, and amphibians. Deer are the common large mammal sightings. Because of their numbers, deer have become nuisances in towns and dangers on roadways. When driving to the trailheads, especially during times of low light, you should lower your speed and watch the roadsides, as well as the road ahead, to reduce the chance of deer collisions.

Black bears also reside in the Empire State. When backpacking, you'll need to take necessary precautions and suspend all foodstuffs, garbage, and smelly accessories. In the Adirondacks, vault containers are required to protect both you and the bears. Although trapped nearly to extinction, beavers again flourish in the state. Their constructions have a tendency to rewrite trails to the frustration of guidebook authors and wet feet of hikers. But the animals' industry improves fisheries and water quality. Moose have been making a comeback since the 1980s. By 1860 they had vanished from the New York landscape. Now the Department of Conservation reports adequate numbers to boast a successful population.

More likely critter encounters include woodchucks, mice, rabbits, raccoons, and muskrats. Songbirds, the state bluebird, migrating kettles of hawks, woodpeckers, loons, ducks, shorebirds, and wild turkeys reward bird-watchers. The cry of the loon is as much a sound of the wilderness here as the howl of the wolf or the coyote in the West. Frogs, toads, efts, newts, salamanders, and slithering snakes can disturb the water and part the grasses. Rattlesnakes find limited habitat in a few of the state's rocky realms. Thriving fish populations claim both warm and cool waters.

Even when the menagerie goes unseen, we can rejoice in the songs, tracks, rustles, splashes, and subtle clues of the life around us. As stewards of the flora and fauna, we need to minimize both our trace and that of our doggie companions when we hike the trails.

Wilderness Restrictions/Regulations

Although this book concentrates primarily on public land offerings, trails across private, trust, and conservancy lands extend hiking opportunities. To continue this privilege, you must assume full responsibility for your own well-being whenever you cross onto privately held land. Heed all posted rules and exercise your best no-trace wilderness manners. Keep to the trail, leave gates as they were found, and police your actions and those of your animal, if indeed pets are allowed. "Pack it in, pack it out."

The text will indicate if and where trails traverse onto these lands. But, occasionally, ownership changes or a landowner may withdraw the privilege of through-travel. Respect such closures. At privately operated resorts or reserves, fees or suggested donations may be requested for the use of their trails.

Summit view on Poke-O-Moonshine Mountain, Adirondack Park ▶

The Nature Conservancy (TNC), a nonprofit organization devoted to the protection of biodiversity, opens its trails to the public for hiking, nature study, and photography. Please note that straying from the trail, hiking with pets, collecting, smoking, picnicking, camping, building fires, swimming, and bicycle riding are forbidden activities in these preserves. With a mission to conserve and preserve the land and its habitats and inhabitants, TNC extends us hiking privileges only where and when such access is compatible with the primary objective. Donations help defray the cost both of maintaining existing preserves and acquiring new ones.

A separate nonprofit entity in the Shawangunks, Mohonk Preserve, similarly protects in perpetuity a tract of prized land in its natural form. This preserve offers hiking and like pursuits and has its own rules and fees.

Trails traversing lands managed by state, county, and federal agencies shape the core of this book. Of the state-operated properties, state park sites (overseen by the New York State Office of Parks, Recreation and Historic Preservation) typically show greater grooming and development and possess more facilities. The trails, however, may not necessarily reflect the same level of civility. A few are overgrown or poorly marked. At most state parks, you can expect to pay a seasonal entrance fee. Many of us who avidly hike and use the outdoors find the purchase of the New York State Parks Empire Passport, an annual day-use pass that provides unlimited access to most state parks, fifty-nine New York State Department of Environmental Conservation (DEC) forest preserve sites, and other lands, easily pays for itself.

The New York State Department of Environmental Conservation manages the vast acreage of state-owned lands, much of it state forests. These encompass planted stands and natural woods open to selective harvests and multiple-use recreation. Backcountry shelters and privies, trail registers, and parking lots are the basic facilities. By contrast, the state forest preserves at Adirondack Park and Catskill Park feature protected woodlands closed to harvest and other revenue-making enterprises but open to various recreational pursuits. State wildlife management areas primarily promote and sustain waterfowl and wildlife populations, with hunting and fishing, bird-watching, and hiking being compatible recreations. Multiple-use areas serve a gamut of year-round recreational users.

Trail parking and use are generally free for DEC lands, although some nature centers and day-use areas require fees. The DEC does have an extensive trailhead registration program. Take the time to sign in and out and comment on the condition of the trail and its markings. The collected information figures into the allotment of funds for trail improvement and expansion.

In a few areas, land agencies issue trail or camp permits to help monitor and manage the trails and to minimize overuse. On DEC lands, single-site stays of longer than three days and camping parties that exceed ten in number do require permits, and

Fungi near the trail to Middle Settlement Lake

Birch-lined trail, Bashakill Wildlife Management Area

these can be picked up at the overseeing DEC office for the particular trail. To protect the integrity of the wild, keep your party size small.

Lean-tos are available first come, first served. Remember, you must share these shelters with other parties. There is no exclusive use. For more detailed rules and regulations, visit the DEC Web page: www.dec.ny.gov.

Trail Navigation

With the predominance of leafy forests, some manner of blazing—paint, diamond, or disk—guides you along most New York trails. The DEC uses both color-coded and user-coded disks to mark routes. In several areas the agency offers independent trail systems for foot, horse, and mountain bike use. On some private lands, blaze patterns may exist for one-directional travel only, so be sure to consult a mapboard or flier before plotting your course. Cairns and stakes are other manners of marking a route. A double-blazing pattern typically warns of a change in direction. Often the top blaze is offset to the right or left to indicate the direction you turn.

Several fine long-distance routes crisscross the state, each with a signature blaze color, including the white Appalachian Trail and the blue North Country Trail.

Because intervals between blazes can vary greatly, make a point to familiarize yourself with the blazing frequency on the trail you are walking. An uncommonly long lapse between blazes may indicate that you have strayed off course, in which case you should backtrack to the last known marker and look again. If reasonable short searches do not turn up the next marker and the trail, the wise course of action is to turn around and return to the trailhead. Autumn adventures require you to be especially alert because fallen leaves can completely conceal the tracked paths.

Backcountry travel includes unavoidable risks that every traveler assumes and must be aware of and respect. Know yourself and your abilities and let independent judgment and common sense be your ultimate guide to safe travel.

AVOIDING THEFT AND VANDALISM

Unattended hiker vehicles are vulnerable to theft and vandalism, but the following steps can minimize your risk:

- When possible, park away from the trailhead at a nearby campground or other facility.
- Do not leave valuables in the vehicle. Place keys and wallet in a button-secured pocket or remote, secure compartment in the pack, where they will not be disturbed until your return.
- Do not leave any visible invitations. Stash everything possible in the trunk, and be sure that any exposed item advertises that it has no value.
- Be suspicious of loiterers, never volunteering the details of your outing.
- Be cautious about the information you supply at the trailhead register. Withhold information such as license plate number and duration of stay until you are safely back at the trailhead. Instead notify a trusted friend of your trip details and notify that friend promptly upon return.

How to Use This Book

Each region begins with an introduction, where you're given a sweeping look at the lay of the land. After this general overview, chapters are presented that feature specific hikes within that region.

To aid in quick decision-making, each hike chapter begins with a hike summary. These short summaries give you a taste of the hiking adventure to follow. You'll learn about the trail terrain and what surprises the route has to offer. Next you'll find the quick, nitty-gritty details of the hike: where the trailhead is located, the nearest town, hike length, approximate hiking time, difficulty rating, elevation change (the difference between a trail's elevation extremes), best hiking season, type of trail terrain, what other trail users you may encounter, trail contacts (for updates on trail conditions), and trail schedules and usage fees.

The approximate hiking times are based on a standard hiking pace of 1.5 to 2 miles per hour, adjusted for terrain and reflecting normal trail conditions. The stated times will get you there and back, but be sure to add time for rest breaks and enjoy-ing the trail's attractions. Although the stated times offer a planning guideline, you should gain a sense of your personal health, capabilities, and hiking style, and make this judgment for yourself. If you're hiking with a group, add enough time for slower members. The amount of carried gear also will influence hiking speed. In all cases, leave enough daylight to accomplish the task safely.

Finding the trailhead gives you dependable directions from a nearby city or town right down to where you'll want to park your car. Following that, the hike description is the meat of the chapter. Detailed and honest, it's the authors' carefully researched impression of the trail. While it's impossible to cover everything, you can rest assured that we won't miss what's important. In Miles and Directions, we provide mileage cues to key junctions and trail name changes, as well as points of interest. The selected benchmarks allow for a quick check on progress and serve as your touchstone for staying on course. At the end of each hike, Hike Information offers local informa-tion sources for learning more about the area and may suggest things to do nearby or places to camp.

Lastly, the Honorable Mentions section at the end of each region identifies hikes that didn't make the cut, for whatever reason. In many cases it's not because they aren't great hikes, but because they're overcrowded or environmentally sensitive to heavy traffic. Be sure to read through these. A jewel might be lurking among them.

A NOTE ON SAFETY

When you enter the wild, you assume the risk and the responsibility for your own safety. You know yourself and your limitations better than anyone. Although this book attempts to alert you to potential dangers, nature is uncertain and trail maintenance can change over time. For safe, responsible travel, you should listen to your inner voice and keep abreast of current outdoor basics. Even outdoor veterans can benefit from a refresher.

How to Use the Maps

For your own purposes, you may wish to copy the directions for the route onto a small sheet to help you while hiking, or photocopy the map and cue sheet to take with you. Otherwise, just slip the whole book in your pack and take it with you. Enjoy your time in the outdoors and remember to pack out what you pack in.

The route map is your guide to each hike. It shows the accessible roads and trails, water, landmarks, towns, and key navigational features. It also distinguishes trails from roads, and paved roads from unpaved roads. The selected route is highlighted.

The included maps are not intended to replace more-detailed agency maps, road maps, state atlases, and/or topographic maps, but they do indicate the general lay of the trail and its attractions to help you visualize and navigate its course.

Map Legend

Transportation

Interstate Highway	=⟨81⟩=
U.S. Highway	⟨9⟩
State Road	⟨177⟩
Local Road	═══
Dirt Road	= = = = =
Featured Trail	▪▪▪▪▪▪▪
Other Trail	- - - - - -
Railroad	⊢—+—+—⊣

Hydrology

Lake/Reservoir	
River/Creek	⌇
Marsh/Swamp	
Waterfall	≋
Spring	⟁

Land Use

State Park	▭
State Border	— ▪ — ▪ —

Symbols

Bridge	⋈
Campground	◮
Camp Site/Shelter	▲
Capital	⊛
City/Town	○
Dam	▬
Mine	⚒
Mountain/Peak	▲
Point of Interest	■
Parking	🅿
Picnic Area	⛉
Tower	⚑
Trailhead (Start)	❺
Viewpoint	◪

Scale

0	Kilometer	1
0	Mile	1

True North
(Magnetic North is
approximately 15.5° East)

N
⊕

Trail Finder

Trail Name	Backpackers	Young Children	Older Children	Dogs	Nature Lovers	History Lovers	Waterfalls	Peak Baggers	Vistas
1. Stone Valley			•				•		
2. Inman Gulf Hiking and Nature Trails		•	•		•				
3. Lakeview Natural Beach Hike		•	•		•				
4. Floodwood Loop	•		•	•	•				
5. Jenkins Mountain Trail			•					•	
6. Poke-O-Moonshine Trail			•					•	•
7. High Falls Loop	•			•	•		•		
8. Van Hoevenberg Trail	•				•			•	•
9. East Branch Ausable River Loop					•		•		•
10. Northville–Placid Trail	•			•					
11. Blue Mountain Trail			•	•	•			•	•
12. Murphy Lake Trail		•	•	•	•				
13. Pharaoh Mountain and Lake Loop	•		•	•	•			•	•
14. Stony Pond Trail	•			•	•				
15. Middle Settlement Lake Hike	•			•	•				
16. West Canada Lakes Wilderness Hike	•				•				
17. Siamese Ponds Hike	•		•	•	•				
18. Tongue Mountain Range Loop	•		•		•			•	•
19. Jockeybush Lake Trail		•	•		•				

Trail Finder

Trail Name	Backpackers	Young Children	Older Children	Dogs	Nature Lovers	History Lovers	Waterfalls	Peak Baggers	Vistas
20. Erie Canal Heritage Trail		•	•			•			
21. Letchworth State Park		•	•			•	•		•
22. Letchworth Trail							•		•
23. Fred J. Cusimano Westside Overland Trail	•			•	•				
24. Allegany State Park, Red House Head- quarters–Eastwood Meadows Loop Hike			•	•	•				
25. Beaver Lake Nature Center		•	•		•				
26. Interloken National Recreation Trail	•		•	•	•				
27. Taughannock Falls State Park		•	•		•		•		
28. Onondaga Trail	•			•					
29. Watkins Glen State Park		•	•			•	•		
30. Buttermilk Falls State Park		•	•				•		
31. Robert H. Treman State Park			•			•	•		•
32. Old Erie Canal Heritage Trail		•	•			•			
33. Beaver Creek Swamp Loop			•	•	•				
34. Wilkinson National Recreation Trail		•	•	•		•			
35. Taconic Crest Trail			•		•				
36. North–South Lake Loop					•				•
37. Indian Head Mountain Loop	•				•			•	•

Trail Finder

Trail Name	Backpackers	Young Children	Older Children	Dogs	Nature Lovers	History Lovers	Waterfalls	Peak Baggers	Vistas
38. Overlook Mountain Hike	•		•					•	•
39. Slide Mountain Loop			•		•	•		•	•
40. Minnewaska State Park Preserve		•	•		•	•			•
41. Bashakill Wildlife Management Area		•	•		•				
42. Taconic State Park			•	•	•				•
43. Appalachian Trail	•			•	•			•	•
44. Breakneck Ridge Trail								•	•
45. Pine Meadow Lake Loop			•		•				
46. West Pond Trail		•	•	•	•				
47. Rocky Point Natural Resources Management Area			•						
48. Fire Island National Seashore	•	•	•		•				
49. Mashomack Preserve		•	•		•				
50. Hither Hills State Park			•		•				

Thousand Islands-
Seaway Region

This Upstate New York region flirts with Canada and unites the Thousand Islands (actually more than 1,800 islands), the Saint Lawrence River Seaway, the eastern shore of Lake Ontario, and the low-lying forests west of the Adirondacks. With all that water, you know boating is big here and fishing, too, but there's plenty of discovery for us foot soldiers as well.

The Indian name for this place means "Garden of the Great Spirit." But the picturesque union of water and woods equally moves the human spirit. The region encompasses gorge and gulf features, shimmering blue expanses, racing waters, wilderness and recreational beaches, island splendor, and a rare "alvar" habitat—an austere barrens with a peculiar linear vegetation pattern. The habitat only occurs within a small arc running from northern Michigan, through southern Ontario, to this remote part of New York.

Raquette River, Stone Valley Recreation Area

History permeates this region and blends the cultures of Native Americans, French, British, and American settlers. More recent arrivals, the Amish have a handful of communities in Saint Lawrence County. Historic battlefields, buildings, and a castle recall the past.

Maple sugaring was important to early area settlers and continues to be a cornerstone to the region's agricultural business. Spring rings in the sugar season. As the sugar maples awaken from winter dormancy, the sap is collected, rendered, and bottled. The tasty products are a year-round enticement. Dairies, wineries, farms, ranches, and apple orchards complete the rural landscape. Maritime economies have both recreational and shipping aspects.

The changeable weather associated with the Great Lakes charges the air with excitement, bringing added intensity to the region along with a long season of winter white. The notorious lake-effect snow is measured in feet, not inches. During the second and third week of October, autumn turns the woods red and yellow, and the waters duplicate the leafy showcase with wavy imposters. The region's backroads and hiking trails are particularly popular in the fall.

1 | Stone Valley

In the towns of Colton, Pierrepont, and Parishville, this moderately difficult wooded trail rounds an exciting 3.2-mile stretch of the Raquette River. Waterfalls, rapids, chutes, scoured potholes, and gorges stir the river, while islands and overhanging cliffs punctuate its course. A hemlock-beech forest with cathedral pines enfolds the offering, and a tannery ruins sits trailside.

Start: At the northwest trailhead off Browns Bridge Road
Distance: 7.8-mile loop, including spur
Approximate hiking time: 4 to 5 hours
Difficulty: Moderate, with some wet or uneven footing and log crossings
Elevation change: The rolling trail shows a 250-foot elevation change.
Trail surface: Woods trail, with linking road stretches
Seasons: Best May through October
Other trail users: Snowshoers, cross-country skiers, and kayakers (during specific power-house scheduled water releases at the dam)
Canine compatibility: Dogs allowed. It is best to leash dogs on roads and during summer high use times to avoid user conflicts.
Land status: Brookfield Power, Saint Lawrence County, and the town of Colton lands, with a few private parcels on the river's east side
Nearest town: Colton

Fees and permits: None required
Schedule: No time restrictions
Maps: Stone Valley Cooperative Recreation Area map (available online, at trailhead registers, or from the Saint Lawrence County Planning Office)
Trail contacts: Saint Lawrence County Planning Department, 48 Court Street, Canton 13617-1194; (315) 379-2292 weekdays only; www.co.st-lawrence.ny.us/Planning/TOCPL.htm
Special considerations: Listen for changes in the sound of the river. Sudden releases of water at the dam can swell the river to dangerous levels and velocities that can trap you and endanger your life. Because horseplay on the rocks can result in tragedy, supervise youngsters and teens. In winter expect icy spots and some risky stretches where an icy slip could land you in the river. Pass respectfully over private lands, heeding any and all postings.

Finding the trailhead: From the intersection of Highway 56 and Highway 68 at the southern end of the hamlet of Colton, go north on Highway 56 for 3.6 miles and turn right (east) onto Browns Bridge Road (County Road 24). Go 0.5 mile and turn right to enter the northwest trailhead parking lot near the powerhouse in 0.1 mile; this site offers the best parking. Find additional access in Colton at the Raquette River bridge. *DeLorme: New York Atlas & Gazetteer:* Page 100 D1.

The Hike

Arrows, blue trail markers, red access trail markers, and small plaques explaining the geologic and cultural history of the area mark this route. The trail rounds the power-house site, following service roads and grassy tracks through open woods, bramble-shrub clearings, and forest plantations. Deer tracks often riddle the soft dirt, and sightings of frogs, hummingbirds, toads, and grouse may cause fingers to point.

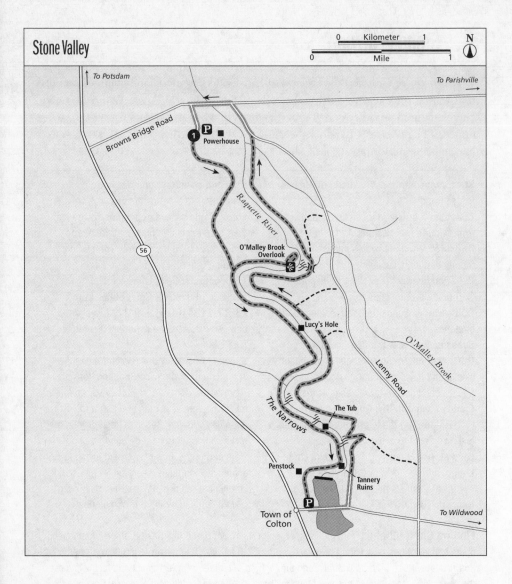

Kilometer

Mile

N

To Potsdam

To Parishville

Browns Bridge Road

1 P Powerhouse

Raquette River

56

O'Malley Brook Overlook

Lucy's Hole

O'Malley Brook

Lenny Road

The Narrows

The Tub

Penstock

Tannery Ruins

P

Town of Colton

To Wildwood

Be alert for a marker pointing you left along an old woods road after a half mile or so. The path descends and rounds toward the river, crossing a soggy drainage where creative stepping may be needed in addition to the corduroys. At a mile the spur to O'Malley Brook Overlook travels a pine-maple slope overlooking a series of beaver dams on a river tributary before reaching a Raquette River overlook and beach. Across the river you will see 15-foot O'Malley Brook Falls. The side trail ends by swinging around a loop.

Beyond the overlook spur, the true river hike begins. It rolls along the wooded slope for a grand upstream tour. Where you first meet the tannin-colored river, it flows broad and slow, coursing between rock and fern banks. Upstream it cuts a more volatile figure as the trail undulates between shore level and 100 feet above the stormy water. At 2 miles pass Lucy's Hole, or "The Gut," a deep pool.

A steep ascent and descent precedes The Narrows, where long bedrock fingers squeeze the water into channels of river fury. Upstream 15- to 18-foot falls, tilted bedrock slabs, worn chutes, and potholes capture the imagination. Side drainages arrive as waterfalls, adding to the bonanza. Above The Tub (a 12-foot-diameter river pothole hidden here by a stone lip), the river spills in serial drops, losing 25 feet in elevation over a 100-foot distance.

As the Raquette River becomes gorgelike just before the power company dam, the trail veers away from the river, climbing above the stone ruins of a tannery. Cross the footbridge over a penstock (a water conduit) and turn left on a dirt road, entering Colton. For the loop, you will cross the road bridge over the Raquette River and take the first left, past the Colton Fire Department. Foot trail resumes at a pair of millstones. As the east shore trail alternates between terrace slope and river level, expect some uneven footing.

The downstream return offers new perspectives on the river. You will skirt a soggy meadow bottomland that separates the path from the river. At the upcoming intersection with a woods road, turn left. Where the trail curves right to edge a bedrock slab at the river, steel anchor pins embedded in the rock echo to the nineteenth century, when lumberjacks floated logs to downstream mills. Side trails branch right to Lenny Road.

Large potholes riddle the bedrock ridge that shapes The Tub. During spring floods, this rock transforms into a roaring cataract of churning stones. After The Narrows, the trail makes a steep uphill charge and travels the upper slope for a spell before plunging back to river level. Plaques identify marble outcrops (common in the Adirondack lowland), glacial erratics, and fossils. Past Lucy's Hole, additional deep pools characterize the Raquette River.

After the O'Malley Brook footbridge, you cross a woods flat on dirt road to pick up the trail on the left. The trail now hugs a terrace 50 feet above the river, before ending at Lenny Road. From there, you will complete the loop via road and road bridge, returning to the trailhead.

Miles and Directions

0.0 Start from the southwest corner of the northwest trailhead parking lot. Follow the marked service road south.

0.1 Turn left on the trail, finding a trail register with brochures.

1.0 Bear right at the trail fork and quickly turn left on the marked O'Malley Brook Overlook spur.

1.5 Return from the overlook spur to the main trail and continue the loop (turning left).

2.0 Reach Lucy's Hole.

3.8 Enter Colton and turn left to cross the road bridge over the Raquette River.

4.0 Turn left on the first paved road and hike past Colton Fire Department to resume on foot trail.

6.3 Cross the O'Malley Brook footbridge.

7.1 At Lenny Road, turn left and walk to Browns Bridge Road, where you'll turn left to cross the river bridge. Turn left on the road near the powerhouse.

7.8 End back at the northwest trailhead.

▶ This trail and the Stone Valley Cooperative Recreational Area owe their existence to the vision, persistence, and energy of Lewis "Lew" Weeks (1920–1999). He spurred like-minded people to preserve this area and build the trail. The Laurentian Chapter of the Adirondack Mountain Club, which continues his work by maintaining the trail, has erected a plaque in Weeks' honor.

Hike Information

Local Information

Saint Lawrence County Chamber of Commerce, 101 Main Street, Canton 13617-1248; (800) 228-7810; http://northcountryguide.com

Local Events/Attractions

Higley Flow State Park on a fettered stretch of the Raquette River south of Colton offers swimming, canoeing, and fishing. Higley Flow State Park, 442 Cold Brook Drive, Colton; (315) 262-2880; http://nysparks.state.ny.us/parks

The annual **Colton Country Family Day** held the third Saturday each July, includes an old-fashioned frog jumping contest, barbecue, band concert, ice cream social, and fireworks. Town of Colton, (315) 262-2810; www.townofcolton.com

Accommodations

Higley Flow State Park campground, open Memorial Day weekend through Labor Day, has 128 campsites. Reservations: (800) 456-2267; www.reserveamerica .com

Organizations

Laurentian Chapter of the Adirondack Mountain Club, http://adklaurentian .org

2 Inman Gulf Hiking and Nature Trails

South of Watertown, three nature and hiking trails line up end-to-end for a single south rim tour, overlooking 5 miles of Inman Gulf. This Tug Hill State Forest area wins over visitors with its ancient river drainage, sheer shale walls, a waterfall, diverse forests, wildflowers, fall foliage, and wildlife.

Start: At the west trailhead (parking area 1)
Distance: 5.5 miles one-way
Approximate hiking time: 2.5 to 3.5 hours one-way
Difficulty: Easy
Elevation change: The trail shows about a 200-foot elevation change.
Trail surface: Earthen path
Seasons: Spring through fall
Other trail users: Mountain bikers, hunters, snowshoers, cross-country skiers (no mountain bikers or skiers allowed on the hike's Oak Rim Trail segment)
Canine compatibility: Dogs permitted but must be under control by leash or voice com-mand (bring water for your dog)
Land status: Department of Environmental Conservation (DEC), except a small private piece along the Oak Rim Trail
Nearest town: Adams Center
Fees and permits: No fees or permits required
Schedule: No restrictions
Maps: DEC Map of the Barnes Corners (online on the DEC Web page under outdoor recre-ation, skiing, Barnes Corners Ski Trails)
Trail contacts: New York State DEC, Region 6, Lowville Office, 7327 State Route 812, Lowville 13367; (315) 376-3521; www.dec.ny.gov
Special considerations: Beware of unstable crumbling shale edges; keep to the trail.

Finding the trailhead: From the intersection of Highway 177 and U.S. Highway 11 at Adams Center south of Watertown, go east on Highway 177 for 6.4 miles and turn north onto Lowe Road at Tremaines Corners. In 1.4 miles bear left and continue 0.2 mile more to Williams Road/Old State Road. There turn right (east) on Williams Road, going another 0.2 mile to reach parking area 1, with space for a half dozen vehicles. Four additional parking lots sit farther east along Williams Road, allowing you to shorten the hike's length or choose an alternate starting point. *DeLorme: New York Atlas & Gazetteer:* Page 84 B1.

The Hike

The geologic feature of Inman Gulf extends 9.6 miles between Barnes Corners and the Sandy Creek confluence in Rodman. This west-to-east (upstream) hike along the south rim offers a restful woods walk, with periodic overlooks of the impressive chasm that measures 250 feet deep. Twisting through the belly, Gulf Stream alternately shows areas of shimmering riffles and still, black pools. DEC trail disks, paint blazes, and cairns variously mark the route. Wooden plaques identify trailside trees. Deer, owl, toad, and raven can dish up surprise encounters.

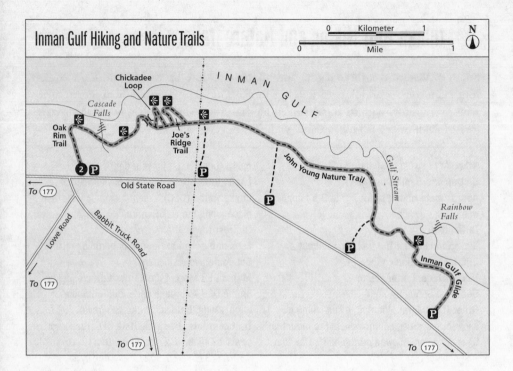

The Oak Rim Trail launches the hike, leading you into a pine-deciduous forest. In moist pockets, jewelweed replaces the woods flora. Where the trail approaches the gulf rim, obtain a quick, restricted look at Inman Gulf. A better view lies just ahead. From the viewpoint's bench seat, you admire the best up-canyon view of the entire hike. For this banner look, the fluted cliffs and steep wooded walls of Inman Gulf meet in a "V." A back rim peeks through the pointed gap.

After a rock-hopping crossing, you will follow a small drainage downstream to overlook Cascade Falls. It plummets in a steep cataract over tiered rock before racing into the gulf. At an ancient red oak, a broad, tree-framed down-canyon view slows steps. Views particularly stir when the gulf dons fall color. More views across and into the twisting gulf urge you onward. Hemlocks claim the rim; oaks cling to the cliff's edge, and mixed deciduous trees fill the gulf.

Chickadee Loop offers a 0.2-mile side trip along a small side ridge and point for a gulf vista of a tight downstream bend and the steep shale cliff of the north wall. Where Chickadee Loop rejoins the main trail, you again have an option of either following the main trail or taking another side trip on Joe's Ridge Trail, which heads left. This 0.3-mile side loop passes through a natural mineral lick, where deer commonly gather, to ascend yet another thin pull-apart ridge (perhaps isolated by the ancient Gulf Stream). This side tour likewise offers a front-row seat to Inman Gulf, while the main trail gets lost in the cheap seats.

The rim-hugging tour then resumes with stolen glances through the hemlock boughs and later through the branchwork of oak, beech, and aspen. Cross an open utility corridor, bypassing the side trail to Williams Road and parking area 2. Rim travel now shows gentle gradients. Brightly colored mushrooms and virtually colorless Indian pipe can sprinkle the forest floor.

After the John Young Nature Trail replaces the Oak Rim Trail as host, you pass through an ice age depression formed when the Gulf Stream flowed at or near the top of the forest plateau. Gulf views become more teasing.

The Inman Gulf Glide brings home the tour. It briefly follows an overgrown woods road, crossing a drainage to return to the rim. Verdant green vegetation claims the southern wall. The highlight on

Inman Gulf, Tug Hill State Forest

this stretch is the tree-framed view of Rainbow Falls. This 60- to 80-foot white veil spills from a treed drainage on the north wall. When full, the waterfall rages.

Later, a lower terrace distances the trail from the gulf. Where the trail curves away from the gulf en route to parking area 5, it passes through a rather uniform plot of mature, planted white and red pines. Because of the plot's forest sameness and no additional gulf views, out-and-back hikers often choose to turn around here, rather than waiting until the parking area to turn back.

Miles and Directions

0.0 Start from the west trailhead (parking area 1); follow the Oak Rim Trail into the woods.

1.4 Cross a bridge, reaching the Chickadee Loop junction. **Option:** Proceed forward on the Oak Rim Trail or turn left on Chickadee Loop, a 0.2-mile crescent-shaped side trail that returns to the Oak Rim Trail farther east.

1.5 Reach the Joe's Ridge Trail junction. **Option:** Proceed forward on Oak Rim Trail or turn left, adding a 0.3-mile side trip on Joe's Ridge Trail.

2.2 Cross a utility corridor, continuing east along the south rim. **Note:** A side trail here leads right to Williams Road and parking area 2.

2.9 Continue forward on John Young Nature Trail.

3.9 Continue forward on Inman Gulf Glide.

4.4 View Rainbow Falls.

5.0 Follow the trail as it curves into a pine plantation en route to parking area 5. **Bailout:** For out-and-back hikers, this site marks the preferred turnaround because the hike no longer overlooks the gulf and because of the uniformity of the plantation.

5.5 End at the easternmost trailhead (parking area 5).

Hike Information

Local Information

The Greater Watertown North Country Chamber of Commerce, 1241 Coffeen Street, Watertown 13601; (315) 788-4400; www.watertownny.com

Local Events/Attractions

Whitewater rafting on the churning Black River in Black River Gorge is a popular area attraction. Rapids bear such descriptive names as "Cruncher" and "Rocket Ride." Outfitters run the river Memorial Day through Columbus Day; May and June have the most powerful flows. You will find links to whitewater outfitters located in Watertown and Dexter through the chamber Web page: www.watertownny.com.

3 Lakeview Natural Beach Hike

In Jefferson County, 20 miles southwest of Watertown, this hike offers a relaxing stroll along a limited-access natural barrier beach on Lake Ontario. The trail sits within 3,461-acre Lakeview Wildlife Management Area and explores a small part of the largest freshwater barrier beach in the state. You will stroll along a natural white-sand beach and spit, view protected vegetated dunes, overlook Floodwood Pond, and spy seabirds.

Start: At beach parking, Southwick Beach State Park

Distance: 6.5 miles out-and-back

Approximate hiking time: 3 to 4 hours

Difficulty: Easy

Elevation change: None

Trail surface: Sand

Seasons: Best for hiking, spring through fall

Other trail users: Birders, fishers, inland hunters

Canine compatibility: Dogs permitted but must be controlled at owner's side by leash or voice command (When entering through the state park, your dog must be leashed and you must have proof of your dog's rabies shots or a current dated collar tag.)

Land status: State park and Department of Environmental Conservation (DEC)

Nearest town: Henderson

Fees and permits: Access to the natural beach hike is via Southwick Beach State Park, a fee area.

Schedule: Daylight hours (State park is seasonal. When the park is gated, access is walk-in only; do not block the entry when parking.)

Maps: Lakeview WMA map (available online: www.dec.ny.gov/docs/regions_pdf/lakeview.pdf)

Trail contacts: New York State DEC, Region 6, 317 Washington Street, Watertown 13601; (315) 785-2261; www.dec.ny.gov

Special considerations: Because this is a natural beach, not a bathing beach, you may not swim, picnic, camp, build fires, or play radios. To protect the vegetated dunes, which are easily damaged, you may only cross at the designated elevated boardwalks. Heed all current posted rules for both the beach and the state park, which gives access to the WMA. Deer and waterfowl hunting occur inland in season.

Finding the trailhead: From Interstate 81, south of Watertown, take exit 40 and head west on Highway 193 for Southwick Beach State Park, reaching the entrance in 8.3 miles. For a beach hike alone—and better parking—start at the state park's beach parking lot. For an inland start, follow the nature trail that heads south at the Southwick Beach entrance station. *DeLorme: New York Atlas & Gazetteer:* Page 83 B5.

The Hike

Ideal for exercise walking, daydreaming, and nature study, this beach hike travels the northern 3-mile spit of Lakeview Wildlife Management Area (WMA). The more remote southern spit is inaccessible, save by boat. The selected hike heads south from the Southwick Beach State Park. During the heyday of the 1920s, this beach bustled with bathhouses, a midway, a dance hall, roller coaster, and ballfield. Now, a much

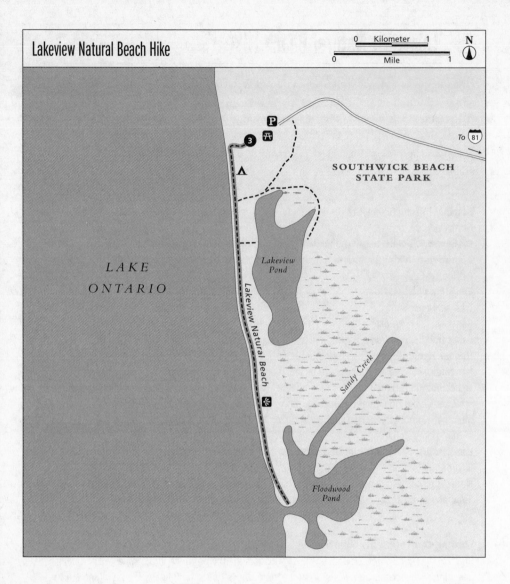

quieter developed beach for swimming and sunbathing abuts the natural spit of the WMA.

The compressed, fine-grained sandy beach embellished by wave-deposited lines of duckweed and tiny mussel shells beckons. Mornings, the cottonwood trees shading the park campground above the beach toss long shadows across the sand. Before long, signs indicate where you leave the developed beach and enter the Lakeview Wildlife Management Area Natural Beach. A low berm or flattish dune now backs the strand, but cottonwoods still claim the back swale.

The first boardwalk over the dune marks the arrival of the nature trail, the Lake Ontario Dune Trail. This nature trail offers an alternative start (or ending for this hike); it begins near the park entrance station, passing among hardwoods. A second trail arriving from the east merges with the nature trail before it reaches the beach. That trail begins at the Lakeview Pond trailhead off Pierrepont Place (west off Highway 3 south of Southwick Beach State Park). It represents yet another start option for this hike and a good option in the off-season.

The rhythmic lapping and tranquil blue of the lake water provide a soothing backdrop for the walk. Storms rolling in across the Great Lake churn out a more exciting stage. A low, flat lake terrain sweeps away to the horizon, as treed shorelines curve away north and south. Across the broad blue expanse, a power plant spews steam. Makeshift wind shelters may dot the beach.

A second walkover leads to Lakeview Pond, and later an elevated platform lifts you above the thicket to view the Sandy Creek wetland. The WMA's Sandy and South Sandy Creeks support steelhead trout and Chinook salmon. White-tailed deer, red fox, and beaver are possible inland wildlife sightings.

Along the beach, Bonaparte gulls bob in the shallows and race along the strand, as terns cut and dive into the water after silvery fish. Eventually the dunes grade higher into humps stabilized by trees and vegetation. Some of the dunes get to be 30 feet high, but there is little loose sand except on the low seaward brow and between the discrete bunches of dune grass. At times small yellow beetles cling to everything, including anyone who lingers too long. Fish carcasses picked bare by gulls and the haphazard boat flotsam alone mar the clean wilderness stage.

The river outlet of Floodwood Pond signals the end for northern spit travel. Across the outlet stretches the inaccessible southern spit. Driftwood-strewn sands and beachgoing red-winged blackbirds precede the outlet. Among the gray weathered driftwood, you may discover tiny cottonwoods taking root or the dizzying tracks of shorebirds. By following the outlet upstream, you can extend the hike as far as the mouth of Floodwood Pond. From this vantage, large beds of reeds shape pond viewing. Now the hike must be reversed; backtrack north along the beach.

Miles and Directions

0.0 Start at beach parking for Southwick Beach State Park. Hike south on the beach from the bathhouse/concession building.

0.2 Enter the Natural Beach area; continue south on the beach spit.

0.5 The nature trail arrives from dunes via boardwalk.

1.0 Reach the walkover to Lakeview Pond.

2.4 Reach the elevated viewing platform at Sandy Creek wetland.

3.2 Reach the Floodwood Pond outlet; backtrack north to beach parking.

6.5 End back at Southwick Beach State Park.

Options

For this hike, you may choose instead to start on the nature trail, which begins near the state park entrance station. You follow the path south, passing in turn an abandoned orchard, some impressive beech trees within a hardwood grove, and a small waterfall at the Filmore Brook crossing. An access path from the Lakeview Pond area arrives on the left, before the hike turns right (west) to arrive at the beach via boardwalk. Keep to the boardwalk to protect sensitive dune habitat. The nature trail joins the beach hike at the 0.5-mile mark. Before starting out on the nature trail, it's a good idea to ask rangers about the trail's condition. You will want to beware of poison ivy. This is especially true when hiking with little ones. Similarly, the nature trail can vary the hike's return.

> ▶ Lake Ontario is the fourteenth-largest lake in the world and the smallest of the Great Lakes in surface area, but it's got depth. The lake's maximum depth exceeds 800 feet.

Additional trails explore the inland area of the WMA, including a 3,800-foot trail to a South Sandy Creek viewing platform. WMA parking areas and a kiosk are reached along Highway 3 south of the state park; review the WMA map on the DEC Web page.

Hike Information

Local Information
The Greater Watertown North Country Chamber of Commerce, 1241 Coffeen Street, Watertown 13601; (315) 788-4400; www.watertownny.com

Local Events/Attractions
You'll find swimming and sunbathing on the adjacent beach of **Southwick Beach State Park.** Southwick Beach State Park, 8119 Southwicks Place, Henderson; (315) 846-5338; http://nysparks.state.ny.us/parks
The 454-mile **Seaway Trail National (and New York State) Scenic Byway** follows the shores of Lakes Ontario and Erie and the Niagara and Saint Lawrence Rivers before drifting into Pennsylvania. The drive passes museums, historic sites, Niagara Falls, lighthouses, trails, natural and recreation areas, farm markets, and wineries. In the trail's vicinity, it follows Highway 3. www.byways.org or www.seawaytrail.com

Accommodations
Southwick Beach State Park campground, open early May through Columbus Day, has one hundred sites. Reservations: (800) 456-2267; www.reserveamerica.com

◀ *Lakeview Natural Beach*

Honorable Mentions

Thousand Island–Seaway Region

A Wellesley Island State Park

Wellesley Island State Park introduces the beauty of the Thousand Islands. Once farmed, this island shows mixed deciduous woods, abandoned field and pasture, rocky shores, and hilltop knolls. Panoramas take in the Saint Lawrence River, Thousand Islands, and Canadian shore. In the southwestern portion of the park, a 600-acre peninsula and nature preserve holds 10 miles of interlocking trails that welcome short excursions. The easy 4-mile Round-the-Peninsula Trail stitches together several of the named paths for a first-rate depiction of the island, its terrain, and locale. Begin at the Minna Anthony Common Nature Center, where maps and brochures are available. The trails are open daylight hours, and park fees are required.

From Watertown, go north on Interstate 81 for 26 miles and take exit 51 for Wellesley Island State Park (after the Thousand Islands Toll Bridge). Following signs, turn right in 0.1 mile, and again turn right onto County Road 100 in another 0.5 mile. Go 0.5 mile more and turn right onto Cross Island Road. The park entrance is in 1.6 miles. Follow the signs to the nature center and trails. *DeLorme: New York Atlas & Gazetteer:* Page 91 B6. For information, contact Wellesley Island State Park, 44927 Cross Island Road, Fineview 13640; (315) 482-2722; http://nysparks.state.ny.us/parks.

B Chaumont Barrens Preserve

Because of its rare and sensitive nature, we have classified this Nature Conservancy preserve northwest of Watertown as an honorable mention, but the natural offering is without peer. Here you will discover a rare alvar landscape, where the austere barrens show an unusual but naturally occurring linear vegetation scheme. Intense glaciation, recurring cycles of flood and drought, and strong winds have shaped this severe landscape of limestone bedrock fissures, marine fossils, rare native grasslands, rubbly moss gardens, and shrub savannas. In North America, only a fistful of alvar sites exist. They occupy an arc from northwest Jefferson County in New York through Ontario, Canada, into northern Michigan.

An easy 2-mile self-guided loop examines the mystery and beauty of this globally significant habitat. Keep to the trail, using stepping-stones where available, and beware of cracks, fissures, and hidden holes. Leave pets at home, and obey The Nature Conservancy's (TNC's) rules and closures that protect this fragile treasure. Summer temperatures can be hot, so carry water. Usually, the trail is open early May through mid-fall from dawn to dusk, but the exact dates depend on the area's flooding cycle.

From Interstate 81 at Watertown, take exit 47/Coffeen Street and follow Highway 12F west for 2 miles. Turn right (north) on Paddy Hill Road/Highway 12E crossing over the river and turning left, staying on Highway 12E all the way to the village of Chaumont (8.4 miles from the Highway 12F junction). In Chaumont take the first right on Morris Track Road/County Road 125; go 3 miles and turn left on unsigned Van Alstyne Road, just beyond a small cemetery on the right. A board with an arrow indicating Chaumont Barrens points out the turn. The preserve entrance and parking are on the left in 1.1 miles; closures are posted at the parking lot. *DeLorme: New York Atlas & Gazetteer*: Page 91 D6. For information, contact The Nature Conservancy, Central and Western New York Office, 1048 University Avenue, Rochester 14607; (585) 546-8030; www.nature.org/wherewework/northamerica/states/newyork.

The Adirondacks

New York's Adirondacks represent a unique mountain range. Unlike the linear ranges elsewhere in the nation or even in the state, these mountains fashion a circular dome 160 miles across and almost a mile high. Although the dome is a geologic youngster, estimated to have formed just 5 million years ago, its composing rocks are ancient. The Adirondacks remained largely untouched by human endeavor, until the wholesale harvest of white pine and eastern hemlock from 1870 to 1890. But this, in turn, sparked fervor for the creation of a wilderness park. The resulting Adirondack Park is a mix of public and private lands, preserving the mountain mystique.

Situated at the transition zone between the eastern deciduous and boreal forest ecosystems, the Adirondacks possess rich flora and fauna. The area encompasses sphagnum bogs, river floodplains, spruce wetlands, agricultural lands, hardwood and conifer forests, and exposed rock realms. The mountains also encompass the creatures feathered, furred, cold-blooded, and scaled that depend on each of these habitats. The region's lengthy isolation kept its inventory of native species, plant and animal, mostly intact.

For seekers of chiseled mountains, remote wooded valleys, crystalline streams, enticing lakes, and expansive views, the Adirondacks fulfill the quest. Occupying the eastern two-thirds of Upstate New York, the six-million-acre Adirondack Park provides a much needed and sought-after outlet for challenge and adventure, renewal and escape. Two visitor information centers, one at Paul Smiths, the other at Newcomb, can help launch you on your way.

The Adirondack High Peaks Region, which encompasses all peaks over 4,000 feet in elevation, receives the greatest amount of boot traffic, but superb trails explore the entire region. You can venture to pristine lakes for fishing or swimming or hike to inspiring streams, cascades, and waterfalls. Other callings include wildflower-dotted beaver meadows, whisper-quiet forests, and thrilling promontories with panoramic views of the lake-and-forest tapestry. The majestic High Peaks can be admired from virtually every corner, and this entire northern locale treats you to one of the showiest fall color changes anywhere.

◀ *Wilcox Lake Wild Forest, Adirondack Park*

4 Floodwood Loop

This easy, although at times soggy, woodland loop in the Adirondack Lakes Region northeast of the hamlet of Tupper Lake strings together prized canoe waters. The trail travels through mature conifer-deciduous woods to stitch together a series of glacial ponds accentuated by rock- and pine-clad islands and floating mats of water lily blooms mid-July to August. Loons, ospreys, herons, frogs, and fish can animate the lakes.

Start: At the western trailhead
Distance: 7.7-mile loop, plus another mile of canoe-carry spurs
Approximate hiking time: 4 to 5.5 hours
Difficulty: Easy because of the flat gradient, but soggy stretches challenge ingenuity
Elevation change: The rolling path has a 100-foot elevation change.
Trail surface: Earthen path, final 0.9 mile on dirt road
Seasons: Best for hiking, spring through fall
Other trail users: Canoeists, hunters, snow-shoers, snowmobilers
Canine compatibility: Dogs permitted but must be controlled at owner's side by leash or voice command

Land status: Department of Environmental Conservation (DEC)
Nearest town: Tupper Lake
Fees and permits: No fees or permits required
Schedule: No time restrictions
Maps: Adirondack Mountain Club (ADK), Adirondack Northern Region map (available at traditional and online bookstores or from the ADK online store: www.adk.org) or National Geographic, Adirondack Park Saranac/Paul Smiths map (available at traditional and online bookstores)
Trail contacts: New York State DEC, Region 5, P.O. Box 296, 1115 State Route 86, Ray Brook, 12977; (518) 897-1200; www.dec.ny.gov

Finding the trailhead: From Tupper Lake travel east on Highway 3 East/Highway 30 North to the split-off in 5.3 miles. There take Highway 30 north for 8.6 miles and turn left (west) on Floodwood Road, bearing left at the fork. The eastern trailhead lies 2.1 miles west of Highway 30, the western trailhead 3 miles west. The western trailhead has better turnout parking; the final 2.3 miles are unpaved. *DeLorme: New York Atlas & Gazetteer:* Page 95 B5.

The Hike

Orange snowmobile markers indicate the start of the loop, while pale yellow canoe-carry disks indicate the spurs to the lakes. By taking full advantage of the canoe carries, this hike visits the shores of seven large ponds and the waters of Fish Creek. Beech, birch, maple, and hemlock overlace the cushiony path, while ferns, hobblebush, oxalis, and club moss decorate the woods floor. A mild gradient, diffused lighting, and scenic snags and logs further contribute to the woods' overall relaxation.

Middle Pond, St. Regis Canoe Area, Adirondack Park ▶

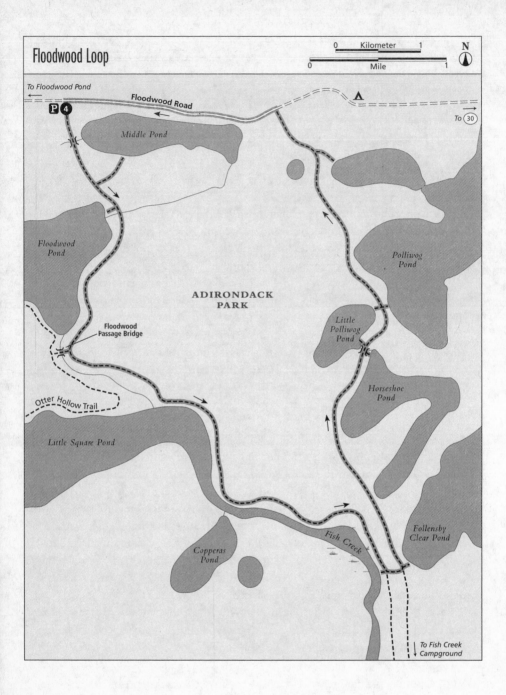

Floodwood Loop

0 —— Kilometer —— 1

0 —— Mile —— 1

N

To Floodwood Pond

Floodwood Road

To 30

P 4

Middle Pond

Floodwood
Pond

ADIRONDACK
PARK

Polliwog
Pond

Little
Polliwog
Pond

Floodwood
Passage Bridge

Horseshoe
Pond

Otter Hollow Trail

Little Square Pond

Fish Creek

Follensby
Clear Pond

Copperas
Pond

To Fish Creek
Campground

The first pond, Middle Pond, presents a charming forest-rimmed crescent, with a conifer-clad island and vast mats of lily pads. During warm weather, approach quietly to avoid spooking turtles that commonly sun on the logs. The second canoe carry to Floodwood Pond is just a short walk beyond, after you resume your travel on the loop.

The hike then drifts from shore, parting an engaging woods. Where wooden palettes formerly eased the crossing of the Middle Pond outlet, beaver activity has raised the waters, short-changing the span. Now you must either wade part way or detour to find an obliging log that allows for a dry crossing. Sphagnum moss typically adorns such soggy sites.

Past a campsite overlooking the steep bank of Floodwood Pond, bear left for the loop; side paths branch to shore. A detour to the Floodwood Passage Bridge finds an attractive lengthy bridge over the Floodwood–Little Square Ponds watery link, which is often log-riddled and flowing with aquatic plants. The tranquil, muddy-bottomed stream hosts schools of fish and the occasional canoe. Across the bridge, Otter Hollow Trail travels the opposite shore, but for this Floodwood Loop hike, backtrack to the junction and head right.

Campsites and privies are tucked along the lakeshores, serving land and water travelers. At Little Square Pond, a marshy peninsula and lily-pad shallows lend character to the long rectangular pond. At a camp flat and fire ring, the loop trail bears right. Trail markers may disappear for a spell, but the path remains good. Hemlocks weave in and out of the mix.

Midway into the loop, you'll come to a three-way junction. Here you can add visits right (west) to Fish Creek, a broad, slow, marshy-sided water, edged by sheep laurel, cranberry, and carnivorous pitcher plants or straight (south) to Fish Creek Campground. En route to Follensby Clear Pond, following the loop left, you will pass a second trail that heads south to Fish Creek Campground and a canoe trail to Follensby Clear Pond, a huge water body with rounded peninsular shores and islands. Conifers dominate its skyline and motorboats can disrupt its calm.

The loop then swings north for the return leg, traversing low glacial ridges. In places, snags open up the cathedral. The deep blue ahead belongs to Horseshoe Pond. But a spruce bog threatens soggy feet before the trail ever puts you within striking distance of Horseshoe, and there is no formal access to this pond. The next official access to a pond comes at the footbridge over the Little Polliwog Pond outlet. North of the outlet bridge, a left leads to the not-so-tiny Little Polliwog Pond, with its marshy far end and jail-like rim of pine snags.

Northbound, the loop next travels the ridge between Little Polliwog and Polliwog Ponds, coming to the canoe carry between the two. Beyond the portage trail, a commonly drowned 20-foot segment of the loop can prove tricky to skirt. Short spurs then access an isolated arm of Polliwog Pond and Middle Pond before the loop exits at Floodwood Road. Turn left on this lightly used dirt road to close the loop.

Miles and Directions

0.0 Start at the western trailhead; follow the trail south for a counterclockwise loop.

0.5 Reach the Middle Pond canoe carry. Head left 0.1 mile to the pond; the loop continues right.

1.8 Reach the Floodwood Passage Bridge junction. Straight continues the loop but first detour right for the bridge overlook.

3.9 Reach a three-pronged junction; head left for Follensby Clear Pond and the loop's continuation. **Options:** A right turn here finds the boardwalk access to Fish Creek. Straight leads to Fish Creek Campground.

6.2 Reach the Polliwog Pond and Little Polliwog Pond canoe carries; continue forward for the loop. **Options:** To the left lies an open-water look at Little Polliwog Pond. To the right is much larger Polliwog Pond.

7.8 Reach Floodwood Road at the eastern trailhead; hike left (west) along the road.

8.7 End at the western trailhead.

Hike Information

Local Information
Saranac Lake Chamber of Commerce, 39 Main Street, Saranac Lake 12983; (800) 347-1992; www.saranaclake.com; or Tupper Lake Chamber of Commerce, 121 Park Street, Box 987, Tupper Lake 12986; (518) 359-3328; www.tupperlakeinfo.com

Local Events/Attractions
On a 31-acre campus, **The Wild Center,** Natural History Museum of the Adirondacks tells the story of the area's natural history through its theaters, hands-on exhibits, live animals, and nature trails. The admission site is open year-round: daily, Memorial Day through Columbus Day; Friday through Monday otherwise and closed major holidays. The Wild Center, Natural History Museum of the Adirondacks, 45 Museum Drive, Tupper Lake 12986; (518) 359-7800; www.wildcenter.org

Canoeing is popular in this region of big natural lakes and on the ponds stitched by Floodwood Loop. Contact the area chambers of commerce.

Accommodations
Fish Creek Pond (DEC) Campground, reached off Highway 30 south of the described trail loop, is open mid-April through Columbus Day and has 355 sites. Reservations: (800) 456-2267; www.reserveamerica.com

Organizations
Adirondack Mountain Club, 814 Goggins Road, Lake George 12845; (518) 668-4447 or (800) 395-8080; www.adk.org

5 Jenkins Mountain Trail

Paul Smiths is one of two visitor interpretive centers (VICs) operated by the Adirondack Park Agency to serve travelers to New York State's six-million-acre Adirondack Park; the other is at Newcomb. At Paul Smiths, nature trails and the Jenkins Mountain Trail encourage the lacing on of hiking boots. Jenkins Mountain Trail, the longest of the site trails, explores forest, glade, and glacial drift before attaining a summit vista. If time is short or you wish to extend your visit, the nature trails introduce mixed forests, meadow openings, and a beaver pond.

Start: At the entrance road to Paul Smiths VIC

Distance: 8.2 miles out-and-back

Approximate hiking time: 4 to 5.5 hours

Difficulty: Moderate due to terrain and gradient

Elevation change: The trail climbs 800 feet to a summit elevation of 2,477 feet.

Trail surface: Service road and rocky or earthen path

Seasons: Best for hiking, summer and fall

Other trail users: Snowshoers, cross-country skiers

Canine compatibility: Leashed dogs permitted (clean up after pet), no dogs in winter

Land status: VIC land

Nearest town: Saranac Lake

Fees and permits: None

Schedule: Building hours: 9:00 a.m. to 5:00 p.m. daily, except Thanksgiving and Christmas; trails: daylight hours

Maps: Paul Smiths Visitor Interpretive Center (VIC) Trail System flier (available at the visitor center or online at the address below)

Trail contacts: Paul Smiths VIC, P.O. Box 3000, 8023 Highway 30, Paul Smiths 12970; (518) 327-3000; www.adkvic.org

Special considerations: There is no camping on VIC land. The lean-tos on the property are day-use-only facilities. There is no bait fishing on VIC waters. Pack in, pack out.

Finding the trailhead: From the Highway 30–Highway 86 junction at Paul Smiths (26 miles north of the hamlet of Tupper Lake, 13 miles west of Saranac Lake), go north on Highway 30 for 0.9 mile and turn left (west) to enter the VIC. *DeLorme: New York Atlas & Gazetteer:* Page 95 A6.

The Hike

Paul Smiths VIC boasts a fine collection of nature trails, but for those with an appetite for greater challenge and a quest to get above it all, the site's Jenkins Mountain Trail may better fill your time. Uphill from the parking lots, this blue-blazed trail follows the gated service road west off the VIC entrance road for just under 2 miles. The road offers a good walking surface and mild grade. Maple, beech, birch, and the occasional conifer shape a semifull canopy. Hobblebush and brambles claim the road shoulder.

Locator boards for cross-country skiers and 0.5-mile incremental markers can assist you in tracking your progress. Where the route crosses over Barnum Brook,

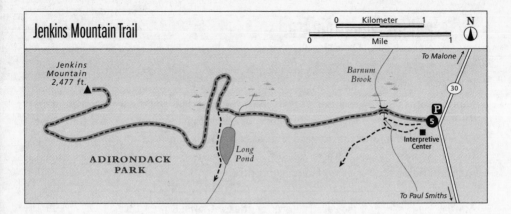

Jenkins Mountain Trail

you'll spy the snag-pierced marsh to your right. The path heading left along the brook's west shore leads to Barnum Brook Trail; keep to the service road.

Past a privy, the hike's foot trail section begins. It traverses a glacial-drift ridge that parts a fern glade from a beaver pond. Beech, maple, and birch clad the ridge. A beaver lodge, a neatly constructed beaver dam, and the north summit of Jenkins Mountain can contribute to views.

Round the point of the glade and continue advancing along and over similar low glacial ridges. Sarsaparilla, fern, and club moss accent the rock-studded forest floor. A few black cherry trees appear in the forest ranks. After crossing a small drainage, the trail enters a long straightaway at the base of Jenkins Mountain. Deer, song-birds, woodpeckers, and toads the size of fingertips can stall your steps for a closer investigation.

Setting up for the final mile, the trail ascends fairly steeply and then enters a switchback between boulders and outcrop ledges. Where the trail hugs the line of Jenkins Mountain Ridge, the grade moderates. Stepping-stones will assist your footing in a small jewelweed meadow.

Just beyond the 4-mile marker, you reach the summit. The summit outcrop presents a 180-degree southwest panorama, with tower-topped Saint Regis Mountain claiming center stage. The Adirondack High Peaks, Long and Black Ponds in the valley bottom, and a rolling wooded expanse complete the view. Fog may lift from the ponds and paint the drainages between the mountains. The return is as you came.

Miles and Directions

0.0 Start from the VIC entrance road; head west on the service road.

0.4 Cross Barnum Brook.

1.6 Reach a trail junction; continue forward on Jenkins Mountain Road. **Note:** The Long Pond Trail (red) heads left here to Long and Black Ponds.

1.8 Foot trail replaces road.

4.1 Reach the summit outcrop; return by same route.

8.2 End back at the trailhead.

Options

The **VIC nature trails** offer alternative or additional hiking. Four easy, interlocking interpretive trails travel mature mixed forest, pine forest, and wetland habitats. The trails range between 0.6 mile and 1.3 miles in length. The 0.6-mile Barnum Brook Trail starts at the entry trailhead. The 1.3-mile Forest Ecology Trail starts midway on the Barnum Brook Trail, the 0.8-mile Heron Marsh Trail starts out the visitor center's back door, and the 0.6-mile Shingle Mill Falls Trail starts off Heron Marsh Trail at the pontoon bridge.

The **Barnum Brook Trail** travels a wide earthen trail and a handsome board-walk and bridge spanning the tea-colored water of Barnum Brook. A dial-a-tree identification wheel and species identification tags introduce a stunning woods of big pines, maple, beech, birch, black cherry, red spruce, and balsam fir. Trail observation decks overlooking Heron Marsh and the mirror-black outlet pool of Barnum Brook will win you over.

The **Forest Ecology Trail** edges Heron Marsh, touring mixed conifer-decidu-ous woods. Its 900-foot boardwalk traverses bog and fen habitats. Initially, tamaracks line the walk; elsewhere sphagnum moss, alder, sedges, cattail, heath, and insect-eating bladderwort, pitcher plant, and sundew engage botanists and photographers. Where the Forest Ecology Trail comes to a junction, go left to meet the Shingle Mill Falls Trail near the pontoon bridge (1.3 miles).

The **Heron Marsh Trail** offers a counterclockwise tour along the shore of exten-sive Heron Marsh. Side loops and spurs lead to marsh vantages and an observation platform. If you are into birding, be sure to carry along your scopes, binoculars, and identification books. An ascent through mature mixed conifers and young deciduous woods returns you to the center.

The **Shingle Mill Falls Trail** rolls along the wooded rim of the open water of Heron Marsh and forms a figure-eight with the Heron Marsh Trail. Cow lilies, pickerelweed, and cattail-sedge islands contribute to views. At the bridge near Heron Marsh Dam, you will overlook Shingle Mill Falls. Spilling over a natural bedrock sill, the falls powered early-day mills. Bittern, heron, osprey, and ducks number among the winged sightings. Beaver-felled trees ring the shore.

Hike Information

Local Information

Saranac Lake Chamber of Commerce, 39 Main Street, Saranac Lake 12983; (800) 347-1992; www.saranaclake.com

Local Events/Attractions

The **Adirondack Scenic Railroad** runs between Saranac Lake and Lake Placid, Memorial Day through Columbus Day. Contact the railroad for scheduled runs. Adirondack Scenic Railroad, Saranac Lake Union Depot, 19 Depot Street, Saranac Lake 12983; (877) 508-6728; www.adirondackrr.com

Accommodations

Meacham Lake (Department of Environmental Conservation) Campground, about 10 miles north on Highway 30, is open mid-May through Columbus Day and has 224 sites. Reservations: (800) 456-2267; www.reserveamerica.com

View from Jenkins Mountain, Paul Smiths Visitor Interpretive Center, Adirondack Park ▶

6 Poke-O-Moonshine Trail

This short, straightforward hike climbs an eastern Adirondack peak, passing through mixed woods and topping outcrops before reaching the rocky summit and a 1917 fire tower, on the National Historic Lookout Register. Granite-gneiss cliffs, mixed forest, a lean-to, and the elevated tower view of the Lake Champlain–High Peaks neighborhood urge hikers skyward. Peregrine falcons judge the peak's cliffs wild enough for nesting.

Start: At the trailhead near Poke-O-Moonshine State Campground, site 14
Distance: 2.4 miles out-and-back
Approximate hiking time: 1.5 to 2 hours
Difficulty: Moderate due to terrain and steep gradient
Elevation change: The trail ascends 1,300 feet to a summit elevation of 2,180 feet.
Trail surface: Rocky or earthen path
Seasons: Best for hiking, late spring through fall
Other trail users: Rock climbers, hunters
Canine compatibility: Dogs permitted but must be controlled at owner's side by leash or voice command
Land status: Department of Environmental Conservation (DEC)
Nearest town: Keeseville
Fees and permits: A day-use or campground fee is charged to park at Poke-O-Moonshine

State Campground.
Schedule: No time restrictions
Maps: Adirondack Mountain Club (ADK), Adirondack Eastern Region map (available at traditional and online bookstores or from the ADK online store: www.adk.org) or National Geographic, Adirondack Park Lake Placid/High Peaks map (available at traditional and online bookstores)
Trail contacts: New York State DEC, Region 5, P.O. Box 296, 1115 Highway 86, Ray Brook 12977; (518) 897-1200; www.dec.ny.gov
Special considerations: Peregrine falcons nest on the mountain cliffs. During peregrine falcon nesting season (April 1 through mid-July), hikers should pass respectfully and climbers may not have access to all routes. Peregrines are territorial and will defend nests, even against humans. Check at the campground about which climbs may be closed.

Finding the trailhead: From the junction of Highway 9N and U.S. Highway 9/Highway 22 in Keeseville, go south on US 9 for 7.2 miles, turning right (west) to enter Poke-O-Moonshine State Campground. From Interstate 87 take exit 33 and go south on US 9 for 3.1 miles to reach the campground. The trail heads west near site 14 at the south end of the campground. *DeLorme: New York Atlas & Gazetteer.* Page 97 A5.

The Hike

This sometimes steep, eroded trail scales the wooded flank of Poke-O-Moonshine Mountain, which owes its peculiar name to a dichotomous profile of fractured cliff and summit rock slabs. To the Algonquin Indians these features suggested a descriptive name, combining the words *pohqui,* meaning "broken," and *moosie,* meaning

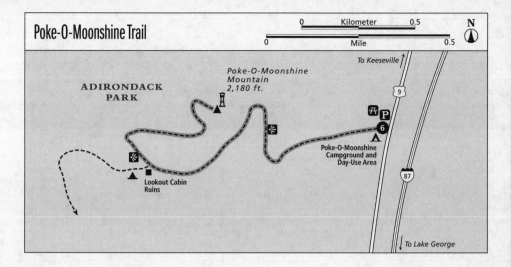

Poke-O-Moonshine Trail

ADIRONDACK
PARK

Poke-O-Moonshine
Mountain
2,180 ft.

To Keeseville

9

6

Poke-O-Moonshine
Campground and
Day-Use Area

87

Lookout Cabin
Ruins

To Lake George

"smooth." Through the passage of time and the inexperienced ear of the white settlers, the Algonquin name eventually corrupted into "Poke-O-Moonshine."

The trail charges steeply up the slope cloaked in sugar maple, birch, and beech.
Oaks, rare interlopers in the Adirondacks, rise among the bigger trees. The side trails
of climbers branch off to round below the cliffs to the right. Sarsaparilla and a few
ferns dot the rock-studded forest floor. Although boots have broadened the trail, the
slope retains its soil, which is not always the case in this region.

The trail veers left at the base of a cliff to top a ledge for an early view of the highway corridor below and the ridges stretched east to Vermont. White pine, hemlock,
striped maple, and oak prefer these rockier reaches. A madrigal of bird whistles, pipes,
and caws competes with the roadway drone.

Where the trail moves inland from the edge of the cliff, so should you. The effects
of weathering combined with the canted surface could cause you to lose your footing. The trail narrows, exhibiting a more moderate grade. Soon it follows a drainage
crowded with nettles, trillium, and red-flowering raspberry. As the drainage steepens,
so does the trail.

In a saddle clearing, a rock fireplace and old foundation hint at the one-time
lookout cabin. If you skirt the site to the left, you will reach the current overnight
lean-to and privy. The trail to the fire tower bears right at the cabin ruins to ascend
an eroded, spring-soaked slope. Infrequent red markers point the way. Just above the
saddle, you will come upon a bald outcrop sloping up to the left. It affords fine views
of ski-run-streaked Whiteface Mountain, as well as a ragged skyline of rounded and
conical peaks. If you are staying overnight at the lean-to, this outcrop is ideal for
stargazing, especially during the annual Perseid meteor showers, which peak August
11 or 12.

▶ In the Adirondacks, nesting peregrines are also found at such sites as Chapel Pond and Whiteface. New York City, with its human-made high-rise structures, is the other major nesting area in the state. The peregrine nest, or scrape, is a shallow gravel depression on a suitable high ledge where three to five eggs are laid. Incubation lasts about one month, and chicks remain at the nest until they fledge about forty-five days later.

Additional outcrops follow, but they neither improve upon nor significantly alter the view. The trail advances in upward spurts. Where it tops out, follow the ridge to the right. You will cut through a corridor of low-stature white birch and striped maple before emerging on the summit outcrop near the tower, which shoots up five flights.

Adopted by a "Friends" group and jointly rehabilitated by volunteers and the DEC, the tower welcomes visitors into the sky. The joint endeavor preserved both the landmark and its fine elevated vantage. Within the tower cab, locator boards identify key features in the panoramic view. In summer, volunteer stewards staff the tower.

The bald summit knob serves vista seekers as well. From here the long, shimmering platter and dark-treed islands of Lake Champlain dominate the view to the east-northeast; Whiteface Mountain rises to the west. Smaller lakes, rural flats, and the ridge and cliffs of Poke-O-Moonshine Mountain complete the panorama. Lichen and mineral leaching streak the cliffs green, orange, and black. Mountain ash grows below the summit. When ready to surrender the mountaintop, the return is as you came.

Miles and Directions

0.0 Start at the trailhead near campsite 14; ascend the forest slope.
0.7 Pass the ruins of the one-time lookout cabin.
1.2 Reach the summit tower; turn around.
2.4 End back at the trailhead.

Hike Information

Local Information

Lake Champlain Visitors Center, 94 Montcalm Street, Suite 1, Ticonderoga 12883; (518) 585-6619 or (866) 843-5253; www.lakechamplainregion.com

◀ *Lookout on Poke-O-Moonshine Mountain, Adirondack Park*

Local Events/Attractions

Noblewood Park, a sixty-three-acre park and nature preserve on Lake Champlain where the Boquet River empties into the lake, offers nature trails, 3,500 feet of sandy beach, 2,500 feet of river frontage, large wetlands, and nesting falcons, all near a virgin forest. Park entrance is off Highway 22 (east of Poke-O-Moonshine). Noblewood Park, Willsboro; www.noblewood.com

Ausable Chasm, 12 miles south of Plattsburgh on US 9 (exit 34 off I-87), offers night lantern tours, boat tours, rafting, tubing, camping, and nature trails among massive 500-million-year-old stone formations. The fee site is open daily, mid-May through Columbus Day, 9:00 a.m. until 4:00 p.m. Ausable Chasm, P.O. Box 390, 2144 US 9, Ausable Chasm 12911; (518) 834-7454; www.ausablechasm.com

Accommodations

Poke-O-Moonshine (DEC) Campground, at the trail's start, is open mid-May through Labor Day and has twenty-five sites. Reservations: (800) 456-2267; www .reserveamerica.com

Organizations

Adirondack Mountain Club, 814 Goggins Road, Lake George 12845; (518) 668-4447 or (800) 395-8080; www.adk.org

BUILT FOR SPEED

The peregrine falcon, a high-nesting hunter built for speed, is an endangered species protected under federal and New York State law. The peregrine falcon population was decimated by DDT, and by the 1960s there were no breeding pairs left in the state. Reintroduction and now natural reproduction are returning these birds to the New York sky. In 1999 nine Adirondack eyries fledged twenty chicks. Adults weigh about two pounds, with adult males being one-third smaller than their female counterparts. The sharp-eyed birds can plunge at speeds of 200 miles per hour, snapping up their feathered prey midflight. When not in diving descent, the 15- to 20-inch birds are recognized by their dark wings, barred pajamas, sideburn eye patches, and sharp talons at the end of "striking" yellow feet.

7 High Falls Loop

This clockwise loop into Five Ponds Wilderness in the Cranberry Lake Region traverses a diverse area of marsh, hardwood forests, conifers, and blowdown, visiting the Dead Creek Flow of Cranberry Lake, High Falls, and the Oswegatchie River drainage. The blowdown is the legacy from the great windstorm of 1995, but the new forest is rapidly returning and thicketlike in places. Wildflowers, wildlife, or a burst of fall color can embellish the journey.

Start: At the eastern trailhead (the Plains Trail)
Distance: 16.8-mile loop, with spurs to overnight shelters
Approximate hiking time: 9 to 11 hours, but you'll move faster when the blackflies are out
Difficulty: Strenuous due to beaver-caused flooding
Elevation change: The trail has a 200-foot elevation change.
Trail surface: Levee, foot trail, old truck grade, and beaver bypasses and dams
Seasons: Best for hiking, late summer and fall
Other trail users: Hunters, snowshoers, cross-country skiers
Canine compatibility: Dogs permitted but must be controlled at owner's side by leash or voice command
Land status: Department of Environmental Conservation (DEC)
Nearest town: Star Lake
Fees and permits: No fees or permits required

Schedule: No time restrictions
Maps: Adirondack Mountain Club (ADK), Adirondack Northern Region map (available at traditional and online bookstores or from the ADK online store: www.adk.org) or National Geographic, Adirondack Park Old Forge/ Oswegatchie map (available at traditional and online bookstores)
Trail contacts: New York State DEC, Region 6, Potsdam Office, 6739 U.S. Highway 11, Potsdam 13676; (315) 265-3090; www.dec.ny.gov
Special considerations: Come prepared for biting insects; netting and repellent are recommended. Avoid after heavy rains or during high water. You will find pit toilets at the overnight shelter sites at Janack's Landing and High Falls. Designated campsites also serve the route. There is no camping within 150 feet of any road, trail, or water, except at the designated sites. The usual DEC rules for camping and permits are enforced.

Finding the trailhead: From the junction of Highway 3 and County Road 61 (the Wanakena turnoff), 8 miles west of Cranberry Lake and 6 miles east of Star Lake, turn south on CR 61 and proceed 1 mile, twice keeping right to cross the Oswegatchie River bridge. Continue east on South Shore Road. You will locate the western trailhead (the High Falls Truck Trail) on a southbound dead-end road in 0.1 mile, its trail parking next to tennis courts in another 0.1 mile, and the eastern trailhead (Plains Trail) 0.4 mile farther. *DeLorme: New York Atlas & Gazetteer:* Page 94 C1.

The Hike

For a clockwise loop, you will follow the Plains Trail. It traces a former logging railroad grade, which later narrows. Young forest frames the route along with wind-

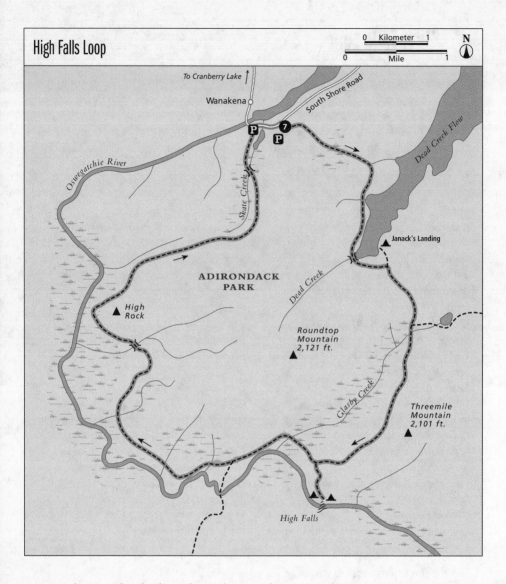

High Falls Loop

To Cranberry Lake

Wanakena

South Shore Road

Oswegatchie River

Skate Creek

Dead Creek Flow

Janack's Landing

ADIRONDACK
PARK

High
Rock

Dead Creek

Roundtop
Mountain
2,121 ft.

Glasby Creek

Threemile
Mountain
2,101 ft.

High Falls

snapped trees. Ahead where the trail parts a beaver marsh, wet spots may require a hop across or navigating via married logs. The snag skyline, blackwater reflections, and clumps of greenery add to viewing; lively birdsongs can serenade the ear.

Where the maples are untouched, you will find a rich, shady cathedral. As the grade edges Dead Creek Flow, part of Cranberry Lake, open-water views alternate with treed buffers. A loon or heron may visit the lake arm. Although the scenery suggests a leisurely Sunday pace, the mosquitoes may call for double time. Spans over the inlet flows keep feet dry, except where beaver-raised waters overflow the log passages.

If taking the detour to Janack's Landing, a rustic boardwalk and trail lead to the

High Falls on the Oswegatchie River, Five Ponds Wilderness, Adirondack Park

landing, its engaging lake view, and its overnight shelter on the peninsular knoll. Lady's slippers seasonally decorate the forest floor. From the landing trail junction, the loop proceeds forward and gradually ascends, passing within a mixed-age woodland of maple, cherry, and birch. Where the trail to Cat Mountain heads left, continue following the loop en route to High Falls.

The loop arcs right and eases down to the Glasby Creek crossing. The creek shows scenic cascades and beaver-broadened segments. The trail traces its east shore in an easy-to-follow bypass along the base of Threemile Mountain. The route can be hot and humid, with an open skyline, snags, thick shrubs, and briers. Continue downstream.

A vast zone of blowdown rubble next claims the loop. Although the trail itself is clear, you have to marvel at the power of the microburst that took place here in 1995. You will remain in the disrupted area until the High Falls junction. There you head left to visit High Falls, a 20-foot-tall cascade near the head of the Oswegatchie River. The tannin-colored water spills between and over the bulging and sloped outcrops of pink granite, streaked by varnish and mottled by lichen. Away from the riotous falls stretches tranquil river. Back in the woods is a shelter.

You will resume the loop, following the High Falls Truck Trail, passing through scenic woods of white pine and mixed hardwoods before entering a tamarack-pine area and, later, a grass meadow. Glasby Creek threads through the meadow and is crossed by a plank bridge. While following the Oswegatchie River downstream, you will gain overlooks and find additional setting changes.

The levee of the truck grade parts two more beaver ponds, but generally the old route allows fast, dry travel. Where the blue-marked Sand Lake Trail heads left, remain on High Falls Truck Trail. Red disks, some remnant and faded, help mark the primary route. More levee and beaver sites follow, and designated campsites are passed where the trail overlooks a horseshoe bend on the Oswegatchie.

The red DEC markers make a more regular appearance as the truck route passes through a recovering forest habitat. In another mile or so, you'll cross an old stone bridge; it sits at a canted-bedrock waterfall on an Oswegatchie tributary. At the truck trail junction beyond the stone bridge, you keep right for the red-marked loop.

▶ In the summer of 2006, the DEC completed the trail between West Inlet and Dead Flow, the final link in the long-distance trail encircling Cranberry Lake, a hike in the 50-mile club.

As the hike completes its passage along the vast Oswegatchie River marsh, it skirts High Rock. After the grade trends northward, the route crosses a pair of brooks and slow-moving Skate Creek to emerge at the barrier and register for the western trailhead. From here you'll return to South Shore Road and follow it east to end back at the Plains Trail parking.

Miles and Directions

0.0 Start from the eastern trailhead; follow the Plains Trail into forest.

3.1 Reach the Janack's Landing junction; proceed forward for loop. **Option:** A 0.2-mile detour left leads to the grassy point of Janack's Landing and its overnight shelter.

4.0 Reach the Cat Mountain junction; follow the red-marked loop as it arcs right.

6.6 Reach the High Falls junction. Hike left to visit the falls, and keep left (upstream) at the fork.

7.0 Reach High Falls; backtrack to the loop and turn left on High Falls Truck Trail.

8.4 Reach the Sand Lake Trail junction; proceed forward, remaining on High Falls Truck Trail.

11.8 Cross an old stone bridge.

12.2 Reach a truck trail junction; keep right for the red-marked loop.

16.2 Reach the barrier/western trailhead; round the gate and hike north to South Shore Road.

16.3 Reach South Shore Road; turn right (east) and follow the road back to your vehicle.

16.8 End at the eastern trailhead.

Hike Information

Local Information
Saint Lawrence County Chamber of Commerce, 101 Main Street, Canton 13617-1248; (877) 228-7810 or (315) 386-4000; www.northcountryguide.com

Local Events/Attractions
Boating and trout fishing are popular on **Cranberry Lake,** a prized water tucked in a 50,000-acre wilderness webbed by trails. This region is also known for its fall foliage drives; contact Saint Lawrence County Chamber of Commerce.

Accommodations
Cranberry Lake (DEC) Campground on Lone Pine Road off Highway 3 in Cranberry Lake Village is open mid-May through mid-October and has 173 sites. For information: (315) 848-2315; reservations: (800) 456-2267; www.reserveamerica .com

Organizations
Adirondack Mountain Club, 814 Goggins Road, Lake George 12845; (518) 668-4447 or (800) 395-8080; www.adk.org

▶ Hunting Season

Hunting is a popular sport in the United States, especially during rifle season in October and November. Hiking is still enjoyable in these months in many areas, but take a few precautions. First, learn when the different hunting seasons start and end in the area in which you'll be hiking. During this time frame, be sure to wear at least a blaze orange hat, and possibly put an orange vest over your pack. Don't be surprised to see hunters in camo outfits carrying bows or muzzleloading rifles around during their season. If you would feel more comfortable without hunters around, hike in national parks and monuments or state and local parks where hunting is not allowed.

8 Van Hoevenberg Trail

In the High Peaks Region, this demanding all-day or overnight hike arriving from the north offers the shortest approach to Mount Marcy—at 5,344 feet, the highest point in New York State. The first recorded ascent came in 1837, and a continuous stream of feet has followed. To the Indians the mountain was known as Tahawus, or "Cloud Splitter," an apt name. If you enlist for the challenge, you'll reap a sweeping High Peaks panorama. Rare arctic-alpine habitat, wildlife, and scenic brooks step up the reward.

Start: At the Loj trailhead
Distance: 14.8 miles out-and-back
Approximate hiking time: 9 to 11 hours
Difficulty: Strenuous due to length, terrain, and gradient
Elevation change: The trail has a 3,200-foot elevation change, attaining Mount Marcy's summit at 5,344 feet.
Trail surface: Rocky or earthen path
Seasons: Best for hiking, summer through fall
Other trail users: Snowshoers, cross-country skiers
Canine compatibility: Leashed dogs permitted (Because this is a well-used trail, leave high-strung dogs at home.)
Land status: Loj (Adirondack Mountain Club) and Department of Environmental Conservation (DEC) land
Nearest town: Lake Placid
Fees and permits: Adirondak Loj charges for trail parking.
Schedule: No time restrictions
Maps: Adirondack Mountain Club (ADK), Adirondack High Peaks Region map (available at traditional and online bookstores or from the ADK online store: www.adk.org) or National Geographic, Adirondack Park Lake Placid/High Peaks map (available at traditional and online bookstores)
Trail contacts: New York State DEC, Region 5, P.O. Box 296, 1115 Highway 86, Ray Brook 12977; (518) 897-1200; www.dec.ny.gov
Special considerations: You have a rock scramble for the final 0.5 mile to the summit. Come prepared for chill winds and cool summit temperatures, and be alert to weather changes. Camp only at the lean-tos or designated tent sites. Camping and fires above 4,000 feet are prohibited. In the High Peaks, all food must be stored in bear vaults (bear-proof containers); suspending food is no longer adequate. The current maximum group size for overnight use is eight, for day use it is fifteen. The DEC asks for your voluntary compliance, keeping off the trail during the mud season in spring.

Finding the trailhead: From the junction of Highway 73 and Highway 86 in the village of Lake Placid, go east on Highway 73 for 3.2 miles and turn right (south) on Adirondak Loj Road. Go 5 miles to reach the entrance station for the Loj. Find the trailhead at the opposite end of the lower parking lot from the High Peaks Visitor Information Center. Because parking lots can fill in summer, off-season and midweek visits are advisable. *DeLorme: New York Atlas & Gazetteer:* Page 96 C2.

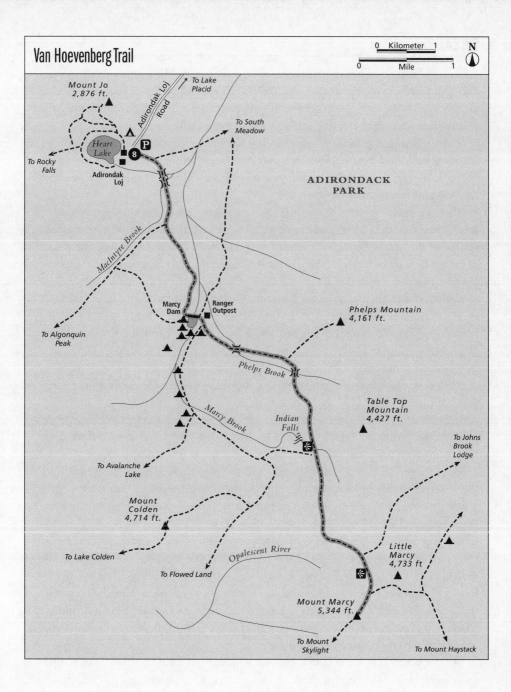

Van Hoevenberg Trail

0 Kilometer 1
0 Mile 1

N

Mount Jo
2,876 ft.

Adirondak Loj Road

To Lake Placid

To South Meadow

Heart Lake

P

8

Adirondak Loj

To Rocky Falls

ADIRONDACK PARK

MacIntyre Brook

Marcy Dam

Ranger Outpost

Phelps Mountain
4,161 ft.

To Algonquin Peak

Phelps Brook

Marcy Brook

Table Top Mountain
4,427 ft.

Indian Falls

To Johns Brook Lodge

To Avalanche Lake

Mount Colden
4,714 ft.

To Lake Colden

Opalescent River

To Flowed Land

Little Marcy
4,733 ft.

Mount Marcy
5,344 ft.

To Mount Skylight

To Mount Haystack

The Hike

Follow the wide, well-trampled blue-marked trail, passing through a mixed conifer-deciduous forest and crossing over the Mr.Van Ski Trail. Ongoing improvements, such as reinforced steps, foot planks, levees, and stepping-stones, have reduced the mire and erosion that once characterized the Van Hoevenberg Trail.

Passing through planted pines, cross the footbridge over the Heart Lake outlet, followed soon after by the footbridge over MacIntyre Brook. Despite the popularity of this hiker highway, wildlife sightings can reward early-morning hikers. Owl, deer, bat, and pine marten may surprise you.

Past the junction with the yellow trail to Algonquin Peak, maple, birch, small beech, hobblebush, and striped maple enfold the way. In another mile you ascend along rushing Marcy Brook, sequestered deep in a draw. Campsites occupy the woods of balsam fir and birch. Ahead the trail crosses the picturesque wooden Marcy Dam. In the past, campers suspended their foodstuffs from the dam, but bears figured out how to haul up the goodies, so take no shortcuts. Comply with the use of bear vaults.

Cross-pond views feature Mount Colden; Avalanche, Phelps, and Table Top Mountains; and the slopes of Wright Peak and Algonquin. Over the shoulder looms Whales Tail Mountain. The popularity of the lean-tos and the ranger station here bring bustle to the area.

Following the rocky terrain of Phelps Brook upstream, you come to the high-water bridge. During low water, cross 500 feet upstream via the rocky streambed itself. The tour continues upstream on the opposite shore, but Phelps Brook slips from sight. At the junction with the red Phelps Mountain Trail, continue forward; dense spruce and fir narrow the aisle.

A mile from the first crossing, you'll cross a bridge back over Phelps Brook, finding a steeper climb and larger rocks. Shortly the trail turns away from the brook, as a winter-use trail continues upstream. Small-stature trees weave an open cathedral. Stone steps and short log ladders help move you along.

Passing designated camp flats, you will cross Marcy Brook upstream from Indian Falls, but there is no hint of the falls at the crossing. For a top-of-the-falls view, you must detour, taking an immediate right on the foot trail heading downstream 100 feet to a broad outcrop washed by the brook at the head of Indian Falls. Here the falls spills through a cliff fissure, which fashions a striking view out to Algonquin and the MacIntyre Range. The hike to Marcy proceeds forward from the crossing, drawing away from the creek, skirting campsites.

At the junction at the 3,600-foot elevation, bear left with the blue disks, temporarily enjoying a more relaxed grade. Bunchberry, moss, and whorled aster carpet the ground. Corduroys span a spring-muddied patch leading to a steep, rocky ascent with stones aligned as stairs.

Summit plaque on Mount Marcy, High Peaks Wilderness, Adirondack Park

In a high meadow you first view imposing Mount Marcy, its open summit outcrop, and the silver snags piercing its fir mantle. Toy-size hikers wind skyward. This eye-opener alerts you to the climb still ahead. Canted exposed outcrops alternate with corduroys as the trail draws into an alpine opening. Views build, with close-by Mount Haystack being particularly arresting.

Because an arctic-alpine habitat claims the upper reaches of Marcy, keep to the prescribed route, now a rock scramble. From the summit plaque, one last scrambling burst tags the top. The view is both glorious and humbling. During summer months, a steward watches over Marcy, educating hikers about this sensitive site.

Views sweep the regal MacIntyre Range, the ridges north to Canada, the Green Mountains of Vermont, Lakes Champlain and Placid, Boreas Ponds, and Lake Tear-of-the-Clouds, the highest lake source of the Hudson River. The Hudson–Saint Lawrence River Divide passes over the top of Mount Marcy. Crystals and lichen adorn the rock. Return as you came.

Miles and Directions

0.0   Start from the Loj trailhead; follow the blue Van Hoevenberg Trail.

1.0   Reach a trail junction; bear left, staying on the blue trail. **Note:** The yellow trail leads to Algonquin Peak.

2.2   Cross wooden Marcy Dam, bear right along the shore, and at the junction in 500 feet, head left for Mount Marcy. **Note:** The trail to the right leads to Avalanche Lake and Lake Colden.

2.5   Cross the high-water bridge on Phelps Brook. (During low water, continue upstream 500 feet to cross on the rocky streambed.)

4.2   Cross Marcy Brook and continue forward. **Option:** Upon crossing, an immediate right leads to an outcrop at the head of Indian Falls in 100 feet.

5.8   Reach a trail junction; head right for Mount Marcy. **Note:** To the left lies Keene Valley.

6.4   Reach the saddle junction; bear right. (Yellow paint blazes and the occasional cairn mark this final leg to the summit.)

7.4   Reach the summit; return by same route.

14.8   End back at the Loj.

Hike Information

Local Information

Lake Placid/Essex County Convention and Visitors Bureau, 2610 Main Street, Suite 2, Lake Placid 12946; (518) 523-2445 or (800) 447-5224; www.lake placid.com

Local Events/Attractions

The **Lake Placid Olympic Center** has a museum of Lake Placid Olympic history and four ice rinks open for hockey, figure, and speed skating, with open evening skating and skate rentals. Olympic Center, 2634 Main Street, Lake Placid 12946; (518) 523-1655; www.orda.org

At **John Brown Farm State Historic Site,** you can tour the last home and burial site of the famed abolitionist. This admission site is open Wednesday through Saturday, 10:00 a.m. to 5:00 p.m.; Sunday 1:00 to 5:00 p.m. 115 John Brown Road, Lake Placid 12946; (518) 523-3900; http://nysparks.state.ny.us

Accommodations

Adirondak Loj has lodge accommodations for forty-six guests and a food service, plus a campground with thirty-four sites, sixteen lean-tos, and three canvas tents. Adirondak Loj reservations and information: (518) 523-3441; e-mail: loj@adk.org

Organizations

Adirondack Mountain Club, 814 Goggins Road, Lake George 12845; (518) 668-4447 or (800) 395-8080; www.adk.org

A LASTING LEGACY

Henry Van Hoevenberg, "Mr. Van," the affable outdoorsman known for his signature leather hat and leather wardrobe, opened the area's first Adirondack Lodge in 1890 and blazed many of the Heart Lake area trails. He laid out the trail to Mount Marcy that now bears his name; it is the most direct and shortest route to the cloud-flirting peak. Van Hoevenberg named Mount Jo, the small but substantial peak rising above Heart Lake, for his bride-to-be, Josephine. He played a key role in shaping the wilderness recreation in the Adirondacks that we know today. The Van Hoevenberg lodge burned down in a forest fire in 1903. The circa-1927 Adirondak Loj was built and named by Melvil Dewey, who preferred this more rustic spelling. He was chairman of the Lake Placid Club, which preceded the Adirondack Mountain Club in ownership of this property and facilities.

9 East Branch Ausable River Loop

Within the private Adirondack Mountain Reserve (or Ausable Club, as it is also known), this rolling hiking trail loop travels the east and west shores of the pristine East Branch Ausable River, with side trips to the elevated vantages at Gothics Window and Indian Head and another to showery Rainbow Falls. Old-growth hemlocks and tranquil woods shape a soothing backdrop.

Start: At the Watchman Hut trailhead
Distance: 9.1-mile loop, including side trips (10.5 miles with the road distance to and from trailhead parking)
Approximate hiking time: 5 to 6.5 hours
Difficulty: Strenuous due to footing and terrain
Elevation change: The trail travels between 1,350 and 2,700 feet above sea level, with the high point at Indian Head.
Trail surface: Earthen and rock-studded woods path
Seasons: Best for hiking, late spring through fall
Other trail users: None
Canine compatibility: Dogs not permitted
Land status: Private reserve land
Nearest town: Lake Placid
Fees and permits: All hikers entering the reserve must register.
Schedule: Daylight hours only
Maps: Adirondack Mountain Club (ADK),

Adirondack High Peaks Region map (available at traditional and online bookstores or from the ADK online store: www.adk.org) or National Geographic, Adirondack Park Lake Placid/High Peaks map (available at traditional and online bookstores)
Trail contacts: New York State Department of Environmental Conservation, Region 5, P.O. Box 296, 1115 Highway 86, Ray Brook, NY 12977; (518) 897-1200; www.dec.ny.gov and Adirondack Trail Improvement Society, P.O. Box 565, Keene Valley 12943; no phone; www.atis-web.com
Special considerations: Reserve rules include no pets, fires, or camping, and no bicycles on Lake Road. Only reserve members may fish or swim. The reserve has protected this site since 1897, so do your part, practicing the no-trace ethic. "ATIS" (Adirondack Trail Improvement Society) markers may help point out trails.

Finding the trailhead: From Keene Valley go south on Highway 73 East for 2.8 miles and turn right (west) onto a gravel road opposite the marked trailhead for Roaring Brook Trail to Giant Mountain. Find the trail parking lot on the left in 0.1 mile; because it often fills, you may need to park along the shoulder of Highway 73 (doing so at your own risk). Do not park anywhere along the gravel road. You must park away from the Ausable Club and not block the club area road with shuttle drop-offs or pick-ups. *DeLorme: New York Atlas & Gazetteer.* Page 96 C3.

From parking, hike west on the gravel road (the surface later changes to pavement) to reach the Ausable Club (0.5 mile). Turn left and descend the road between the tennis courts. Beyond member parking, reach the register and the Watchman Hut at 0.7 mile.

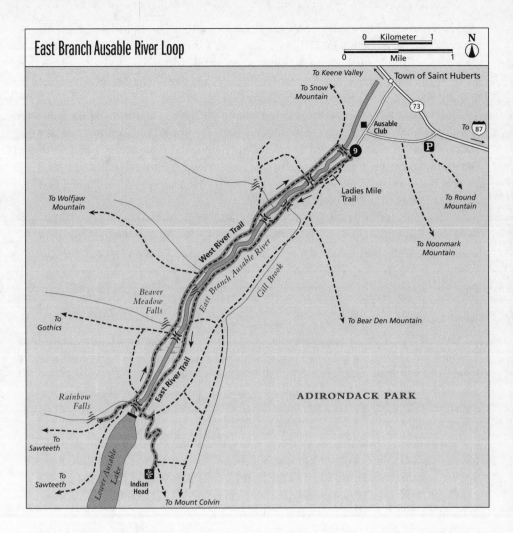

East Branch Ausable River

West River Trail

East River Trail

Gill Brook

To Keene Valley

To Snow
Mountain

Town of Saint Huberts

Ausable
Club

73

To 87

9

Ladies Mile
Trail

To Wolfjaw
Mountain

To Round
Mountain

To Noonmark
Mountain

Beaver
Meadow
Falls

To
Gothics

To Bear Den Mountain

ADIRONDACK PARK

Rainbow
Falls

To
Sawteeth

To
Sawteeth

Lower Ausable Lake

Indian
Head

To Mount Colvin

The Hike

You follow the Ladies Mile Trail into hemlock-beech woods, keeping right at junctions to reach the river trails upstream at a bridge. Clockwise, forgo crossing, continuing upstream along the east bank; the west bank holds the loop's return. The East Branch is a clean-coursing mountain water, reflecting the hues of the rocks it bathes. Mossy stones stud the east bank trail.

After crossing the footbridge over Gill Brook, you next cross a reserve road and ascend through a high-canopy forest. The trail rounds below an isolated outcrop, gathering views of Wolfjaw Mountain. Where the trail travels an old-growth hemlock plateau, you draw some 200 feet above the river before a quick, difficult descent.

On the lower slope you overlook a double river falls. In a pinched gorge the upper 20-foot falls feeds a lower 6-foot falls, with a surging channel between and a dark pool at the exodus. Back on the elevated riverbank, you pass room-size boulders, briefly parallel a pipe that draws water for the club, and pass a river bridge. Upstream you'll spy the ragged Gothics–Sawteeth skyline.

Beaver Meadow soon claims the river bottom, braiding the stream. Below Bullock Dam, Leach Bridge spans the river at the outlet to Lower Ausable Lake. The lake waters and boathouse are closed to the general public, and shore access is limited to the marked trails. Here you cross the bridge for the loop, but to top Indian Head for an overlook, remain on the east shore, coming out at the main reserve road. You'll find the marked trail to Indian Head off this road.

En route to Indian Head, a 115-foot spur heads right to Gothics Window, offering a tree-framed look at the rugged Gothics and high-peak amphitheater. The main trail climbs, with short ladder segments at steep stretches. Taking a right at a three-way junction puts you atop Indian Head—a broad, flat outcrop with a spectacular view surpassed only by the view from the Indian's brow below. Nippletop, Colvin, the curved platters of Upper and Lower Ausable Lakes, the Sawteeth, Gothics, and Wolfjaws fashion the stage.

Back at Leach Bridge, you cross the river. Views stretch to the Mount Colvin–Sawteeth gateway at the head of Lower Ausable Lake. Adding the left spur to Rainbow Falls, you find sheer cliffs, the 150-foot misty shower, and a greenery-filled box canyon. When sun-kissed, a rainbow spectrum autographs the falls. When you return to Leach Bridge, hike the West River Trail downstream, passing the trail to Lost Lookout.

The shoreline ramble takes you over rocks, below the cliffs, and through shady spruce-hardwood forest. The trail eases, traversing a beech flat and raised dike. Eastern views span the alder meadow to the Bear Den–Dial Mountain ridge. You cross a couple of drainages and pass a ladder ascent to the Gothics to reach Beaver Meadow Falls, an 80-foot falls splashing over tiered cliff.

Past the double falls on the East Branch, the trail drifts from the river into a realm of old-growth hemlock. Stay on the West River Trail, crossing paired logs over a pretty brook with a 10-foot cascade in a rocky slot. The trail next descends a steep ridge.

Where the trail bottoms out, the West River Trail veers left. You'll hike past a spur on the right to Canyon Bridge and ones to the left to Pyramid Brook and a falls mostly swallowed by rocks. Downstream the trail is again at river level, taking you past another river bridge. Where the West River Trail merges with the Nature Trail, 300-year-old hemlocks grace the hike. You do cross the next river bridge to close the loop and angle through the reserve to Watchman Hut.

Lower Ausable Lake, Adirondack Mountain Reserve ▶

Miles and Directions

0.0 Start at the Watchman Hut trailhead. Hike the dirt road past the hut, entering Adirondack Mountain Reserve at the rustic gate, and in 100 feet turn right on the signed Ladies Mile Trail.

0.2 Reach the Ladies Mile loop junction; head right.

0.4 Reach the trail junction; proceed forward (upstream) 500 feet to reach the river trails at a bridge. Continue forward on the east shore trail. **Note:** The Ladies Mile Trail loops left at 0.4 mile.

1.0 Cross Gill Brook footbridge; turn left, following this side brook upstream to cross a reserve road and ascend.

1.8 Overlook a double falls on the river.

2.2 Reach a junction; bear right, staying along the east bank. **Note:** To the left is the main reserve road.

2.3 Reach a junction; keep left. **Note:** Path heading right leads to the river bridge to Beaver Meadow Falls.

2.8 View Bullock Dam, a plank-topped log stretched the length of the river.

3.3 Reach Leach Bridge and the river loop return junction. **Side trip:** To add the Indian Head overlook, postpone crossing and remain on the east shore. Ascend sharply left, turn right near a storage shed, and ascend 50 yards on a gravel road to emerge at the main reserve road in 0.1 mile. Follow the main reserve road left 500 feet to the marked trail to Indian Head. Take the indicated trail and stay left, contouring and switching back up the slope. At 3.6 miles a 115-foot spur heads right to Gothics Window. The main trail climbs. At a three-way junction, go right 0.1 mile to top Indian Head (4.2 miles). Backtrack to Leach Bridge.

5.1 Cross Leach Bridge to the west shore junction; the loop's return is to the right. **Side trip:** To add a visit to Rainbow Falls, turn left. At the dam bear right and, shortly after, again bear right to reach Rainbow Falls (5.3 miles). Return to the river loop at Leach Bridge.

5.6 Reach Leach Bridge; hike the west shore trail downstream.

6.8 View Beaver Meadow Falls.

8.0 Reach a junction; proceed forward and remain on the West River Trail at junctions that quickly follow. **Note:** Downhill to the right is Canyon Bridge, largest of the river footbridges.

8.4 Reach another bridge junction; continue straight on the West River Trail as it merges with the Nature Trail.

9.0 Cross the river bridge; turn left (downstream) and veer right into the woods.

9.1 End at Watchman Hut. To return to your car, ascend through club grounds and turn right.

Hike Information

Local Information

Lake Placid/Essex County Convention and Visitors Bureau, 2610 Main Street, Suite 2, Lake Placid 12946; (518) 523-2445 or (800) 447-5224; www.lake placid.com

Local Events/Attractions

The **Adirondack History Center Museum,** open weekends Memorial Day weekend through Columbus Day, is a classic small-town museum in the old school building at the corner of Highway 9N and Hand Avenue in Elizabethtown. The collection records two centuries in Essex County and is paired with a traditional colonial garden of plants, herbs, and flowers. Contact Essex County Historical Society, (518) 873-6466; www.adkhistorycenter.org.

Organizations

Adirondack Mountain Club, 814 Goggins Road, Lake George 12845; (518) 668-4447 or (800) 395-8080; www.adk.org

▶ Getting into Shape

Unless you want to be sore—and possibly have to shorten your trip or vacation—be sure to get in shape before a big hike. If you're terribly out of shape, start a walking program early, preferably eight weeks in advance. Start with a fifteen-minute walk during your lunch hour or after work and gradually increase your walking time to an hour. You should also increase your elevation gain. Walking briskly up hills really strengthens your leg muscles and gets your heart rate up. If you work in a storied office building, take the stairs instead of the elevator. If you prefer going to a gym, walk the treadmill or use a stair machine. You can further increase your strength and endurance by walking with a loaded backpack. Stationary exercises you might consider are squats, leg lifts, sit-ups, and push-ups. Other good ways to get in shape include biking, running, aerobics, and, of course, short hikes. Stretching before and after a hike keeps muscles flexible and helps avoid injuries.

10 Northville-Placid Trail

Built in 1922 by the Adirondack Mountain Club, this 133-mile-long isolated wilderness route journeys through the rugged splendor of the Adirondacks between Northville and Lake Placid. It takes an average of two to three weeks to hike. The southern two-thirds rolls to obtain a top elevation of 3,008 feet at Central Plateau, south of Long Lake, the largest water body on the trail. The northern portion twists through valleys parting trailless high peaks to end at Averyville Road near Lake Placid. The trail's pristine wilds, solitude, picturesque waters, fall foliage, and spur trails to ponds and peaks continually reward.

Start: At the Upper Benson trailhead (north of Northville) to forgo the trail's initial road miles (In the future, the Northville–Placid Trail out of Northville will be routed off the roadway.)

Distance: 122.8 miles one-way when starting at Upper Benson

Approximate hiking time: 10 to 15 days for entire 122.8 miles but options for short samplings

Difficulty: Strenuous due to length, terrain, and grade

Elevation change: From its southern terminus at Upper Benson, the trail travels from an elevation of 1,300 feet to a high of 3,000 feet at Central Plateau (4.6 miles south of Long Lake). The hike's northern end at Averyville Road is at 2,000 feet.

Trail surface: Rocky and earthen path, logging tote roads, and primary roads

Seasons: Best for hiking, late spring through fall

Other trail users: Hunters

Canine compatibility: Dogs permitted (leashing recommended)

Land status: Department of Environmental Conservation (DEC) and private land

Nearest town: Northville or Lake Placid

Fees and permits: You must secure a camping permit from the area DEC office if your group number exceeds ten or if you plan to use the same campsite for more than three nights.

Schedule: No time restrictions

Maps: Adirondack Mountain Club (ADK),

Northville–Placid Trail map and book (available at traditional and online bookstores or from the ADK online store: www.adk.org) or National Geographic, Adirondack Park Northville/ Raquette Lake and Lake Placid/High Peaks maps (available at traditional and online bookstores)

Trail contacts: New York State DEC, Region 5, P.O. Box 1316, 701 South Main Street, Northville, 12134; (518) 863-4545; www.dec.ny.gov

Special considerations: Through-hikers need to work out the logistics for getting adequate food and supplies, plan what to do in case of an emergency, and arrange for transportation at the end of the trail. Expect rocky, difficult conditions. Despite blue-disk and Northville–Placid Logo markers and regular DEC maintenance, strong map and compass skills will ease travel. Because beaver activity can force reroutes, keep alert while tracking blazes. The trail traverses public lands for the most part. Where it crosses private lands, some logging may occur; keep to the trail and respect any posted rules. Again, nature can sometimes get ahead of trail crews, so be careful out there.

Although some thirty lean-tos on or just off the trail offer convenient, dry overnight waysides, a tent remains standard equipment. Because lean-tos cannot be reserved, chancing that you will be the first to arrive and claim the lean-to for the night is both unwise and an unnecessary wilderness risk.

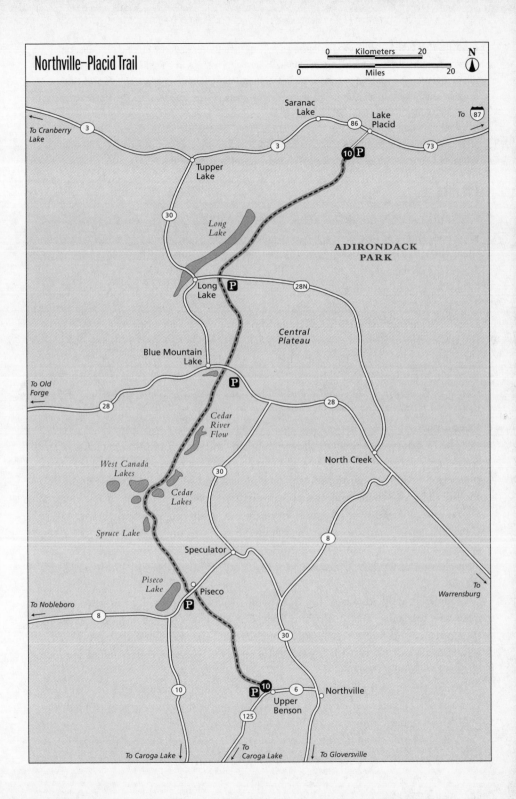

Northville–Placid Trail

Kilometers
0   20

Miles
0   20

N

To Cranberry Lake

3

Saranac Lake

86

Lake Placid

To 87

3

Tupper Lake

73

30

10 P

Long Lake

ADIRONDACK PARK

Long Lake

P

28N

Central Plateau

Blue Mountain Lake

P

To Old Forge

28

28

Cedar River Flow

North Creek

West Canada Lakes

30

Cedar Lakes

Spruce Lake

8

Speculator

To Warrensburg

Piseco Lake

Piseco

To Nobleboro

8

P

30

10

6

Northville

10

P

10

Upper Benson

125

To Caroga Lake

To Caroga Lake

To Gloversville

Finding the trailhead: From Northville go 4.1 miles north on Highway 30 and turn west on Benson Road (County Road 6), a paved road. Following the signs in 5.6 miles, turn right onto a dirt road and quickly take a second right. In 0.6 mile, near Trailhead Lodge, turn left onto Godfrey Road to reach the trail register in 0.5 mile; parking precedes the trail on the right. *DeLorme: New York Atlas & Gazetteer.* Page 79 C6.

Find the northern terminus at the junction of Averyville and Old Military Roads. Reach the junction by going south on Old Military Road from Highway 86 or west on Averyville Road from the village of Lake Placid. *DeLorme: New York Atlas & Gazetteer.* Page 96 B2.

The Hike

The route typically travels through low- and middle-elevation forests along drainages, past lakes, and over low passes. Expect more rugged conditions when passing through the wilderness interior. Spurs present opportunities to view additional ponds or to ascend peaks for vistas. Otherwise, your admiration of the Adirondack Mountains comes by way of gaps in the tree cover.

Three primary crossroads—Highway 8 near Piseco, Highway 28/30 at Lake Durant (near Blue Mountain Lake), and Highway 28N near Long Lake—break the route into four disproportionate segments. From Upper Benson to Highway 8 covers a distance of 22.2 miles, from Highway 8 to Highway 28/30 covers 47.8 miles, from Highway 28/30 to Highway 28N covers 15.2 miles, and from Highway 28N to the intersection of Averyville and Old Military Roads covers a distance of 37.6 miles. These routes, along with some secondary crossroads, suggest likely resupply or exit points.

The first quarter of the tour shows gentle ups and downs, crossing branches of the Sacandaga River and numerous brooks and creeks. Beaver ponds, lakes, and meadows punctuate travel through the mostly deciduous woods of the Southern Adirondack foothills. The lakes here tend to support trout.

A series of large wild lakes and virgin forests in the popular Spruce Lake–West Canada Lakes–Cedar Lakes area highlight the trek's second leg. The remote lakes, while enchanting in beauty, remain quiet, stilled by acid rain. Some lakes show not a ripple or a dragonfly. Only the mournful call of an occasional loon breaks the silence.

This long, wild stretch of the Northville–Placid Trail provides unrivaled escape from the workaday world. Pristine West Canada Lakes Wilderness Area with its spruce-hardwood forests remained untouched until this trail opened its gates. Cedar River Road, a dirt access road within Moose River Recreation Area, offers another chance to resupply or exit.

Along the third trail segment, you will find a rolling woods excursion that takes you past several lakes before claiming the hike's high point and dipping to Highway 28N. Views remain limited as the hike proceeds north.

A lengthy stretch along the eastern shore of Long Lake launches the final leg. A half-dozen lean-tos dot the shore, hinting at the lake's popularity. Land ownership at the lake is mixed; the trail primarily travels public lands, skirting private parcels. From Long Lake you will pass through forest to reach Cold River, an exciting, crystalline Adirondack waterway guiding you upstream into the High Peaks area. The trail passes lakes, following Roaring Brook and Moose Creek (side drainages of the Cold River) upstream, where you cross over a pass entering the Upper Chubb River drainage. The short spur to Wanika Falls puts a sterling imprint on the tour, and you'll find the last lean-to on the Northville–Placid along this waterfall spur.

Wildlife sightings, wildflowers, autumn hues, and echoes to the past all contribute to a lifetime memory of hiking the Northville–Placid Trail. Undeniably the Northville–Placid Trail belongs in any survey book of the state's premier trails. But because spatial constraints here limit the detail we can provide, if you plan to through-trail hike or even just make short excursions on the Northville–Placid Trail, be sure to purchase the latest maps and a good guidebook specific to the trail. Markers can disappear over time, and nature can rewrite your course. You'll be venturing into a remote area, where you'll want as many clues as possible to navigate the trail safely. In this unforgiving terrain, there is no such thing as overkill. Get the best maps and information possible.

Miles and Directions

0.0 Start from the southern (Upper Benson) trailhead; head north.

16.2 Reach Whitehouse Crossing; cross the suspension bridge.

22.2 Reach Highway 8 near its intersection with County Road 24 (Old Piseco Road); follow CR 24 north.

24.3 Pass the Piseco Post Office.

34.8 Reach Spruce Lake; travel the east shore.

40.5 Reach the West Canada Creek lean-to as you enter West Canada Lakes Wilderness Area.

48.2 Reach Cedar Lake.

57.8 Pass Wakely Dam; remain on Cedar River Road, continuing northbound.

64.4 Leave Cedar River Road at McCanes Resort, turning left.

70.0 Cross Highway 28/30 near Lake Durant Public Campground.

74.6 Reach Tirrell Pond; travel the west shore.

85.2 Cross Highway 28N; hike Tarbell Road north.

87.0 Follow Long Lake's east shore.

97.7 Pass Shattuck Clearing.

98.4 Cross the first of back-to-back suspension bridges over Moose Creek and the Cold River to follow the Cold River upstream along the north bank.

109.7 Pass the Duck Hole dam.

115.2 Pass the Wanika Falls spur, which heads right.

121.6 Emerge at Averyville Road near a parking area; follow Averyville Road right.

122.8 End near the Averyville Road–Old Military Road intersection (the official end).

Hike Information

Local Information

Lake Placid/Essex County Convention and Visitors Bureau, 2610 Main Street, Suite 2, Lake Placid 12946; (518) 523-2445 or (800) 447-5224; www.lakeplacid.com or **Hamilton County Department of Economic Development and Tourism,** South Shore Road, P.O. Box 57, Lake Pleasant 12108; (800) 648-5239; www .hamiltoncounty.com

Local Events/Attractions

Adirondack Saddle Tours offers horseback riding in the Adirondack woods. The company's most popular rides are the half-day rides to Moss Lake, Cascade Lake, or Cascade Falls. Helmets are available. Adirondack Saddle Tours, 5 Uncas Road, Eagle Bay 13331; (315) 357-4499 or (877) 795-7488; www.adkhorse.com

Organizations

Adirondack Mountain Club, 814 Goggins Road, Lake George 12845; (518) 668-4447 or (800) 395-8080; www.adk.org

11 Blue Mountain Trail

Above the east shore of Blue Mountain Lake, this quick, steep summit ascent reaches a fire tower, retired from duty but open for public viewing, and a cherished 360-degree Central Adirondack view. Besides the sweeping vistas, the trail offers an attractive fir-spruce forest and the historic summit benchmark placed by Verplanck Colvin. Colvin, an important early surveyor, helped open the Adirondacks to the public.

Start: At the Blue Mountain Trail trailhead

Distance: 4 miles out-and-back

Approximate hiking time: 2 to 3 hours

Difficulty: Moderate due to the sharp elevation gain

Elevation change: The trail travels between 2,200 feet at the trailhead and a summit elevation of 3,759 feet.

Trail surface: Worn rock path with surface hardening and stone step improvements

Seasons: Best for hiking, spring through fall

Other trail users: Snowshoers

Canine compatibility: Dogs permitted (Leash your dog because the first part of the trail is on private land and because of the trail's popularity and the narrowness of the travel aisle.)

Land status: Department of Environmental Conservation (DEC) and private land

Nearest town: Blue Mountain Lake (or Indian Lake or Long Lake)

Fees and permits: No fees or permits required

Schedule: No time restrictions

Maps: Adirondack Mountain Club (ADK), Adirondack Central Region map (available at traditional and online bookstores or from the ADK online store: www.adk.org) or National Geographic, Adirondack Park Northville/Raquette Lake map (available at traditional and online bookstores); interpretive brochure (generally available at nature brochure box on the trail)

Trail contacts: New York State DEC, Region 5, P.O. Box 1316, 701 South Main Street, Northville 12134; (518) 863-4545; www.dec.ny.gov

Special considerations: After rainstorms, the worn bed of the rocky trail can become a runoff channel, so watch your footing.

Finding the trailhead: From the intersection of Highways 28, 30, and 28N in the hamlet of Blue Mountain Lake, go north on Highway 30/Highway 28N for 1.4 miles and turn right (east) for the marked trailhead parking lot for the Blue Mountain and Tirrell Pond Trails. *DeLorme: New York Atlas & Gazetteer:* Page 87 B5.

The Hike

From the trailhead parking lot, follow the red disks of the Blue Mountain Trail. Yellow disks now mark the northbound Tirrell Pond Trail, which used to be red as well. This color change eliminates the risk of confusion. The first half of the trail shows refinements of stone steps and parallel plank walks designed to minimize erosion. The second half shows the eroded bare rock of the historic trail, naked of any topsoil.

The highly accessible Blue Mountain interpretive trail ascends the namesake peak that looms above the east shore of Blue Mountain Lake. Because of the trail's convenient location and relatively short length, it offers newcomers a quick snapshot of the

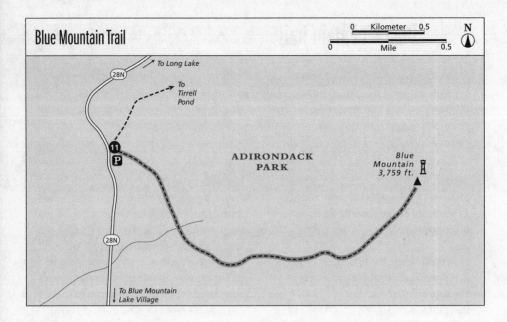

0   Kilometer   0.5

N

0   Mile   0.5

To Long Lake

28N

To
Tirrell
Pond

11

P

ADIRONDACK
PARK

Blue
Mountain
3,759 ft.

28N

To Blue Mountain
Lake Village

challenge and wilderness discovery of the Adirondacks. A box near the trail register, a short distance into the trail, contains interpretive brochures, but the popularity of this trail can draw down the supply. Numbered features along the trail correspond to numbered descriptions in the brochure. Donations collected at the trail's iron ranger (a fee-deposit post) go directly to trail improvement.

Tall maple, black cherry, and birch weave the overhead canopy, with fern, viburnum, striped maple, and brambles filling out the woods. Where the trail briefly levels, big birch trees, both yellow and white, claim the way. Many of these birches germinated following the blowdown of 1950. What has come to be known as the Great Appalachian Wind Storm of 1950 impacted 424,000 acres in the forest preserve.

At the upcoming brook crossing, a small cascade sheets over canted rock. Ahead you can see where trail improvements of hardening and stone steps are gradually overcoming the trail's problems of erosion trenches and soggy spots. At times snags open the canopy, but the trail remains semishaded. At the next brook crossing, both forest and trail undergo a character change. A higher-elevation forest of spruce, fir, birch, and mountain ash now claims the peak, while the trail narrows, steepens, and grows increasingly rocky.

Steep rock outcrops next advance the trail. On the descent, you will need to dig in with the toes of your boots here. After rains this section can become a full-fledged creek, with racing water spilling down, around, and over the rocks. At the trail's sides, clintonia, bunchberry, oxalis, and club moss grow. In another half mile, canted bedrock offers a more moderate climb through tight stands of picturesque fir and spruce.

The bald summit outcrop holds the five-story steel-frame observatory. The public may ascend the fire tower, but numbers are limited on the structure at any one time.

Blue Mountain Trail, Blue Mountain Wild Forest, Adirondack Park

Erected in 1917, the tower was restored by a volunteer committee in 1994, and the DEC has since restored the tower cab for public use. Viewing from the cab is through open steel grids. Summit views sweep Whiteface, Algonquin, Colden, and Marcy Peaks; Blue Mountain, Eagle, Utowana, and Durant Lakes; Minnow, Mud, South, and Tirrell Ponds; and Blue Ridge—a bold tapestry of forests, ridges, peaks, and lakes. On autumn mornings, handkerchiefs of fog lift from the cobalt platters and drift across the gold, green, and red of the lake basins.

Other summit structures include a cell tower and a DEC communication station. A few paces north of the 35-foot fire tower, you will discover the summit markings placed by Verplanck Colvin. In the 1870s Colvin's men shot off bright explosions here so that the Adirondack survey teams could triangulate on the peak. The return descent is as you came.

Miles and Directions

0.0 Start from the Blue Mountain trailhead; head generally east on the red trail.

0.7 Cross a brook.

2.0 Reach the summit outcrop and fire tower; return by the same route.

4.0 End back at the Blue Mountain trailhead.

Options

You might choose to hike the 3.3-mile Tirrell Pond Trail, which shares the same trailhead parking area. This yellow-marked wooded trail journeys north before turning east, passing at the northern foot of Blue Mountain. It follows private roads and intersects the Northville–Placid Trail north of Tirrell Pond. Lean-tos occupy the north and south ends of the pond. The pond's beach and views of Tirrell Mountain engage visitors.

Hike Information

Local Information
Hamilton County Department of Economic Development and Tourism, South Shore Road, P.O. Box 57, Lake Pleasant 12108; (800) 648-5239; www.hamilton county.com

Local Events/Attractions
The **Adirondack Museum** in the hamlet of Blue Mountain Lake has twenty buildings on a thirty-two-acre campus filled with exhibits that unfold the story of life, work, transportation, and recreation in the Adirondacks since the early 1800s. The site is noted for its historical boat collection. Events fill out the museum calendar, including the annual Rustic Fair in September. The museum is open daily 10:00

STORM OF THE CENTURY

The Great Appalachian Wind Storm of November 1950, a cyclonic Nor'easter, cut a swath of fear and destruction across the Appalachians, impacting twenty-two eastern and Midwest states and killing more than 300 people before entering Canada. In New York, punishing winds and rain toppled trees, cut power, raised coastal waters, and swamped banks. This storm of the century, the largest recorded windstorm in the Adirondacks, wreaked havoc on more than 400,000 acres. Before the century was out, though, a second megablow smacked the Adirondacks on July 15, 1995. The declared microburst (a downdraft that causes an outburst at surface level) downed hundreds of thousands of trees, killing five, clogging and wiping out trails, and stranding ninety hikers and canoeists. It prompted the biggest rescue effort in New York State Department of Environmental Conservation history. Although the 1995 storm occupies only a fraction of the 1950 storm footprint, it left 38,000 acres with more than 60 percent downed trees and another 109,000 acres with 30 to 60 percent of trees down. The High Falls area (Hike 7) perhaps best reveals the legacy and the recovery.

a.m. to 5:00 p.m., late May through mid–October. Admission is charged. Adirondack Museum, P.O. Box 99, Blue Mountain Lake 12812; (518) 352-7311; www.adkmuseum.org

Accommodations

Lake Durant (DEC) Campground, about 4 miles south on Highway 30/Highway 28, is open mid-May through Columbus Day and has sixty-one sites. Reservations: (800) 456-2267; www.reserveamerica.com

Organizations

Adirondack Mountain Club, 814 Goggins Road, Lake George 12845; (518) 668-4447 or (800) 395-8080; www.adk.org

▶ Hiking with Your Dog

Bringing your furry friend with you is always more fun than leaving him behind. Our canine pals make great trail buddies because they never complain and always make good company.

Before you plan outdoor adventures with your dog, make sure he's in shape for the trail. Take him on your daily runs or walks. Also, be sure he has a firm grasp of the basics of canine etiquette and behavior, and that he can sit, lie down, stay, and come on command. Purchase collapsible water and dog food bowls for your dog. If you are hiking on rocky terrain or in the snow, you can purchase footwear for your dog that will protect his feet from cuts and bruises.

Once on the trail, keep your dog under control. You can buy a flexi-lead that allows your dog to go exploring along the trail, while allowing you the ability to reel him in should another hiker approach or should he decide to chase a rabbit. Always obey leash laws and be sure to bury your dog's waste or pack it in resealable plastic bags.

12 Murphy Lake Trail

North of Northville, this easy hike along a time-worn, centuries-old road accesses three sparkling lakes—Bennett, Middle, and Murphy—cradled in the quiet wooded beauty of the Southern Adirondacks. Fishing, camping, a historic settlement site, loons, and colorful fall foliage all help sell the trail. Because of its gentle grade and multiple stops, it makes a fine first backpack for the family.

Start: At the Creek Road trailhead

Distance: 9.4 miles out-and-back

Approximate hiking time: 5 to 6 hours

Difficulty: Easy

Elevation change: From a trailhead elevation of 940 feet, the trail tops the 1,600-foot mark while rounding Middle Lake. It then dips to Murphy Lake at 1,473 feet.

Trail surface: Earthen or grassy old road

Seasons: Best for hiking, spring through fall

Other trail users: Hunters, mountain bikers, snowmobilers, snowshoers, cross-country skiers

Canine compatibility: Dogs permitted (leashing recommended)

Land status: Department of Environmental Conservation (DEC)

Nearest town: Wells

Fees and permits: No fees or permits required

Schedule: No time restrictions

Maps: Adirondack Mountain Club (ADK), Adirondack Southern Region map (available at traditional and online bookstores or from the ADK online store: www.adk.org) or National Geographic, Adirondack Park Lake George/Great Sacandaga map (available at traditional and online bookstores)

Trail contacts: New York State DEC, Region 5, P.O. Box 1316, 701 South Main Street, Northville 12134; (518) 863-4545; www.dec.ny.gov

Special considerations: During the fall hunting season, it's best to avoid the area or, at least, wear bright-colored clothing. Although snowmobilers can use the trail, their use is generally light because the trail is not long.

Finding the trailhead: From Sacandaga Campground and Day-use Area (3.4 miles south of Wells), go south on Highway 30 for 5 miles and turn left (east) onto Creek Road. From Northville find the turn for Creek Road 3 miles north of the Highway 30 bridge over the Sacandaga River. The marked trailhead is left off Creek Road in 2.2 miles; parking is on the broad road shoulder. *DeLorme: New York Atlas & Gazetteer:* Page 79 B7.

The Hike

This trail heads north along a former road, ascending with a steady, moderate grade past the register. It probes a tall forest of white pine, hemlock, oak, maple, ash, birch, and aspen. Various ferns, sarsaparilla, and sugarscoop spot the understory. Mossy boulders and logs lend interest to the forest floor. In places the old road is worn deep into the terrain.

Before long, the greenery all but vanishes from the forest floor. Where the incline flattens, big white pines shade the route and soften the road with their discarded needles. The hike next passes a remnant rock wall and rounds a barrier. This trail is closed to all motorized travel except for snowmobiles. The snowmobile markers perform double duty, guiding hikers in the off-season.

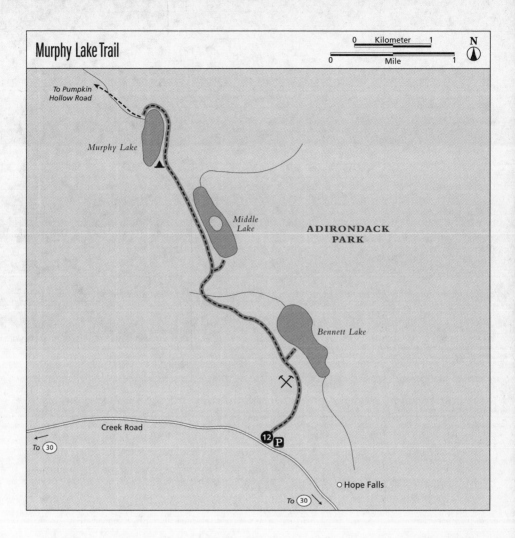

0 Kilometer 1

0 Mile 1

N

To Pumpkin Hollow Road

Murphy Lake

Middle Lake

ADIRONDACK PARK

Bennett Lake

Creek Road

To 30

12 P

○ Hope Falls

To 30

The trail then dips away. At about a mile, you may discern some exposed red soil, hinting at a turn-of-the-twentieth-century ferric oxide (paint pigment) mine. Although trees and leaf mat have reclaimed the mining settlement, you still may notice unusual mounds, cellar holes, or rusting debris.

A pair of cairns on the right funnels you down a wide trail to Bennett Lake, a camp flat, and a privy. The elongated oval of Bennett Lake rests below a rolling wooded ridge. Aquatic grasses and plants adorn its shallow edge, while insect chirrs enliven the air. A small boot-compressed beach offers lake access.

A moderate, rocky ascent from the Bennett Lake basin continues the hike. Toad, red eft, gray squirrel, and grouse may grow your wildlife tally. From somewhere on the lake, the haunting cry of a loon can usually be heard.

Where the trail passes between two low ridges, the comfortable earthen bed

Bennett Lake, Wilcox Lake Wild Forest, Adirondack Park

returns, and more greenery spreads beneath the trees. At a small drainage, you may encounter a mud hole; bridges typically span the larger runoffs.

After the trail tops out, a side trail veers right, passing through a hemlock grove to reach a Middle Lake campsite. A muddy shoreline with a few logs for footing offers a lake perspective that presents a small island topped by white pines and a large central island that deceives visitors into thinking it is the far shore.

The primary trail then contours the slope 200 feet above Middle Lake. Small-diameter trees choke out meaningful views, but the sparkling blue water provides a grand canvas for the leafy boughs. Slowly, the trail inches toward the lake, where a second unmarked spur ventures 200 feet to the right, reaching Middle Lake at another campsite. Here, too, a log-strewn, marshy shore greets you. Views feature the north end of the big central island and a scenic rounded hill with western cliffs. Aquatic grasses, pickerelweed (arrowhead), and water lilies adorn the shallows.

The trailbed alternately shows grass, rock, and earthen stretches as you continue to round Middle Lake. Before leaving the lake, you will find a couple of open views. After a woods ascent, the trail crosses a rocky drainage and curves right to meet Murphy Lake at the lean-to, where an outcrop slopes to the water. The reflecting waters of Murphy Lake and the enfolding, rounded, tree-mantled hills with their cliff outcrops hold a signature charm, dazzling in autumn attire.

A marked foot trail continues past the lean-to. It travels counterclockwise halfway around the lake, passing campsites, lake accesses, and coves thick with pickerelweed.

The trail rolls just above shore, rounding through meadow, hemlock stand, and leafy woods. The natural rock-and-log dam at the outlet signals the end of the lakeshore trek and the turnaround for this hike. But a footpath continues north from the dam to Pumpkin Hollow Road. (See options)

Miles and Directions

0.0 Start from the Creek Road trailhead; head north.

1.4 Reach the Bennett Lake spur.

2.7 Reach Middle Lake.

3.9 Reach the Murphy Lake lean-to.

4.7 Reach the natural dam; turn around, backtracking your steps.

9.4 End at the Creek Road trailhead.

Options

If you spot a second vehicle at the Pumpkin Hollow Road trailhead, this hike can be walked as a 7.6-mile shuttle. From the natural rock-and-log dam, you would continue north on the foot trail following the outlet to reach the northern trailhead in 2.9 miles. Pumpkin Hollow Road is reached east off Highway 30 a couple of miles south of Sacandaga Campground. Find the trailhead on the right off Pumpkin Hollow Road in 1.6 miles. *DeLorme: New York Atlas & Gazetteer.* Page 79 B7.

Hike Information

Local Information
Hamilton County Department of Economic Development and Tourism, South Shore Road, P.O. Box 57, Lake Pleasant 12108; (800) 648-5239; www.hamiltoncounty.com

Local Events/Attractions
With a surface area of 42 square miles and 125 miles of shoreline, **Sacandaga Lake** invites with liquid recreation: fishing, kayaking, canoeing, sailing, boating, and beaches; www.visitsacandaga.com

Accommodations
Sacandaga (DEC) Campground, south of Wells, is open mid-May through Columbus Day and has 143 sites. It was one of the first two campgrounds built in the forest preserve. Reservations: (800) 456-2267; www.reserveamerica.com

Organizations
Adirondack Mountain Club, 814 Goggins Road, Lake George 12845; (518) 668-4447 or (800) 395-8080; www.adk.org

13 Pharaoh Mountain and Lake Loop

In the Schroon Lake area of the Eastern Adirondacks, this all-day or overnight hike tags the summit of Pharaoh Mountain and encircles large, deep Pharaoh Lake, touring mixed forest and wetland meadows. Summit and shore vistas, swimming and trout fishing, an expansive marsh, convenient overnight lean-tos, prized solitude, and fall color swell this Pharaoh's treasure cache.

Start: At the official Crane Pond trailhead

Distance: 18.1-mile lasso-shaped hike

Approximate hiking time: 9.5 to 12 hours

Difficulty: Strenuous due to distance and terrain

Elevation change: The trail has a 1,500-foot elevation change, with the high point atop Pharaoh Mountain, elevation 2,556 feet.

Trail surface: Earthen, rocky, and meadow trails; woods road; and plank walk

Seasons: Best for hiking, late spring through fall

Other trail users: Hunters

Canine compatibility: Dogs permitted

Land status: Department of Environmental Conservation (DEC)

Nearest town: Schroon Lake

Fees and permits: No fees or permits required

Schedule: No time restrictions

Maps: Adirondack Mountain Club (ADK), Adirondack Eastern Region map (available at traditional and online bookstores or from the ADK online store: www.adk.org) or National Geographic, Adirondack Park Lake George/Great Sacandaga map (available at traditional and online bookstores)

Trail contacts: New York State DEC, Region 5, P.O. Box 220, 232 Golf Course Road, Warrensburg 12885; (518) 623-1200; www.dec.ny.gov

Special considerations: There can be some soggy obstacles along Alder Creek; watch for bypasses and changes in bypasses.

Finding the trailhead: From the Highway 74/U.S. Highway 9 junction (0.1 mile east of Interstate 87), go south on US 9 for 0.6 mile and turn left (east) onto Alder Meadow Road toward Schroon Lake Airport. In 2 miles bear left on Crane Pond Road and go 1.4 miles east, reaching a parking area on the left; en route, the road changes to gravel. *DeLorme: New York Atlas & Gazetteer:* Page 88 B4.

The Hike

You first hike the retired stretch of Crane Pond Road to Pharaoh Lake Wilderness. The road narrows and changes to dirt, offering an easy tree-shaded avenue. As you parallel Alder Creek upstream, outcrops, a dark hollow, and wetlands vary viewing. At road's end, you arrive at the old Crane Pond trailhead. Cross the bridge over the watery link between Crane and Alder Ponds. Meadowy islands adorn the more-vegetated Alder Pond. Now proceed on an older woods road as it gently ascends into a hemlock-birch woods filled out by maples, firs, and 4-foot-diameter white pines.

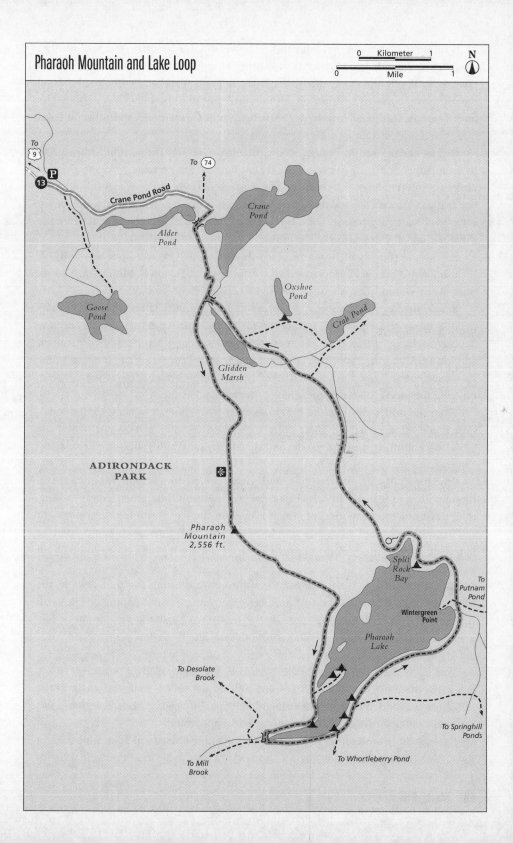

Pharaoh Mountain and Lake Loop

0   Kilometer   1

0   Mile   1

N

To 9

13

P

To 74

Crane Pond Road

Crane
Pond

Alder
Pond

Goose
Pond

Oxshoe
Pond

Crab Pond

Glidden
Marsh

**ADIRONDACK
PARK**

Pharaoh
Mountain
2,556 ft.

Split
Rock
Bay

To
Putnam
Pond

Wintergreen
Point

Pharaoh
Lake

To Desolate
Brook

To Mill
Brook

To Whortleberry Pond

To Springhill
Ponds

Bear right at the loop junction to first top Pharaoh Mountain. You will skirt an elbow pond of Glidden Marsh before passing behind a low ridge, where foot trail takes over. Slowly the climb intensifies. After an angling ascent, bedrock slabs shape a more vertical charge up Pharaoh Mountain. Aspen and mountain ash disperse the open forest. A northwest view finds Desolate Swamp, Goose Pond, and Schroon Lake. Top Pharaoh Mountain near an old mining adit.

Before striking south, straight across the crown, mount the summit outcrops to piece together a 270-degree view—a fantastic landscape of rolling ridges, rounded peaks, and myriad lakes and marshes. The western outcrop (to your right) holds survey markers; one dates back to 1896. On descent, another outcrop bids you over for a southern view of Pharaoh Lake, big and glistening, with its rock islands, irregular shoreline, and encompassing wilderness.

Rocks and roots complicate the steep descent, which zigs and pitches south off the mountain. Areas of bedrock open views northeast to Treadway Mountain. A plank walk over a wet meadow then leads to the lake. Bear right, counterclockwise.

Yellow markers point the way to peninsula lean-tos in 0.25 mile. The peninsula's rocky end invites swimming, fishing, daydreaming, and stargazing. As you resume counterclockwise, yellow disks also mark the lake loop. An outcrop pushes the trail up and inland. Along the shore you encounter additional lean-tos or the spurs to them. Pass above the shallow, pinched outlet bay to cross a footbridge. Beaver-peeled sticks can clog the brook; frogs and mergansers stir the bay.

From the outlet crossing, the trail pulls away from shore, traversing a corridor of spruce and reindeer lichen. Next up is an inviting lakeside lean-to, christened the "Pharaoh Hilton" by past guests. Beyond the Springhill Ponds Trail, you follow along a quiet bay.

Outcrops can lure you lakeside, and views stretch to Pharaoh Mountain. You round a lily-pad bay and from a log bridge can admire Wintergreen Point—a long, thin, treed outcrop separating the main lake from the bay. Past a trail heading right to Putnam Pond, a red secondary trail leads 0.1 mile to Wintergreen Point. The lake trail drifts from shore into deciduous woodland filled out by midstory hobblebush and striped maple.

Ahead is Split Rock Bay, named for a distinctive offshore feature. Views to the southwest span Pharaoh Lake to Number 8 and Little Stevens Mountains. A small ridge offers a farewell lake view before the trail turns right and ascends away. The grade is steep, the terrain rocky, and the woods deciduous; yellow remains the guiding color.

You travel the outskirts of beaver wetlands, variously filled in with vegetation. Rock-free stretches ease the slow descent. Still on the yellow trail, you arrive at the east shore of Glidden Marsh at its snag-riddled end. Lily pads, cattails, islands of grass and rock, and open water later alter the marsh's appearance.

Round east behind a low ridge, returning to Glidden Marsh, and continue straight past a blue trail junction to return to Crane Pond. You will round the west shore of a snag-riddled meadow basin, before crossing the footbridge over the dark outlet of Glidden Marsh to close the loop. A right returns you to the trailhead.

Miles and Directions

0.0 Start from the official Crane Pond trailhead; hike the retired road stretch east.

0.8 Pass the Goose Pond trailhead.

1.5 Take the bypass trail left to skirt a flooded site.

1.8 Reach the old Crane Pond trailhead (at road's end); follow red markers, crossing the split-level bridge over the outlet linking Crane and Alder Ponds.

2.4 Reach the loop junction; head right, counterclockwise.

4.7 Reach Pharaoh Mountain summit; head south straight across the crown.

6.3 Reach Pharaoh Lake. You'll encircle it counterclockwise.

7.2 Reach the peninsula spur; detour left to the peninsula and its lean-tos.

8.7 Cross the outlet bridge, coming to a junction. Follow the yellow markers uphill to the left, soon hiking on a soft woods road.

9.3 Bypass the "Pharaoh Hilton" lean-to and keep left where the Springhill Ponds Trail heads right.

10.5 Reach a camp flat; turn right, ascending to round the steep rocky slope above a lily-pad bay.

11.0 Bypass the trail that heads right to Putnam Pond, reaching the Wintergreen Point spur; continue on the lake trail. **Option:** A 0.1-mile detour leads to the Point.

12.0 Round Split Rock Bay.

14.7 Reach a junction; continue straight on the yellow trail to Glidden Marsh.

15.3 Reach a blue-trail junction; continue straight for Crane Pond.

15.7 Close the loop; turn right to return to the old trailhead.

16.3 Reach the old Crane Pond trailhead.

18.1 End at the official trailhead.

Options

An alternative start to the Pharaoh Mountain and Lake Loop would be to take the 2.8-mile blue Long Swing Trail that heads south from Highway 74 just west of the Paradox Lake Campground road. It comes out on the retired stretch of Crane Pond Road 0.1 mile northwest of the old trailhead. This would give you a 20.3-mile round-trip hike. *DeLorme: New York Atlas & Gazetteer*: Page 89 B4.

Hike Information

Local Information

Lake Champlain Visitors Center, 94 Montcalm Street, Suite 1, Ticonderoga 12883; (518) 585-6619 or (866) 843-5253; www.lakechamplainregion.com

Pharaoh Mountain summit, Pharaoh Lake Wilderness, Adirondack Park

Local Events/Attractions

Fort Ticonderoga National Historic Landmark offers costumed interpreters, guided tours, historical collections, and musket-firing demonstrations at the restored military fortress, a critical Lake Champlain/Lake George defense during the French and Indian and Revolutionary Wars. The fee site is open daily, early May to mid-October, 9:00 a.m. to 5:00 p.m. Fort Ticonderoga, P.O. Box 390, Ticonderoga 12883; (518) 585-2821; www.fort-ticonderoga.org

Accommodations

Paradox Lake (DEC) Campground, about 4 miles east of the U.S. Highway 9/Highway 74 junction, is open mid-May through Columbus Day and has fifty-eight sites. Reservations: (800) 456-2267; www.reserveamerica.com

Organizations

Adirondack Mountain Club, 814 Goggins Road, Lake George 12845; (518) 668-4447 or (800) 395-8080; www.adk.org

14 Stony Pond Trail

This Adirondack Park trail north of Irishtown and Minerva traverses varied terrain to visit Stony Pond along with its neighbors: Little and Big Sherman Ponds to the south, and Center Pond to the north. A hardwood and conifer forest, beaver sites, and fall foliage complement the serenity of the blue ponds.

Start: At the Highway 28N trailhead
Distance: 8.8 miles out-and-back
Approximate hiking time: 4.5 to 6 hours
Difficulty: Moderate
Elevation change: The trail has a 100-foot elevation change.
Trail surface: Earthen path, woods road
Seasons: Best for hiking, spring through fall
Other trail users: Hunters, snowmobilers, snowshoers, cross-country skiers
Canine compatibility: Dogs permitted
Land status: Department of Environmental Conservation (DEC)
Nearest town: Chestertown

Fees and permits: No fees or permits required
Schedule: No time restrictions
Maps: Adirondack Mountain Club (ADK), Adirondack Central Region map (available at traditional and online bookstores or from the ADK online store: www.adk.org) or National Geographic, Adirondack Park Northville/ Raquette Lake map (available at traditional and online bookstores)
Trail contacts: New York State DEC, Region 5, P.O. Box 220, 232 Golf Course Road, Warrensburg 12885; (518) 623-1200; www.dec.ny.gov
Special considerations: Beaver activity can muddle, muddy, or rewrite the trail.

Finding the trailhead: Find the trailhead east off Highway 28N, 3.9 miles north of its intersection with Olmstedville Road in Minerva and 2.8 miles south of Hewitt Lake Club Road in Aiden Lair. Parking is roadside; a DEC sign indicates the trail. *DeLorme: New York Atlas & Gazetteer.* Page 88 B1.

The Hike

The trail wears a single track down the middle of the woods road that leads east, away from Highway 28N. Yellow snowmobile and red-disk markers help indicate this route, which slowly ascends. Fir, spruce, tamarack, birch, maple, beech, and hobble-bush frame the travel aisle. Beyond a site that appears to have been quarried, you'll proceed forward, passing first a private trail to a small pond and then a closed woods road, both on the right.

The trail tops out and slowly descends, passing an area of domino-tumbled rocks. You cross Deer Creek headwaters just below a beaver dam; sometimes the engineer can be spied. Here you have the uncommon experience of being at eye level with the resulting pond. Cross via the dam or on a makeshift array of limbs, or simply give in and wade.

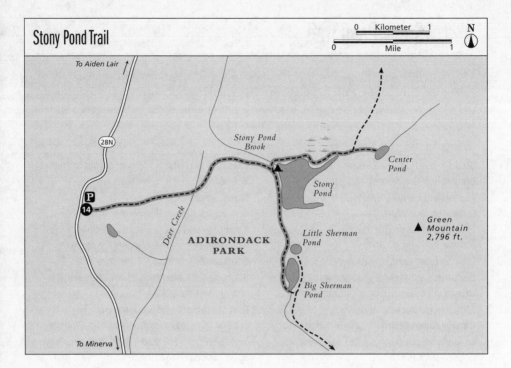

Stony Pond Trail

0   Kilometer   1

0   Mile   1

N

To Aiden Lair

28N

Stony Pond
Brook

Center
Pond

P
14

Deer Creek

Stony
Pond

ADIRONDACK
PARK

Little Sherman
Pond

Green
Mountain
2,796 ft.

Big Sherman
Pond

To Minerva

A slow ascent follows. Low spruce and hemlock trees grow roadside. In half a mile follow the beaver bypass, heading right for drier footing. Where the bypass returns to the snowmobile trail, follow Stony Pond Brook upstream to Stony Pond, a quiet enchantress with a wooded rim, Green Mountain rising to the east, a flat island, and nearshore rocks. Because its lean-to looks out at the pond, you can enjoy this image until shut-eye.

From the lean-to, trails head around the pond in both directions. To the left, a stone-and-log crossing of the Stony Pond outlet leads to Center Pond, with Barnes and Hewitt Ponds beyond. But first head right for Sherman Ponds. Follow the orange or red disks, tracing a line where the hardwood slope and conifer shore meet. The trail takes you below some noteworthy 100-foot-tall vertical gray cliffs showing block fracturing, mossy ledges, and a whitewash of lichen.

Eventually the trail climbs away to the right to follow the snowmobile branch that heads toward Sherman Ponds. Another snowmobile route heads left. Before long, the trail descends to Little Sherman Pond, enlarged by beaver-elevated waters. A left spur leads to the marshy shore. The primary trail bears right, rimming the lake through woods. Green Mountain adds to skyline views. Snowmobile and red-disk markers still show the way.

Skirt the shallow neck joining Little and Big Sherman Ponds. Snags rim the main lake body. You'll gain views of a wooded peninsula as the trail progresses, and skirt a campsite before veering away from the pond. Although the trail continues along Big Sherman, for this hike turn back at the outlet, returning to the Stony Pond lean-to.

To visit Center Pond, cross the Stony Pond outlet at the pond outlet and follow the trail as it drifts above and away from shore to round the wooded slope. You'll overlook the gorgelike channel of an inlet brook before hopping across the inlet. Briefly the trail becomes wetter, with sphagnum moss growing beneath the fir and spruce branches; trail markers are sporadic.

At the next small brook, look for the trail to jog downstream to an easy crossing point. Stony Pond is but a 100-foot spur away. The trail returns upstream, contouring the slope above a beaver pond and later a larger pond with reflections of the near-shore snags and trees. At the upcoming junction, you'll follow the yellow trail right to Center Pond.

A steep climb and descent through a similar forest leads to Center Pond. You arrive at a narrow opening in the shrubby shoreline ring that otherwise limits access. This pond is about a quarter of the size of Stony Pond but offers nice solitude. Mergansers may peel off the pond upon approach of the boot. Return to Stony Pond and then backtrack to Highway 28N.

Miles and Directions

0.0 Start from the Highway 28N trailhead; head east.

1.1 Cross Deer Creek headwaters.

2.0 Reach the Stony Pond lean-to; round the lake to the right to continue to Sherman Ponds.

3.2 Reach Big Sherman Pond's outlet; backtrack to the Stony Pond lean-to.

4.4 Reach the lean-to again and cross Stony Pond's outlet.

5.3 Reach a junction; head right on the yellow trail to Center Pond. **Note:** Straight on the red trail leads to Barnes and Hewitt Ponds.

5.6 Reach Center Pond; return to Stony Pond and the Highway 28N trailhead.

8.8 End at the Highway 28N trailhead.

Hike Information

Local Information

Lake Placid/Essex County Convention and Visitors Bureau, 2610 Main Street, Suite 2, Lake Placid 12946; (518) 523-2445 or (800) 447-5224; www.lake placid.com

Local Events/Attractions

The garnet is the New York State gemstone. At **Garnet Mine Tours,** a family-owned and -operated mine at Gore Mountain since 1878, visitors can strike color—deep red. Tours and gem-cutting demonstrations provide a sense of history. The fee site is open daily late June through early October. Garnet Mine Tours, P.O. Box 30, North River 12856; (518) 251-2706; www.garnetminetours.com

Organizations

Adirondack Mountain Club, 814 Goggins Road, Lake George 12845; (518) 668-4447 or (800) 395-8080; www.adk.org

15 Middle Settlement Lake Hike

Southwest of Old Forge, this all-day or overnight rolling meander through the forests and meadows of Ha-De-Ron-Dah Wilderness visits prized lakes. Wildlife sightings, wilderness quiet, and a complete escape from the trappings of civilization make this a special outing. Because beaver activity and the trail's sometimes sparse markings can compound the challenge, you'll need to keep your wilderness skills sharp.

Start: At the southern Middle Settlement Lake trailhead
Distance: 15.2-mile lasso-shaped hike, including spurs to Middle Branch Lake and Grass Pond
Approximate hiking time: 8 to 10 hours
Difficulty: Strenuous because of areas of awkward footing and lack of markers
Elevation change: The trail passes from a low point of 1,650 feet at Stony Creek to a high point of 1,800 feet.
Trail surface: Time-reclaimed earthen and grassy logging roads, foot trail, and boardwalk
Seasons: Best for hiking, late spring through fall
Other trail users: Hunters, snowshoers, cross-country skiers
Canine compatibility: Dogs permitted but must be controlled at owner's side by leash or voice command
Land status: Department of Environmental Conservation (DEC) land and private land (at trail's start)
Nearest town: Old Forge
Fees and permits: No fees or permits required
Schedule: No time restrictions
Maps: Adirondack Mountain Club (ADK), Adirondack West-Central Region map (available at traditional and online bookstores or from the ADK online store: www.adk.org) or National Geographic, Adirondack Park Old Forge/Oswegatchie map (available at traditional and online bookstores)
Trail contacts: New York State DEC, Region 6, Herkimer Office, 225 North Main Street, Herkimer 13350; (315) 866-6330; www.dec .ny.gov
Special considerations: You should possess good map and trail detective skills. Be aware that in places the trail markers can grow scarce or disappear altogether or may not adhere to color scheme. Beaver-caused wet passages may require ingenuity. Keep to the initial trail easement, respecting private property.

Finding the trailhead: From Old Forge go 6.4 miles southwest on Highway 28 and turn right at the signed easement for the trails to Ha-De-Ron-Dah Wilderness and Middle Settlement Lake. Go 0.5 mile north on the gravel road to find parking on the right; the arrow for the trail is just beyond it on the left. *DeLorme: New York Atlas & Gazetteer:* Page 85 C7.

The Hike

A forest of maple, birch, beech, and viburnum engages eyes as you travel the conservation easement and Copper Lake Road, following yellow markers weaving into the wilderness. Periodic postings indicate the wild forest preserve.

Cross small, braided Stony Creek and ascend to the loop junction. Go left, clockwise, now passing beneath big black cherry trees. The trail continues its rolling mean-

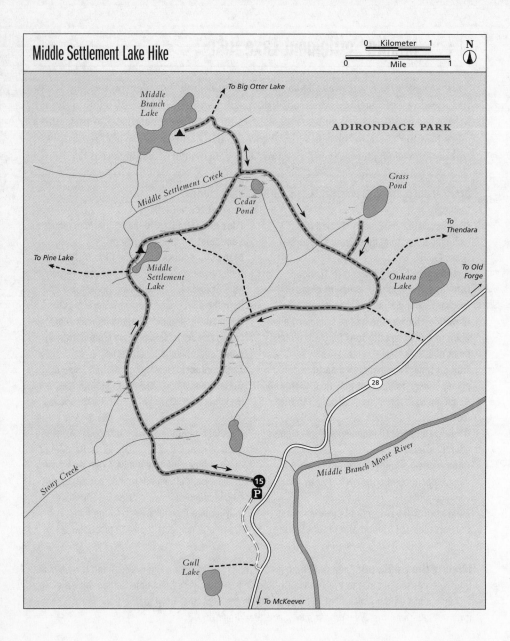

der, crossing small brooks and soggy bottoms of sphagnum moss. You must be attentive to footing and markers.

After a couple of miles, you'll descend to round the southwestern arm of Middle Settlement Lake, where cross-lake views can include a large beaver lodge, lily-pad clusters, evergreen points, islands, and the large open-water lake. Ruffed grouse, owl, deer, beaver, mink, toad, frog, and red eft contribute lively interludes.

WHAT'S IN A NAME?

Middle Settlement Lake takes its name from an early colony of John Brown. This John Brown, though, was not the famed abolitionist, but a land speculator in the Old Forge area. He attempted to subdivide his lands and attract farmers to the region, but the stern climate and poor soils thwarted his plans and led to the abandonment of his settlements. The wilderness's name, Ha-De-Ron-Dah, attempts to more accurately reflect the Iroquois term for "bark-eater," previously interpreted as "Adirondack." Adirondack (Ha-De-Ron-Dah) is the disparaging name the Iroquois gave to their Algonquin neighbors because they would eat the inside of the bark of the white pine during times of food scarcity.

Cross the inlet on either of two beaver dams within easy reach. Afterward stay low to the water before pulling away from shore and coming to a trail junction. Bear right, following yellow disks to the Middle Settlement lean-to. After crossing the outlet on rocks and boot-polished logs, you reach the shelter, atop a 10-foot-high outcrop overlooking the main body of Middle Settlement Lake. The lake's shimmery depths may suggest a swim.

The loop resumes north, rounding the wooded shore with the hummocky floor on a well-traveled path. Among the gargantuan boulders at the end of the lake, meet a blue trail and bear left, staying along the drainage. A soggy meadow passage precedes the stone-stepping crossing (or high-water wading) of the outlet of Cedar Pond. Ahead you will glimpse Cedar Pond, a mosaic of open water and soggy shrub islands. Spruce, maple, and birch compose the forest.

Where red disks take over as the loop markers, detour left on the yellow trail to add a visit to Middle Branch Lake. This detour shows marked climbs and pitches. Go about a mile and turn left to reach the shelter, which occupies a small point overlooking the long water body of Middle Branch Lake. During rainstorms you can pass time reading sagas penned in the lean-to's journal.

Back on the clockwise loop, the trail, sometimes marshy or rocky, rolls through open woods. Stones ease your crossing of the dark-ale water of the Grass Pond outlet. In another half mile, look for the yellow trail angling left to the pond. En route to Grass Pond, close-growing beech and striped maples may crowd the trail. You'll arrive at a camp flat between the spruce woods and meadow shore, but the pond requires a bushwhacking approach.

Back on the loop, a tranquil woods stroll unrolls before you. Where yellow markers again show the way, you travel on boardwalk through a wet bottomland near the state lands boundary. Keep to the yellow trail, now wide, flat, and easy, bypassing the trail to the popular Scusa Access and later one to Middle Settlement Lake. The route grows less broad and less refined. Nearing a beaver pond, turn left, cross atop the earthen dam, and again turn left to travel along the wooded edge of the floodplain meadow.

Before long, you will turn right onto an overgrown woods road; the tracked trail usually remains visible beneath the masking ferns. Although the isolation of this section engages, the hike requires greater attention to avoid straying off trail. Bottom areas can be soggy, even in August.

The overgrown roadbed then curves away from the Middle Settlement Creek floodplain. Where hardwoods prevail, rocks and leaves replace the fern wade. Now keep watch for the path on the right, where you'll veer off the woods road to quickly close the loop. From the loop junction, proceed straight toward Copper Lake Road, retracing your steps to the trailhead.

Miles and Directions

0.0 Start from the southern Middle Settlement Lake trailhead. Follow the arrow and yellow markers, around a metal gate and along the conservation easement across paper company land.

0.7 Meet narrow dirt Copper Lake Road; follow it left.

1.1 Reach a junction; turn right off Copper Lake Road onto an established footpath.

1.3 Reach the loop junction; head left. **Aside:** Before continuing, observe how and from where the return leg of the loop arrives. It may help when navigating the end of the trail.

2.7 Descend to round the southwestern arm of Middle Settlement Lake.

3.1 Reach a junction; bear right, still following yellow disks. **Note:** To the left leads to Lost and Pine Lakes.

3.5 Reach the Middle Settlement Lake lean-to.

3.8 Reach a junction; bear left, staying along the drainage. **Note:** Uphill to the right lies the blue trail to Highway 28 (a more-established access).

4.8 Reach a junction; detour left on the yellow trail to Middle Branch Lake before continuing the loop on the red trail straight ahead.

6.0 Follow the left spur to the shelter.

6.3 Reach the Middle Branch Lake shelter; backtrack to the loop at the 4.8-mile junction.

7.8 Resume the clockwise loop, now following red markers. **Bailout:** Backtrack to the trailhead, forgoing the remainder of the loop, for a 12.6-mile out-and-back hike.

9.1 Cross the Grass Pond outlet.

9.5 Detour left to Grass Pond.

10.0 Reach Grass Pond; backtrack to the loop.

10.5 Resume the clockwise loop, turning left. **Bailout:** Because the route ahead becomes trickier to follow, you may choose instead to backtrack the loop and return to the trailhead for a 17-mile out-and-back trek.

10.8 Reach a junction; follow the yellow trail forward to traverse a boardwalk.

11.0 Reach a junction; proceed forward on the yellow trail. **Note:** A left here finds Highway 28 and the popular Scusa Access.

11.9 Reach a junction; follow the yellow markers ahead. **Note:** The blue trail heading right leads to Middle Settlement Lake.

12.3 Cross a beaver dam; turn left to travel at the wooded edge of the floodplain meadow.

Boardwalk on the Brown Tract Trail, Ha-de-Ron-Da Wilderness, Adirondack Park

12.6   Turn right, following an overgrown woods road.

13.9   Veer right, returning to the loop junction. Continue straight for Copper Lake Road.

14.1   Turn left onto Copper Lake Road.

14.5   Turn right off Copper Lake Road, retracing the easement to the trailhead.

15.2   End back at the southern trailhead.

Hike Information

Local Information

Old Forge New York Tourist Information Center, Old Forge 13420; (315) 369–6983; www.oldforgeny.com

Local Events/Attractions

Just outside Old Forge, **McCauley Mountain Scenic Chairlift Rides** carry you to the mountaintop for scenic viewing of the surrounding lakes and peaks. The fee lift is open daily (except Wednesday) late June through Labor Day, and then weekends through Columbus Day. Contact (315) 369-3225; www.oldforgeny.com/mccauley.htm.

Moose River white-water rafting is another popular Old Forge draw, with easy trips on the Middle Moose River (May through September) and challenging Class V trips on the Lower Moose (April only). Visit Moose River Rafting Center, on

Highway 28, 4 miles south of Old Forge, or contact Whitewater Challengers, (800) 443-RAFT (7238); www.whitewaterchallengers.com.

Accommodations

Nicks Lake (DEC) Campground, off Highway 28 west of Old Forge, is open early May through Columbus Day and has 112 sites. Reservations: (800) 456-2267; www.reserveamerica.com

Organizations

Adirondack Mountain Club, 814 Goggins Road, Lake George 12845; (518) 668-4447 or (800) 395-8080; www.adk.org

16 West Canada Lakes Wilderness Hike

In Moose River Recreation Area in the west-central Adirondacks, this designated wilderness encompasses one of the last regional wilds to be opened to foot travel and human visitorship. This overnight outing or demanding all-day hike travels to the core of the West Canada Lakes Wilderness, passing through conifer-hardwood forest and meadow breaks to visit three pristine lakes: Falls Pond, Brooktrout, and West. From the trail, you can access the trans-Adirondack Northville–Placid Trail or visit such other celebrated features as Spruce Lake and Cedar Lakes.

Start: At the Brooktrout Lake trailhead
Distance: 18.2 miles out-and-back, including the Falls Pond detour
Approximate hiking time: 9 to 11.5 hours
Difficulty: Strenuous due to length
Elevation change: The trail has a 550-foot elevation change.
Trail surface: Earthen or grassy foot trail and retired logging roads, outcrop
Seasons: Best for hiking, Memorial Day weekend through fall
Other trail users: Hunters
Canine compatibility: Dogs permitted (leashing recommended)
Land status: Department of Environmental Conservation (DEC)

Nearest town: Inlet
Fees and permits: None, but drivers entering Moose River Recreation Area must register upon entering
Schedule: No time restrictions
Maps: Adirondack Mountain Club (ADK), Adirondack West-Central Region map (available at traditional and online bookstores or from the ADK online store: www.adk.org) or National Geographic, Adirondack Park Northville/Raquette Lake map (available at traditional and online bookstores)
Trail contacts: New York State DEC, Region 5, P.O. Box 1316, 701 South Main Street, Northville 12134; (518) 863-4545; www.dec.ny.gov

Finding the trailhead: From central Inlet go southeast on Highway 28 for 0.8 mile and turn south onto Limekiln Road for Moose River Recreation Area. Go 1.8 miles, turn left, and register for the recreation area. Continue east on the wide improved dirt road (15 miles per hour), following signs to Otter Brook. In 11.4 miles you'll cross the Otter Brook bridge and follow the signs to Brooktrout Lake (right). Find the trailhead on the left in 0.9 mile and parking for a dozen vehicles. *DeLorme: New York Atlas & Gazetteer:* Page 86 C3.

The Hike

The trail ascends steadily, overlooking a series of beaver ponds. Boughs of maple, spruce, birch, and beech interlace overhead; sarsaparilla, ferns, whorled aster, and brambles edge the lane.

Detour right on the yellow-marked trail to Falls Pond. You'll travel scenic fir-spruce woods, edge the outlet meadow, and cross the outcrop at the head of the meadow before reaching the lake outlet, a campsite, and an outcrop view. Falls Pond, a mountain beauty with an irregular shoreline, enchants with outcrop points and

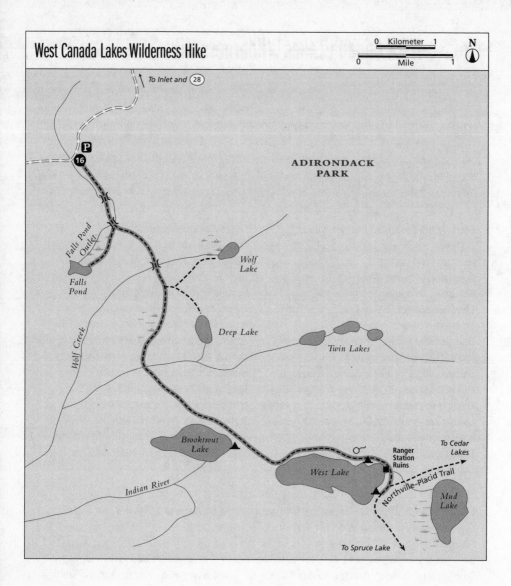

0   Kilometer   1

0   Mile   1

N

To Inlet and (28)

P

16

ADIRONDACK PARK

Falls Pond Outlet

Falls Pond

Wolf Creek

Wolf Lake

Deep Lake

Twin Lakes

Brooktrout Lake

West Lake

Ranger Station Ruins

To Cedar Lakes

Northville–Placid Trail

Indian River

Mud Lake

To Spruce Lake

islands, an evergreen rim, and enfolding leafy hillsides.

On the main trail, outcrops open up the trail corridor, while dense, low-growing spruce and fir squeeze it. By August's last days, the leaves show the onset of change, with orange, yellow, red, and maroon hues. The trail rolls to cross the bridge over the Wolf Lake outlet, coming to a junction. You may opt to explore the path on the left, which takes you to two additional lakes: Deep and Wolf, each within a mile of the trail. For this hike alone, though, continue forward.

The main trail passes over exposed bedrock (slippery when wet) and among young deciduous trees. A cairn points you onto the lower edge of the outcrop, which then leads to trail. Paired planks cross wet spots and meadow habitats. Blue gentian and sunlit nodding cotton grass adorn meadow swaths in late summer. At a beaver pond, you might spy the industrious furball.

Later you will lose all trace of the old road, as well as such niceties as the wetland foot planks, but more yellow disks show the way. Cross the Deep Lake outlet atop stones. Past a scenic cluster of mossy boulders and logs, keep left, traversing a spruce bog. Here the trail becomes muddied both literally and figuratively; beware of impostor paths. At a rise, hobblebush and young beech frisk passersby.

The trail then contours the wooded slope above Brooktrout Lake—a gleam in the basin. Because the wilderness trail is removed from the lakes, you must take advantage of all side trails to camp flats and lean-tos to admire the waters. At the Brooktrout Lake lean-to, side trails venture to the lake and a boulder-and-marsh shore. Although the legacy of acid rain still silences these remote lakes, their beauty is uncompromised.

Past the lean-to, bear left, rounding away from the lake. You'll cross over a rise to tour above the meadow basin at the upper extent of West Lake. At a trail sign near a split boulder, a spur leads to a lakeside camp, where views span the lake to Pillsbury

Ranger station ruins, West Canada Lakes Wilderness Area, Adirondack Park

Peak. The rolling trail now contours the forested slope above West Lake. Beyond piped spring water, you'll reach the first of two West Lake lean-tos. Spurs branch to the bouldery lakeshore.

Continue rounding the lake to the southeast, crossing rotting footboards in wet meadow. Where the trail returns to woods, beautiful carpets of oxalis complement the curvature of the trail. After crossing the outlet bridge and bypassing the historic dump from the former rangers' cabin, find a junction post in the meadow.

Here you meet the blue Northville–Placid Trail. A left leads to Cedar Lakes. Go right for the second West Lake lean-to, this hike's turnaround point. A cross and an old rock foundation sit near the junction. The cross commemorates the rangers' cabin that stood here but no longer conformed to "wilderness." The ruin is what's left of the fireplace from French Louie's cabin; it preceded the rangers' cabin.

The West Lake lean-to looks out at West Lake, its bouldery shore, a string of rocks concluding at a small rock island, and an attractive rolling wooded terrain. Return as you came, or check out some other lakes.

Miles and Directions

0.0 Start from the Brooktrout Lake trailhead; round the barrier to follow a retired logging road.

1.2 Cross a small logging bridge.

1.5 Reach a junction; detour right to Falls Pond.

2.0 Reach Falls Pond; return to the main trail.

2.5 Reach the main trail; turn right.

3.2 Cross the bridge over the Wolf Lake outlet. Ahead 200 yards, reach a junction and proceed forward. **Option:** The trail on the left leads to Deep and Wolf Lakes, reaching Deep Lake in 0.9 mile or Wolf Lake in 1 mile. Wetlands and beaver flooding can create a soggy trek to the latter.

5.5 Pass a scenic cluster of mossy boulders and logs; keep left, traversing a spruce bog.

6.5 Reach the Brooktrout Lake lean-to; hike past the lean-to and bear left away from the lake, following red and yellow disks.

8.9 Reach the first West Lake lean-to.

9.4 Meet Northville–Placid Trail; head right and then bear right at the next junction.

9.6 Reach the second West Lake lean-to; return to the trailhead.

18.2 End at the Brooktrout Lake trailhead.

Hike Information

Local Information

Old Forge New York Tourist Information Center, Old Forge; (315) 369-6983; www.oldforgeny.com

Local Events/Attractions

The **Old Forge Mountain Bike Trail System** between Old Forge and Eagle Bay in the Adirondack Forest Preserve incorporates 100 miles of interlocking mountain bike trails, fun rides for the entire family. Contact the Old Forge tourist information center.

Accommodations

Limekiln Lake (DEC) Campground, off Limekiln Road en route to the trailhead, is open mid-May through Columbus Day and has 271 sites. Reservations: (800) 456-2267; www.reserveamerica.com

Organizations

Adirondack Mountain Club, 814 Goggins Road, Lake George 12845; (518) 668-4447 or (800) 395-8080; www.adk.org

▶ Water

Even in frigid conditions, you need at least two quarts of water a day to function efficiently. Add heat and taxing terrain and you can bump that figure up to one gallon. That's simply a base to work from—your metabolism and your level of conditioning can raise or lower that amount. Unless you know your level, assume that you need one gallon of water a day. Now, where do you plan on getting the water?

The easiest solution is to bring water with you. Natural water sources can be loaded with intestinal disturbers, such as bacteria, viruses, and fertilizers. *Giardia lamblia,* the most common of these disturbers, is a protozoan parasite that lives part of its life cycle as a cyst in water sources. The parasite spreads when mammals defecate in water sources. Once ingested, *Giardia* can induce cramping, diarrhea, vomiting, and fatigue within two days to two weeks after ingestion. If you believe you've contracted giardiasis, see a doctor immediately, as it is treatable with prescription drugs.

17 Siamese Ponds Hike

This easy all-day or backpack hike travels a scenic low-elevation Central Adirondack forest, parallels the East Branch Sacandaga River, and visits a large wilderness pond. The hike follows the historic 1800s Bakers Mills–North River Stagecoach Route and travels a wild area suitable for beaver, bear, mink, otter, grouse, and other woodland creatures. Autumn brings rustling palettes of fire.

Start: At the Siamese Ponds Highway 8 trailhead
Distance: 12 miles out-and-back
Approximate hiking time: 6 to 8 hours
Difficulty: Easy
Elevation change: This trail has a 500-foot elevation change. From a trailhead elevation of 1,800 feet, the trail ascends 200 feet before descending to a river elevation of 1,600 feet and ultimately climbing to Siamese Ponds at 2,118 feet.
Trail surface: Earthen path, stage route, old road
Seasons: Best for hiking, spring through fall
Other trail users: Hunters
Canine compatibility: Dogs permitted

Land status: Department of Environmental Conservation (DEC)
Nearest town: Wells
Fees and permits: No fees or permits required
Schedule: No time restrictions
Maps: Adirondack Mountain Club (ADK), Adirondack Central Region map (available at traditional and online bookstores or from the ADK online store: www.adk.org) or National Geographic, Adirondack Park Northville/ Raquette Lake map (available at traditional and online bookstores)
Trail contacts: New York State DEC, Region 5, P.O. Box 220, 232 Golf Course Road, Warrensburg 12885; (518) 623-1200; www.dec.ny.gov

Finding the trailhead: From Bakers Mills (south of Wevertown), go 3.8 miles south on Highway 8; a small DEC sign marks the trail's large gravel parking lot on the west side of the highway. *DeLorme: New York Atlas & Gazetteer:* Page 88 D1.

The Hike

Ideal for a family backpack or your very first backpack outing, this trail journeys west into Siamese Ponds Wilderness, initially ascending on a former roadbed through an arbor of young birch, aspen, and maple. The blue-disk trail markers are few in number, but little needed. In places rocks riddle the bed. Ferns, hobblebush, and sarsaparilla contribute to the woodland understory; jewelweed, the moist drainages.

The grade eases as the trail parallels a small drainage upstream, crossing over the low shoulder of Eleventh Mountain. From here the historic stagecoach route carries your boots, and the trail descends. The forest's spatial order and changing mix of trees lend visual diversity. After a mile, firs and spruce fill out the complex, and black cherry trees make an appearance. In meadow clearings, you may discover joe-pye weed, aster, and dogwood.

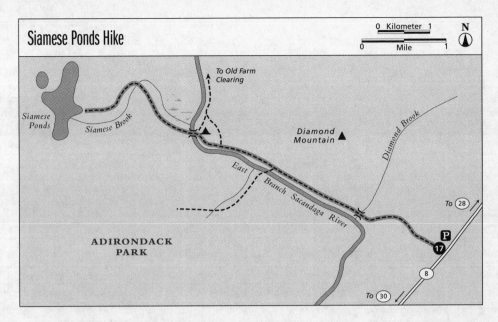

Siamese Ponds Hike

0 Kilometer 1

0 Mile 1

N

Siamese Ponds

Siamese Brook

To Old Farm Clearing

Diamond Mountain

Diamond Brook

East Branch Sacandaga River

To 28

P

17

8

ADIRONDACK PARK

To 30

The stage route levels off along the riparian corridor of the East Branch Sacandaga River. At the Diamond Brook bridge crossing, budding biologists often kneel on the bank in search of tiny fry, crayfish, and mud puppies. Goldenrod, brambles, and low alders contribute to the riparian meadow bordering the trail. At the plank bridge ahead, look for Diamond Mountain to the right. Woodland travel resumes within 100 feet of the river.

The trail briefly tags the herb-and-forb riverbank for an open look at the shallow 50-foot-wide river marked by occasional riffles, rocks, and bedrock. Its mood varies widely from times of high water to times of low water. The mild-grade earthen trail frees eyes to enjoy the setting, perhaps even to spy a bear slogging across the river—something we were fortunate enough to do.

After the trail draws farther from the river, it becomes more rolling. Abandoned apple trees and a younger, more open woods hint at a former farm. Afterward, the trail drifts back toward the river.

At the fork, bear left for Siamese Ponds. You'll follow a former road grade as it dips to a drainage crossing and returns to the wooded riverbench for occasional views. When you reach the suspension bridge over the East Branch Sacandaga, cross to continue toward the ponds. On the east bank (before you cross), a lopsided lean-to overlooks the water. This rain-tight lodging comes complete with table, fireplace, and functional privy. A connecting spur to the Old Farm Trail passes in front of the lean-to; avoid taking it.

The suspension bridge affords fine up- and downstream views of the East Branch Sacandaga River. As you step off the bridge, continue straight ahead. Side spurs branch to camp flats and shore. The trail rolls and then dips, coming to a small runoff meadow where a pair of hewn logs aid crossing. A rock-riddled ascent follows, but easy travel

East Branch Sacandaga River on the Siamese Ponds Trail, Siamese Ponds Wilderness, Adirondack Park

resumes with an earthen bed and nothing more strenuous than a moderate grade. Fir, spruce, birch, hemlock, and striped and sugar maples shade the way, with a fickle showing of ground cover.

After crossing Siamese Brook, you assume a more continuous rocky ascent. Where a few boulders dot the slope, the trees can exceed 18 inches in diameter and the trail becomes more rolling. Woodpecker, grouse, or red eft may divert your eyes. The trail then passes campsites, descending to Siamese Ponds.

Shaped like an amoeba, the primary pond has a bouldery and sandy beach at its point of access. Humped-back conifer-deciduous hills, including Hayden Mountain to the north, overlook the pond. Aquatic vegetation spots its shallow edge. To round the shore for new perspectives or to reach Upper Siamese Pond requires bushwhacking. When ready, you'll return as you came.

Miles and Directions

0.0 Start from the Siamese Ponds Highway 8 trailhead; head west.

0.4 Cross the shoulder of Eleventh Mountain.

1.5 Cross Diamond Brook bridge.

3.5	Reach a fork; bear left on a former road grade for Siamese Ponds. **Note:** The old stage-coach route continues to the right toward the Old Farm trailhead.
3.9	Cross the East Branch Sacandaga River suspension bridge.
4.9	Cross Siamese Brook atop rocks.
6.0	Reach Siamese Ponds; return to the trailhead.
12.0	End back at the Highway 8 trailhead.

Hike Information

Local Information

Adirondacks Speculator Region Chamber of Commerce (on Highway 30 and Highway 8), P.O. Box 184, Speculator 12164; (518) 548-4521; www.speculator chamber.com

Local Events/Attractions

The **Speculator Region** (southwest of Siamese Ponds) is noted for its fishing. Lakes, ponds, and rivers produce catches of smallmouth bass, trout, salmon, and walleye. Contact the chamber for details and for outlets where fishing licenses are sold.

Organizations

Adirondack Mountain Club, 814 Goggins Road, Lake George 12845; (518) 668-4447 or (800) 395-8080; www.adk.org

18 Tongue Mountain Range Loop

Northeast of Bolton Landing, this demanding loop tags five summits of the peninsular Tongue Mountain Range for unsurpassed looks at the Lake George countryside. It then dips to lake level and visits Point of Tongue before returning along Northwest Bay. Although the trail's signature offering is its spectacular lake, island, and ridge views, diverse woods, colorful fall foliage, marsh, cliffs, vernal pools, and wildlife sightings will further reward your raising a sweat.

Start: At the Clay Meadow trailhead
Distance: 14-mile lasso-shaped hike
Approximate hiking time: 8 to 10 hours
Difficulty: Strenuous due to terrain and elevation gains and losses
Elevation change: This peak-tagging trail has a 1,500-foot elevation change, with the low point at Montcalm Point (Point of Tongue), and the high point at the Fifth Peak lean-to (1,813 feet).
Trail surface: Woods road, rocky and earthen path
Seasons: Best for hiking, spring through fall
Other trail users: Hunters
Canine compatibility: Dogs permitted
Land status: Department of Environmental Conservation (DEC)
Nearest town: Bolton Landing
Fees and permits: No fees or permits required

Schedule: No time restrictions
Maps: Adirondack Mountain Club (ADK), Adirondack Eastern Region map (available at traditional and online bookstores or from the ADK online store: www.adk.org) or National Geographic, Adirondack Park Lake George/Great Sacandaga map (available at traditional and online bookstores)
Trail contacts: New York State DEC, Region 5, P.O. Box 220, 232 Golf Course Road, Warrensburg 12885; (518) 623-1200; www.dec.ny.gov
Special considerations: The trail has steep pitches that may require hand assists. Markers may be few and faint in places, so keep a careful watch for them. Carry adequate drinking water, and beware: Rattlesnakes live in this rugged terrain.

Finding the trailhead: From Interstate 87 take exit 24 and head east toward Bolton Landing. In 5 miles turn north on Highway 9N and go 4.4 miles to find head-in parking on the east side of the highway at the old quarry pond. You'll find the Clay Meadow trailhead just south of the parking lot; the trail heads east. *DeLorme: New York Atlas & Gazetteer:* Page 89 C5.

The Hike

You travel a time-softened woods road through a conifer plantation and across a wetland boardwalk to reach the loop junction. Common wetland sightings include white-tailed deer, frogs, and herons. For the clockwise loop, bear left toward Fifth Peak lean-to on a steadily ascending woods road, sometimes rocky and rootbound.

In 1995 a severe windstorm gleaned some of the bigger framing hemlock, beech, and maple. Where the trail grows steeper, look for it to switchback to the left, where it rounds below mossy outcrop cliffs on a scenic hemlock-birch plateau.

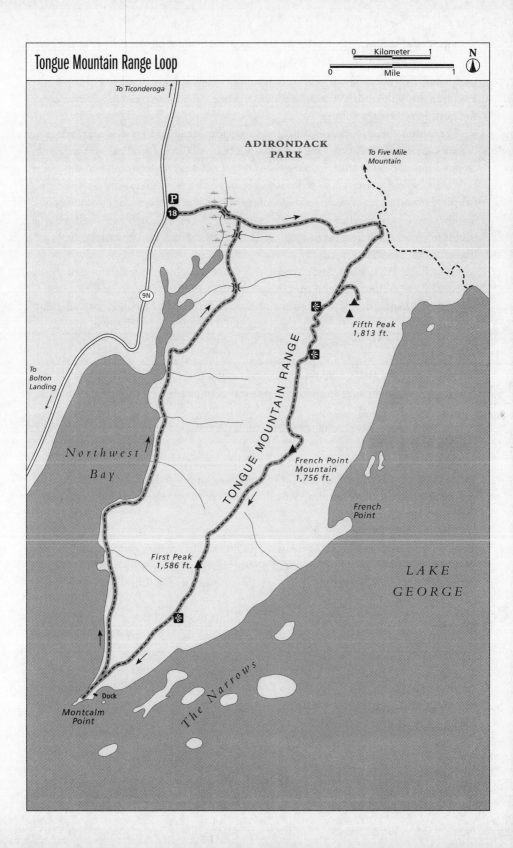

Tongue Mountain Range Loop

0 Kilometer 1

0 Mile 1

N

To Ticonderoga

ADIRONDACK PARK

To Five Mile Mountain

P 18

9N

To Bolton Landing

Fifth Peak 1,813 ft.

TONGUE MOUNTAIN RANGE

Northwest Bay

French Point Mountain 1,756 ft.

French Point

First Peak 1,586 ft.

LAKE GEORGE

The Narrows

Dock

Montcalm Point

The ascent resumes to the saddle junction. Turn right for the loop, continuing toward the Fifth Peak lean-to, and stay right for a pleasant rolling hike to the shelter junction. A half-mile out-and-back detour with yellow markers leads left to the Fifth Peak lean-to, with its dry overnight wayside, privy, and an open outcrop delivering a southern Lake George vantage.

The primary trail journeys south along a narrow, less-used foot trail, descending a hemlock-pine slope to reach a moist deciduous bottom. On Fourth Peak you top outcrops within an old fire zone, hinted at by silver snags. Views stretch south and west.

At the base of an outcrop, a trail marker points left. Briefly contour the slope then sharply descend right, easing over rocks, coming to a notch. Again climb from maple-hemlock woods to a piney crest, with overlooks of Lake George and the forested islands from South Sacrament to Floating Battery Island and with cross-lake views of Black and Erebus Mountains.

Atop Third Peak, you'll find a steep pitch before climbing to another open view. The trail then pitches, rolls, and streaks up French Point Mountain for the best views of the hike. Open outcrop vantages line up. Looks encompass French Point (a peninsula extending into Lake George), the many treed islands of The Narrows, the chain of islands stretching north, and the ridges and mountains rolling east.

Round a small cairn and descend past a vernal pool to an outcrop view of Northwest Bay and First Peak—the final summit conquest separated by a 400-foot elevation drop and a matching gain. The trail shows a similar pitch-and-climb character, passing through an oak and grass habitat. Where the path again overlooks the steep eastern flank, views laud the narrow lake, the dark humped-back ridges, and the jigsaw puzzle of islands.

Atop First Peak awaits a 180-degree Lake George vista. The trail now hugs the east side of the ridge, passing among oak, hickory, and ash. Later two small bumps add views toward Bolton Landing. Ahead the trail opens up, descending and offering views of Montcalm Point.

After the trail curves west into hemlock-deciduous woods, you come to a junction. Here the loop bears right. A detour left follows blue markers to Montcalm Point (Point of Tongue). It travels the forested peninsula to the point, which extends views to Lake George and Northwest Bay, as well as an outcrop that calls to swimmers and sunbathers.

Resume the loop north, passing through moist woodland along Northwest Bay, heading toward Clay Meadow. The trail rolls to and from shore, rounding shallow coves and cutting across points. You will cross an ash swale (formerly a beaver pond) before the trail drifts away into mixed woods. A spur branches to a viewpoint of the marshy head of Northwest Bay. Ahead find passing looks at the marsh grass, lily pads, and stands of red maple and cedar.

At a footbridge, the trail heads inland for a steady half-mile ascent. You'll return once more to the marsh's edge before crossing another footbridge to close the loop. Backtrack to the trailhead.

Miles and Directions

0.0 Start from the Clay Meadow trailhead; follow blue disks along a woods road.

0.4 Reach the loop junction; bear left, following red disks uphill.

1.3 Look for the trail to switchback left.

1.9 Reach the saddle junction; turn right and keep right, heading toward the Fifth Peak lean-to.

2.4 Reach the Shelter junction; turn left.

2.6 Reach the Fifth Peak lean-to and vantage; return to the loop and turn left.

3.5 Look at the base of an outcrop for the trail marker, pointing you left.

3.9 Reach Third Peak.

4.9 Reach French Point Mountain.

6.0 Reach First Peak.

7.6 Follow the trail as it curves west into hemlock-deciduous woods.

8.0 Reach a junction. Detour left to Montcalm Point (Point of Tongue) before resuming the loop, which heads right here.

8.4 Reach Montcalm Point; return to the loop and bear left.

10.4 Cross an ash swale (formerly a beaver pond).

11.8 Pass a spur to the marshy upper bay.

12.0 Cross a drainage footbridge; ascend inland on trail.

13.6 Close the loop; backtrack left to the trailhead.

14.0 End at the Clay Meadow trailhead.

Hike Information

Local Information
Warren County Tourism Department, 1340 Highway 9, Municipal Center, Lake George 12845; (800) 95-VISIT, ext. 143; www.visitlakegeorge.com

Local Events/Attractions
Lake George is noted for its fishing and boating. Charter cruises and steamboat tours are popular, offering leisurely introductions to the lake. Contact the county tourism department for names of operators.

Accommodations
Rogers Rock (DEC) Campground, about 20 miles north on Highway 9N, is open early May through Columbus Day and has 332 sites. Reservations: (800) 456-2267; www.reserveamerica.com

Organizations
Adirondack Mountain Club, 814 Goggins Road, Lake George 12845; (518) 668-4447 or (800) 395-8080; www.adk.org

19 Jockeybush Lake Trail

This easy climb through rich mixed forest follows the outlet drainage to Jockeybush Lake, attractive, cold, and deep. Although the hike is short and the lake is small, the offering is big with its fishing, woods flora, and calm. This trail is ideal to cap off the day or to tuck into a busy travel schedule.

Start: At the Jockeybush Lake trailhead

Distance: 2.2 miles out-and-back

Approximate hiking time: 1.5 to 2 hours

Difficulty: Easy

Elevation change: The trail has a 250-foot elevation change.

Trail surface: Earthen path, sometimes muddy or rocky

Seasons: Best for hiking, spring through fall

Other trail users: Hunters, snowmobilers, snowshoers, cross-country skiers

Canine compatibility: Dogs permitted (leashing recommended)

Land status: Department of Environmental Conservation (DEC)

Nearest town: Gloversville

Fees and permits: No fees or permits required

Schedule: No time restrictions

Maps: Adirondack Mountain Club (ADK), Adirondack Southern Region map (available at traditional and online bookstores or from the ADK online store: www.adk.org) or National Geographic, Adirondack Park Northville/Raquette Lake map (available at traditional and online bookstores)

Trail contacts: New York State DEC, Region 5, P.O. Box 1316, 701 South Main Street, Northville 12134; (518) 863-4545; www.dec.ny.gov

Special considerations: Expect some soggy reaches. Because the lake access is limited, this trail is best hiked when there are few or no other vehicles at the trailhead.

Finding the trailhead: From the junction of Highway 29A and Highway 10 in the village of Caroga Lake, go north on Highway 10 for 14.6 miles, passing through the village of Canada Lake and the small hamlet of Arietta. Find the marked trailhead and paved parking area on the left side of Highway 10, across from a lily pond. A register is on the left at the hike's start. *DeLorme: New York Atlas & Gazetteer*: Page 78 B4.

The Hike

You'll head west, ascending into woods and following the orange snowmobile markers. The mixed-age, multistory forest of white pine, hemlock, birch, black cherry, maple, and beech, along with hobblebush and ferns, weaves an enchanting study. Sunlight filters through the branches, and a breeze often lilts through the woods. Soon a pair of grand hemlocks stand sentinel.

At a mud hole crossing, a disorganized scatter of logs left over from an old corduroy helps keep your feet dry. The trail now travels the north shore above the outlet brook. Early in the hiking season, side drainages also can complicate travel. Most times, though, the foot trail presents a pleasant, meandering tour.

Next you'll make a stone-stepping crossing over the 10-foot-wide, clear-flowing

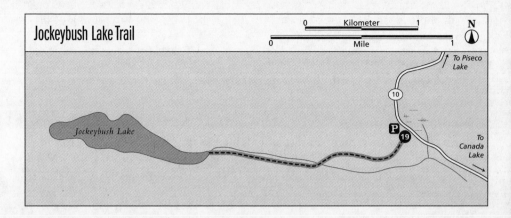

Jockeybush Lake Trail

outlet brook. High water, though, could require you to wade. A mossy cascade accentuates the outlet where the brook washes over outcrop. Where the trail grows rockier with muddy pockets, evasive paths can disguise the true trail. In this stretch, just keep the outlet brook to your right. Before long, the trail and brook become more closely paired, and hemlocks wane from the south-bank forest.

As you ascend the ridge to the lake basin, you again find a good earthen path. Arriving at the lake, you cross the beaver dam at the outlet, now crowded with silver logs, to reach a shoreline outcrop. It presents an open view spanning the length of this long, deep lake and takes in the shrub banks and enfolding conifer-deciduous rims. Regularly stocked with fish, Jockeybush Lake offers anglers a challenge, if not always success. Local anglers typically carry in a fishing tube or small raft to escape the shrubby entanglements of shore.

A campsite sits above the outcrop. To round the shore to the main body of the lake requires some determination and a bit of bushwhacking through thick spruce and hobblebush. Frogs and toads dwell lakeside, while insect hatches lift from the lake surface. You'll likely choose to linger awhile before surrendering the lake view. Once ready, the return is back the way you came.

Miles and Directions

0.0   Start from the Jockeybush Lake trailhead; ascend west.

0.4   Cross the outlet brook.

1.1   Reach Jockeybush Lake; return by the same route.

2.2   End at the Jockeybush Lake trailhead.

Hike Information

Local Information

Hamilton County Department of Economic Development and Tourism,

South Shore Road, P.O. Box 57, Lake Pleasant 12108; (518) 548-3076 or (800) 648-5239; www.hamiltoncounty.com

Local Events/Attractions

Piseco Lake, to the north of Jockeybush Lake, is a popular center for fishing and camping.

Accommodations

Poplar Point, Little Sand Point, and Point Comfort (DEC) Campgrounds on the north side of Piseco Lake, 8 miles north on Highway 10, are open early May through Columbus Day and have a total of 175 sites. Reservations: (800) 456-2267; www.reserveamerica.com

Organizations

Adirondack Mountain Club, 814 Goggins Road, Lake George 12845; (518) 668-4447 or (800) 395-8080; www.adk.org

INCREDIBLE ADIRONDAK PARK

Adirondack Park is the outcome of one of the oldest conservation efforts in the nation. Verplanck Colvin's early survey work and reports to the legislature on the Adirondacks laid the groundwork for this wild area to receive permanent protection. In 1885 the New York State legislature passed the act that created both the Adirondack and Catskill Forest Preserves. It declared that the state-owned lands in eight Adirondack and three Catskill counties should "be forever kept as wild forest lands." Then, in 1892 legislators stretched the boundaries of these special places to include neighboring private lands, forming Adirondack and Catskill Parks. The forward-thinking conservation movement culminated in 1895, when the "Forever Wild" Amendment was written into the New York State Constitution, bolstering up and sealing the protection.

Today, at six million acres, Adirondack Park is the largest intact publicly protected land in the continental United States, outside of Alaska. To grasp its size, Adirondack Park exceeds the combined land areas of the big boys: Yellowstone, Yosemite, Everglades, and Grand Canyon National Parks. Although the protective legislation for the Adirondacks has faced challenges over the past one hundred years, it has endured. Besides pristine forests, Adirondack Park enfolds more than 8,000 square miles of mountains, including forty high peaks topping the 4,000-foot elevation; more than 2,000 lakes and ponds; and more than 1,500 miles of river. Taking you to and through this bonanza, more than 2,000 miles of hiking trails web Adirondack Park.

Honorable Mentions

The Adirondacks

C Grass River Wild Forest Hike

About 15 miles south of Canton, Grass River Wild Forest offers a 2,900-foot-long all-ability trail leading to the nearly 100-foot plunge of Lampson Falls and gathering views of rapids, deep pools, and cascades. Mixed forest, meadow shores, wildlife, and solitude help the river wash away stress. For a longer exploration, you can take a 3-mile out-and-back hike following the well-tracked paths downstream along the east shore of the river from the falls to a former bridge site, where an island still divides the Grass River flow (1.5 miles). From there, a more informal trail continues north (downstream) along the east bank. Future plans call to develop the river trail all the way from Lampson Falls north to Harper's Falls on the North Branch Grass River.

From Cranberry Lake Village, go west on Highway 3 for 19.9 miles. There turn north toward DeGrasse on County Road 27 (DeGrasse Fine Road). Bear right in 0.8 mile; go another 7.6 miles and turn right at a T junction in DeGrasse, remaining on CR 27. Go 4.3 miles from DeGrasse to find the DEC sign for Grass River Wild Forest on the left. *DeLorme: New York Atlas & Gazetteer:* Page 93 A7. Contact New York State Department of Environmental Conservation (DEC), Region 6, 317 Washington Street, Watertown 13601; (315) 785-2261; www.dec.ny.gov.

D Indian Pass-Lake Colden Loop

In the MacIntyre Mountain Range of Adirondack Park, this grueling boulder-and-mud obstacle course passes through typical Adirondack splendor: mixed forests, shining waters, meadows, and great views. Beware, though—the loop includes the notoriously difficult Cold Brook Pass, and the missing trail markers sometimes leave you on your own. But sterling views of Wallface Cliff and the Adirondack High Peaks, chill-blue lakes, and crystalline brooks counter the physical and mental challenge and, sometimes, torment of the trail.

So muster up some steely determination, and gather maps and your best back-country travel skills and aids, if you plan to hit this 15.9-mile loop. Starting at the Upper Works trailhead, the loop swings clockwise past Henderson Lake, along Indian Pass Brook past Wallface Peak, and then up and over the MacIntyre Mountains at Cold Brook Pass. The route then curls back, visiting Colden Lake, Flowed Ponds, and Calamity Brook. The loop is best hiked in summer and fall. Avoid during high water because of the boulder-hopping passage along and across Indian Pass Brook and the many side brook crossings. Even under the best conditions, this stretch threatens a cracked tailbone if you lose your footing. For a map, use the Adirondack Mountain Club, High Peaks Region map and/or the National Geographic, Adirondack Park Lake Placid/High Peaks map.

From the Highway 30–Highway 28N junction in Long Lake, go east on Highway 28N for 18 miles. There turn left on County Road 2 (seasonally maintained), bearing left at the intersection in 0.4 mile. In another 0.8 mile turn left on County Road 25 toward Tahawus, following the road to where it dead-ends at the Upper Works trailhead (another 9.5 miles). Trailhead parking and the trail's start and end are all state easements on private land. *DeLorme: New York Atlas & Gazetteer.* Page 96 D1. Contact New York State Department of Environmental Conservation, Region 5, P.O. Box 296, 1115 Highway 86, Ray Brook 12977; (518) 897-1200; www.dec.ny.gov.

E Camp Santanoni Trail

In the Newcomb Area, this trail journeys 5 miles (10 miles out-and-back) along carriage road to a classic Adirondack Great Camp, a National Historic Landmark. In the late nineteenth and early twentieth centuries, these camps offered luxury vacation getaways to the elite of the city. Camp Santanoni belonged to the Pruyn family of Albany. It included a working farm that provided meat, fruit, and dairy for the vacationers and the large, woodsy lakeside mansion on Newcomb Lake.

The main lodge dates to 1893, designed by noted architect Robert H. Robertson. A common roof and extensive porches adjoin the sleeping and common living areas of this large, dark log complex. Stone fireplaces and rustic limb-fashioned doors

Santanoni Farm, Lake George Wild Forest, Adirondack Forest Preserve

add to its charm. The Great Camp came into the state's hands in 1972. Much of it is undisturbed, with restoration and preservation ongoing to keep this emblem of the past for generations to come. The carriageway trail extends an enjoyable and comfortable woods stroll to the camp. The leafy boughs of mixed hardwoods decorate the roadside and weave a picturesque cathedral. In summer, a horse carriage (a private tour) may share the way, harkening back to the era of the Great Camp.

The trail's marked turnoff is north off Highway 28N at the west end of Newcomb, east of the Newcomb Visitor Interpretive Center (VIC). The Department of Environmental Conservation (DEC) trailhead and parking are just up the road near the camp's Gateway Arch. *DeLorme: New York Atlas & Gazetteer*: Page 87 A7. You can obtain brochures and trail information at the Newcomb VIC or contact New York State DEC, Region 5, P.O. Box 296, 1115 Highway 86, Ray Brook 12977; (518) 897-1200; www.dec.ny.gov.

F Goodnow Mountain Trail

Also in the Newcomb Area, this self-guided hiking trail in the Huntington Wildlife Forest, privately owned by the College of Environmental Science and Forestry (ESF) in Syracuse, offers one of the most manageable and popular climbs in the Adirondacks. Beech, birch, and maple, along with a few hemlocks and white pines, shape the woodland setting. The trail leads to the nine-story restored 1922 lookout tower and partially open summit that extend grand forest, basin, and High Peaks–Hudson River views. You can enjoy Adirondack wilds as far as the eye can see, but use the tower at your own risk, and beware of high winds. Historic structures from the Archer and Anna Huntington estate: foundations, a well, and an old horse barn add to discovery. The 3.8-mile out-and-back hike has a moderate gradient. Dogs must be leashed and you must obey all ESF rules. Arrows and interpretive posts keyed to the ESF trail brochure keep you on track.

Locate the marked trail and its parking south off Highway 28N, 1.5 miles west of the Newcomb Visitor Interpretive Center and about 12 miles east of Long Lake. *DeLorme: New York Atlas & Gazetteer*: Page 87 A7. Contact the State University of New York (SUNY) College of Environmental Science and Forestry, 1 Forestry Drive, Syracuse 13210; (315) 470-6644 or (315) 470-6500; www.esf.edu.

G Whetstone Gulf State Park

South of Lowville, Whetstone Creek cuts a 380-foot-deep, 3-mile-long gash into this 2,100-acre park on the eastern edge of the Tug Hill Plateau. The park's North and South Trails shape a 6-mile rim loop, overlooking the gulf. Picturesque Whetstone Creek, dramatic sandstone-shale cliffs, fossils, a falls, and wildflowers nudge you forward. You pass through either a pine woods intermixed with oak, maple, beech, and birch or a pine plantation. Whetstone Creek makes a hairpin turn in a sheer cliff bowl. In a squeezed gorge at the head of the gulf, the creek tumbles furiously in serial cascades that grade from 2 feet high at the top to 40 feet high at the bottom. You must be off the trail by 6:00 p.m., and no one may start a hike after 3:00 p.m. Leashed dogs are allowed, but owners must present proof of each animal's rabies shot.

From central Lowville, go south on Highway 26 for 6.1 miles and turn right (northwest) onto West Road (County Road 29). Go 0.2 mile and turn left, entering the state park. Find the trailhead near the beach house/swimming area. *DeLorme: New York Atlas & Gazetteer:* Page 84 C4. Contact Whetstone Gulf State Park, RD 2, Box 69, Lowville 13367; (315) 376-6630; http://nysparks.state.ny.us/parks.

H Gleasmans Falls Trail

East of Lowville, you will find a relaxing stroll through magnificent woods and meadow clearings to an outcrop overlooking this picturesque stepped falls on the Independence River. The 6.5-mile out-and-back trail journeys past the stone ruins of a sawmill and a beaver pond and welcomes nature study. At the first rocky access to the Independence River, the river pulses through a gorge shaped by outcrops, cliffs, and boulders—an exciting union of cascades, deep pools, dark water, and gneiss (metamorphic rock). Pockets of ferns adorn the gorge. The view at the end of the trail overlooks the upper cascade of Gleasmans Falls, which shows the greatest drop of 12 feet. Overall, the waterfall plunges 50 to 60 feet over a 0.2-mile distance. Flat stretches interrupt the half-dozen stepped cascades.

From Highway 12/Highway 26 in Lowville, turn east on River Street, which becomes Number Four Road (County Road 26), upon leaving town. In 4.1 miles turn left, staying on Number Four Road for another 4.8 miles. Turn right onto Erie Canal Road, go 2.5 miles, and turn left onto McPhilmy Road, a single-lane dirt road. In 0.2 mile turn left onto Beach Mill Road, a narrower dirt road with limited shoulder for turnouts; reduce speed. Where this road forks in 0.9 mile, stay left and go another 2 miles to reach the trailhead at road's end. *DeLorme: New York Atlas & Gazetteer:* Page 85 B5. Contact New York State Department of Environmental Conservation, Region 6, 317 Washington Street, Watertown 13601; (315) 785-2261; www.dec.ny.gov.

I Peaked Mountain Trail

In Siamese Ponds Wilderness, this split-personality trail joins an easy hike to Peaked Mountain Pond with a rugged summit ascent of Peaked Mountain. The final 0.3 mile to the summit laughs at gravity, uniting boot-skidding, steep dirt surfaces and severe bare-rock inclines—all the more tricky on descent. For anyone uninitiated with the rugged nature of the Adirondacks, this summit approach shouts a loud, clear "howdy!" Exposed summit outcrops among the low-growing spruce unfold a 270-degree view; obtaining northern views requires more effort. Best views sweep the immediate neighborhood with Peaked Mountain Pond, the meadows, Big and Little Thirteenth Lakes, and Slide and Hour Pond Mountains. Far-reaching views round up the Adirondack High Peaks and Vermont Green Mountains. Ravens offer noisy commentary while vultures drift on thermals. Lake, brook, pond, forest, and meadow habitats enfold the trail, which travels 6 miles out and back. Best time to hike the trail is summer and fall; wet weather increases the summit challenge.

At the hamlet of North River on Highway 28 (12 miles east of Indian Lake), turn south on Thirteenth Lake Road for Siamese Ponds Wilderness/Thirteenth Lake. Go 3.3 miles and turn right onto improved-dirt Beach Road to reach the wilderness entry and trailhead parking in another 0.5 mile. *DeLorme: New York Atlas & Gazetteer.* Page 88 C1. Contact New York State Department of Environmental Conservation, Region 5, P.O. Box 220, 232 Golf Course Road, Warrensburg 12885; (518) 623-1200; www.dec.ny.gov.

J Black Mountain Loop

This 7-mile lasso-shaped trail tops Black Mountain, the tallest mountain above Lake George, for a superb panorama of the lake region, with its open water, islands, and bumpy ridges; eastern looks strain to Vermont. Counterclockwise, the hike pairs a fairly steep assault on the mountain with a tempered, switchbacking descent. Mountaintop views unite Lake George; Elephant and Sugarloaf Mountains; Main, Harbor, and Vicars Islands; Five Mile Mountain; and the northern Tongue Mountain Range. You'll find superb viewing from the outcrop nose at the abandoned fire tower. The hike's descent builds on these views. Keep alert for where this trail loops back east at the base of the mountain. Rangers report this is a trouble spot for many hikers.

Ponds and beaver marshes put a stamp on the tour. At the base of the mountain, you'll travel the north shore of Black Mountain Pond, an open water with a broad meadow shore of leatherleaf and other marsh shrubs. Fish tap the surface, leaving ever-widening rings. Next up is Round Pond, which resembles the first pond but with a broader marsh shore and small silvered snags. Lapland Pond completes the roll call. Meadow, beaver marsh, and woods carry the hike home.

From the junction of Highway 74 and Highway 22 at Ticonderoga, go 17 miles south on Highway 22, turning west on County Road 6 for Huletts Landing. In 2.5 miles turn south on Pike Brook Road, finding the gravel parking lot for the trailhead on the right in 0.8 mile. *DeLorme: New York Atlas & Gazetteer.* Page 89 D6. Contact New York State Department of Environmental Conservation, Region 5, P.O. Box 220, 232 Golf Course Road, Warrensburg 12885; (518) 623-1200; www.dec.ny.gov.

Niagara Frontier

At the northwestern extreme of New York State, the Niagara Frontier claims an inspired location between two Great Lakes: Erie to the west and Ontario to the north. The Alleghenies nudge from the south while the Finger Lakes Region shapes the frontier's eastern border. Two famous rivers punctuated by raging falls, the Niagara and the Genesee, sign the landscape with a flourish. The Seneca Indians who dwelt here were known as the "Keepers of the Western Door."

The isolation and protection afforded by the Great Lakes and the Niagara River shaped this region's history. Archives reveal a restless history of contention, expansion, and escape. Native peoples battled over this land long before white settlement.

Tour boat, Erie Canal Heritage Trail, Lockport

Contentions continued with the arrival of the French, the British, and the Americans. The French and Indian Wars of the 1750s and the War of 1812 were particularly heated here. The Erie Canal linking the Atlantic Ocean to the Great Lakes pushed the western frontier beyond this region's borders, bringing a booming commerce and an end to isolation. In the years leading up to the Civil War, the Underground Railroad, firmly established in the Niagara Frontier, helped fleeing slaves as they tackled the final leg north to Canada.

Buffalo and Rochester are the major cities, and agriculture, industry, and tourism are the big callings for this area. Father Hennepin, a French Recollect priest who was among the first to explore the area, popularized Niagara Falls in his 1683 published travel account, and the curiosity and wonder associated with Niagara Falls have never ceased. Less flashy landscapes of lowland forest, plain, and swamp hold their own appeal and discovery. The deep incision of the Genesee River Gorge, centerpiece to Letchworth State Park, is an undeniable star. Glacial activity gouged out this attraction.

As far as weather is concerned, with two Great Lakes for neighbors, this region is no stranger to lake-effect winds or winter snowstorms. Hiking is a three-season sport.

20 Erie Canal Heritage Trail

Between Lockport and Rochester, the retired towpath of the Erie Canal, a national recreation trail, traces the past and provides an attractive, carefree avenue for hiking, cycling, jogging, and exercise walking. Working features of the historic canal, canalside museums, lowland forest, rural scenes, greenway parks, and the historic communities that emerged and burgeoned with the canal bring to life the era's exciting story.

Start: At the Lockport trailhead
Distance: 55 miles point-to-point between Lockport and Henpeck Park
Approximate hiking time: Dependent on distance traveled, anywhere from 1 hour to 4 or 5 days
Difficulty: Easy
Elevation change: The trail is flat, at about 550 feet above sea level.
Trail surface: Paved, crushed limestone, stone dust, or natural surface
Seasons: Best for hiking, spring through fall
Other trail users: Cyclists, joggers, snowshoers, cross-country skiers
Canine compatibility: Leashed dogs permitted
Land status: Public lands
Nearest town: Lockport
Fees and permits: No fees or permits required

Schedule: Dawn to dusk
Maps: Canalway Trail map (available from the New York State Canal Corporation)
Trail contacts: New York State Canal Corporation, 200 Southern Boulevard, P.O. Box 189, Albany 12201-0189; (800) 422-1825 or (800) 422-6254; www.nyscanals.gov
Special considerations: Because the sun can be harsh and there is little or no drinking water available along the trail, carry plenty of drinking water for both you and your pets. Several greenways have picnic tables, serving boaters and trail users. A few have chemical toilets, but the canal trail could use more public facilities for through-trail travelers. Beware of poison ivy growing along the trail's sides. Bicycle rentals are available at Lockport, Brockport, and Spencerport.

Finding the trailhead: Find the western terminus at Locks 34 and 35 in downtown Lockport at the corner of Cottage and Main Streets, opposite the Lockport Municipal Building and Visitor Center, where brochures are available. *DeLorme: New York Atlas & Gazetteer:* Page 69 C6.

Multiple north-south roadways cross the canal trail, providing convenient access to or egress from the route. The eastern terminus is at Henpeck Park on Highway 386 in the town of Greece. DeLorme: New York Atlas & Gazetteer: Page 71 C7.

The Hike

In the nineteenth century the Erie Canal linked the Hudson River to the Great Lakes, opening the remote western hinterlands to settlement and commerce. Today the historic canal serves recreationist, naturalist, and historian, offering a gentle escape from the settled, commercial world it fostered. The communities that sprang up along the canal continue to provide services to canal travelers.

Locks 34 and 35, Erie Canal Heritage Trail, Lockport

Making a west-to-east journey along the northern towpath, you descend along Locks 34 and 35, where impressive gates of wood and steel close at an angle, sealed by the force of the water. Chambers fill and empty in fifteen minutes. Boats rise to head west, drop to head east. Where the trail crosses the grate of a thundering spillway, interpretive signs explain the operation and history of the canal. The Canal Museum, also located here, deepens the story with historic photographs, artifacts, and personal accounts of the great engineering feat.

Dubbed the "Long Level," the canal tour from here to Rochester is lock-free. You pass through tree-shaded Upson Park and skirt the New York State Canal Corporation maintenance yard, before towpath travel begins in earnest. Ensnared by wild grape and poison ivy, a border of locust, mulberry (recalling an early venture into the silk industry), box elder, willow, and cottonwood shades travelers. Queen Anne's lace, chicory, daisy, black-eyed Susan, tiger lily, and a dozen other wildflowers shower the trailside in color. Long open stretches occur later.

Orchards, cornfields, and cropland; farmhouses and silos; and historic homes complete the canal surroundings. In this flat terrain, the height of the towpath levee is adequate to provide an overview. A marina and a few primitive boat docks access the 60-foot-wide canal. Muggy summer days have found local boys—advisable or not—splashing about in the green murk. Gulls, kingfishers, swallows, and herons share the corridor.

Small towns mark off travel: Gasport (5 miles), Middleport (11 miles), Medina (15 miles), Albion (25 miles), Holley (36 miles), Brockport (42 miles), and Spencerport (50 miles). Typically, the heart of each town sits on the south side of the canal. At many, freshly painted lift bridges facilitate boat traffic and link the canal towpath to town. Attractive brick buildings with old-style business fronts and side murals depicting the canal era characterize more than a few.

Elsewhere single-lane bridges span the canal and towpath; all date back to the 1910s. East of Medina, the trail passes over Culvert Road, the only road that travels under the Erie Canal.

East past Gallop Road Bridge, the towpath halts, putting you onto Canal Road for 0.2 mile. The tour then resumes on the northern towpath, where a canal breach feeds a lake on the south shore.

East past Brockport and Adams Basin, the tree border fills out, casting shadows and closing out views. The trail landscape blinks from rural to rural-suburban. At Canal and Union in Spencerport, you may detour to Towpath Park on the south shore—another likely stopping point.

The selected hike ends on the east side of the Highway 386 bridge at the town of Greece's Henpeck Park. In the 1800s, Henpeck (the port of South Greece) boasted a grocery, post office, school, apple dryhouse, two doctors, and a community of twenty-five homes. Eastbound from here, the towpath is again paved but quickly grows more urban with some critical road crossings. Although it is not ideal for hikers, cyclists may continue. The canal route ends at Lock 32 Park (off Highway 65 in Rochester), 63 miles from Lockport.

Miles and Directions

0.0 Start from the western (Lockport) trailhead; follow the northern towpath east. **Side trip:** To set the stage, detour to the Canal Museum for a bit of history.

5.0 Reach Gasport.

11.0 Reach Middleport.

15.0 Reach Medina.

17.0 Cross over Culvert Road.

25.0 Reach Albion.

36.0 Reach Holley.

42.0 Reach Brockport.

50.0 Reach Spencerport. **Side trip** or **Bailout:** At Canal and Union in Spencerport, you may detour to Towpath Park on the south shore. This greenway with tables and benches suggests a potential stopping point.

55.0 End at Henpeck Park in the town of Greece.

Options

▶ **Ripley's Believe It or Not!** recognizes Culvert Road, the only road that passes under the Erie Canal. This 1823-built road shows a stone block construction and dripping archway. Culvert Road runs north-south between Highway 31 (Telegraph Road) and Portage Road east of Medina. *DeLorme: New York Atlas & Gazetteer: Page 70 C2.*

Continuing the canal tour east another 8 miles from Henpeck Park to Rochester, the towpath is now paved. At Long Pond Road cross over the road bridge, following Erie Canal Heritage Trail markers, to resume eastbound travel along the south shore. The canal tour is now mostly an urban bike lane. The route parallels Highway 390 and requires a crossing of Highway 31 (a feat of patience and good timing). More city road crossings and a railroad overpass follow. Travel flips to the north canal bank at Genesee River Valley Park and continues so until you reach the Lock 32 Canal Park (off Highway 65). Painted blue and gold, Lock 32 and its gatehouse colorfully mark the end of the Long Level.

Hike Information

Local Information

Niagara Tourism and Convention Corporation, 345 Third Street, Suite 605, Niagara Falls 14303; (716) 282-8992 or (877) FALLS US (325-5787); www.niagara-usa.com/region_canal.html

Local Events/Attractions

One block from the Lockport Lock, the **Erie Canal Discovery Center,** open daily

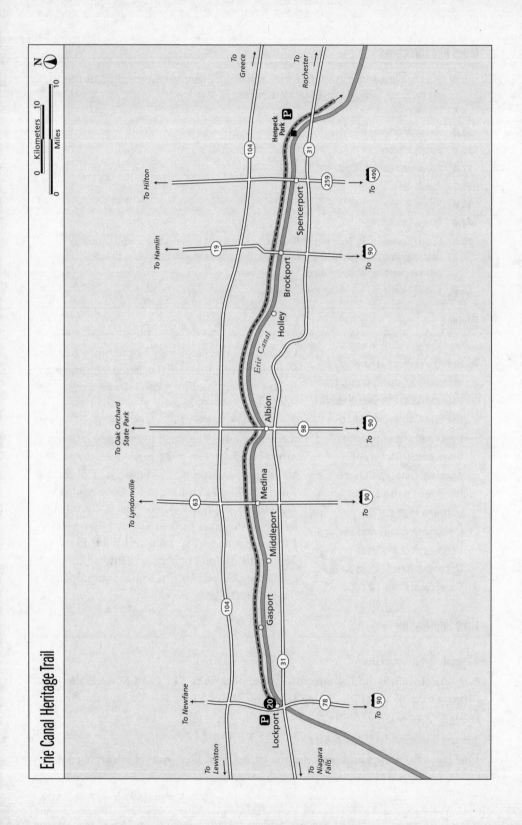

Erie Canal Heritage Trail

N

Kilometers 10
0
Miles
0   10

To Greece

To Rochester

31

Henpeck Park [P]

104

To Hilton

Spencerport

259

To 490

To Hamlin

19

Brockport

To 90

Holley

Erie Canal

To Oak Orchard State Park

Albion

98

To 90

Medina

To Lyndonville

63

Middleport

To 90

Gasport

104

To Newfane

31

Lockport

[P] 20

78

To 90

To Lewiston

To Niagara Falls

May through October, celebrates the great endeavor of the Erie Canal and Lockport's own supporting role through video, exhibits, and a mural. The Erie Canal Discovery Center, 24 Church Street, Lockport; www.eriecanaldiscoverycenter.org.

In Medina, the **Medina Railroad Museum** in the old New York Central freight depot holds exhibits, models, and dioramas devoted to railroading history. An excursion train departs the depot traveling through canal country. Museum hours are Tuesday through Sunday, 11:00 a.m. to 5:00 p.m.; call for train schedules. Medina Railroad Museum, 530 West Avenue, Medina 14103; (585) 798-6106; www.railroadmuseum .net

Accommodations

Nearly two dozen B&Bs or quaint inns sit in the historic towns along this section of the canal. Contact Niagara Tourism and Convention Corporation.

Organizations

Parks & Trails New York helps promote, expand, and protect trails, parks, and open spaces statewide and prints and sells a cycling guide to the Erie Canal. Parks & Trails New York, 29 Elk Street, Albany 12207; (518) 434-1583; www.ptny.org

▶ Ticks

Ticks can carry diseases such as Rocky Mountain spotted fever and Lyme disease. The best defense is, of course, prevention. If you know you're going to be hiking through an area littered with ticks, wear long pants and a long-sleeved shirt. You can apply a permethrin repellent to your clothing and a Deet repellent to exposed skin. At the end of your hike, do a spot check for ticks (and insects in general). If you do find a tick, coat the insect with petroleum jelly or tree sap to cut off its air supply. The tick should release its hold, but if it doesn't, grab the head of the tick firmly—with a pair of tweezers if you have them— and gently pull it away from the skin with a twisting motion. Clean the affected area with an antibacterial cleanser and then apply triple antibiotic ointment. Monitor the area for a few days. If irritation persists or a white spot develops, see a doctor for possible infection.

21 Letchworth State Park

South of Rochester, Letchworth State Park enfolds the 17-mile-long Genesee River Gorge, three major waterfalls, elegant side-creek falls, and 400- to 600-foot-tall sheer sandstone-shale cliffs. Numbered trails explore the developed park of the western rim. The park's celebrated Gorge Trail salutes canyon rim and waterfall features. The Mary Jemison Trail opens a chapter of early Seneca Indian history. Centerpiece to the area is the historic Glen Iris Inn.

Start: At the Gorge Trail's upper trailhead
Distance: 7.8 miles one-way
Approximate hiking time: 4 to 5.5 hours
Difficulty: Moderate, due to stairs and some uneven footing
Elevation change: The rolling trail has a 300-foot elevation change.
Trail surface: Earthen forest path
Seasons: Best for hiking, spring through fall
Other trail users: None
Canine compatibility: Leashed dogs (with proof of rabies shot) permitted on short lead (Because this is a busy trail, it is best to leave high-strung and rambunctious dogs at home.)
Land status: State park

Nearest town: Mount Morris
Fees and permits: Park admission fee
Schedule: Daylight hours for trails
Maps: Letchworth State Park map
Trail contacts: Letchworth State Park, 1 Letchworth State Park, Castille 14427; (585) 493-3600; http://nysparks.state.ny.us/parks
Special considerations: The park allows spring turkey hunting and deer hunting during season, October to December; wearing orange is recommended for hiker safety during deer season. Keep to the trails and keep well back of the cliffs because of undermining and unstable, crumbling edges.

Finding the trailhead: From the Highway 36–Highway 408 junction in the village of Mount Morris, go north on Highway 36 for 1.1 miles and turn left, reaching the Mount Morris entrance to the state park in 0.4 mile. From this entrance, proceed 15.8 miles south to the Gorge Trail upper trailhead; it is 0.4 mile north of the park's southern entrance. *DeLorme: New York Atlas & Gazetteer:* Page 57 D4.

The Hike

The popular Gorge Trail (Trail 1) represents the premier hiking trail within the developed park. This downstream stroll begins at the upper trailhead, passing under the railroad bridge. The first rim vista overlooks the 70-foot horseshoe drop of Upper Falls. A plume of mist shoots up and out from the white rushing fury, nurturing the green cloak of the eastern wall. Only the heavy railroad footings from High Bridge steal from the natural wonder and photographer's image.

As the well-groomed trail continues, it presents new perspectives. Basswood, maple, oak, and spruce overhang the route; poison ivy drapes the edging stone wall

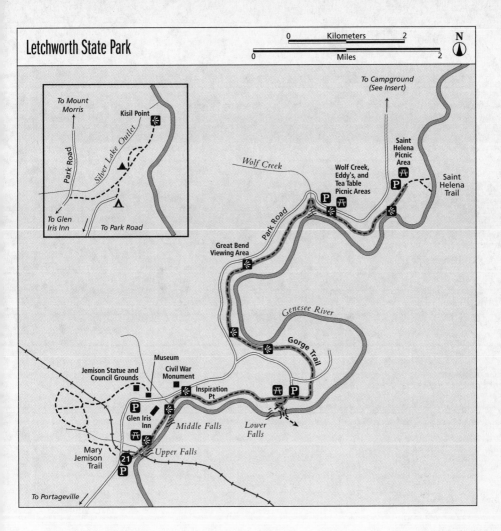

Letchworth State Park

0 — Kilometers — 2
0 — Miles — 2

N

To Mount Morris

Kisil Point

Park Road

Silver Lake Outlet

To Glen Iris Inn

To Park Road

To Campground (See Insert)

Saint Helena Picnic Area

Saint Helena Trail

Wolf Creek

Wolf Creek, Eddy's, and Tea Table Picnic Areas

Park Road

Great Bend Viewing Area

Genesee River

Gorge Trail

Museum

Jemison Statue and Council Grounds

Civil War Monument

Inspiration Pt

Glen Iris Inn

Middle Falls

Lower Falls

Mary Jemison Trail

Upper Falls

21

To Portageville

and slope to the river. As the trail skirts a landscaped day-use area, it offers downstream looks at the delicate streamers of a side-creek falls and the bulging west cliff.

Next up you gain a side perspective on a waterfall of Niagara proportion—Middle Falls. A viewing deck below Glen Iris Inn serves up a grand look at this 107-foot-high, 285-foot-wide waterfall, which thunders over an abrupt river ledge. Next you follow the yellow blazes up and away from the inn, where the trail frequently travels the thin woods-and-grass buffer between the rim and the park road. After passing through a mixed evergreen stand planted in 1917, look for an obelisk dedicated to New York's First Dragoons of the Civil War on a roadway island.

At the roadside vista dubbed Inspiration Point, you gather an upstream view of Middle and Upper Falls and High Bridge. Interpretive signs now mark the tour, and views come piecemeal. The trail descends the rim's tiers. In another mile you come

to the side trail that descends 127 steps to Lower Falls. A broad vista deck, a river bridge, and a 0.1-mile upstream spur present this 50- to 60-foot waterfall that shows a slight crescent curvature along with an entourage of cascades. At the bridge, you can examine the platy shale and sandstone seams of the cliff.

You then retrace your steps uphill to resume the downstream hike, skirting below the Lower Falls day-use area. Hemlock and beech offer a rich shade. After the Gorge Trail turns away from the rim, bear right to pass a restaurant and again travel near the park road, where you will share roadside vistas with motorists, now overlooking Big Bend. Copper-gilded vultures soar on the thermals.

At the designated Great Bend Viewing Area, you will overlook the dizzying 550-foot cliffs, scoured bowl, and muddy green Genesee River. Afterward, the trail descends fairly steeply, crossing a footbridge over a charming side water. Still the trail flip-flops from rim to road. The beauty of Wolf Creek later complements the trail. Here you can admire the eroded and fluted river cliffs, the broad Genesee River, and twisting Wolf Creek Falls in its own narrow canyon.

Next up you skirt the picnic areas of Wolf Creek, Tea Table, and Saint Helena, with their rustic stone-and-slab tables. The Gorge Trail stops at the lower Saint Helena Picnic Area, where it meets the Saint Helena Trail, Trail 13.

Miles and Directions

0.0 Start from the Gorge Trail upper trailhead. Cross the park road from the upper trailhead parking lot, pass under the railroad bridge, and follow rockwork steps downhill to the gorge rim. Turn left (downstream).

0.2 Reach the Upper Falls view.

0.7 Reach the Middle Falls viewing deck.

1.4 Reach Inspiration Point.

2.4 Take the spur to the right to the Lower Falls area.

2.8 Reach the Lower Falls vantages; return to rim trail travel.

3.2 Resume downstream rim travel, skirting the Lower Falls picnic area.

3.5 After the Gorge Trail turns away from the rim, reach a junction and bear right, skirting a restaurant to again travel near the park road.

4.2 Reach a roadside vantage.

4.7 Reach another roadside vantage.

5.6 Reach Great Bend Viewing Area.

6.6 Cross Wolf Creek.

7.8 End at the Saint Helena Trail (Trail 13) in the lower Saint Helena Picnic Area. **Option:** You may continue on the Saint Helena Trail, which forks in 0.1 mile. Each branch then leads 0.2 mile to the river shore and an interior view of the Gorge.

◀ *Middle Falls, Letchworth State Park*

Options

While at the park, here are a couple of other trails to investigate:

The 2.8-mile knot-shaped **Kisil Point Trail** (Trail 18) travels a canyon jut, Kisil Point Ridge, to overlook Silver Lake Outlet and the Genesee River farther downstream from the Gorge Trail. The hike begins from a roadside trailhead near the Highbanks Campground entrance or near Campground Loop 100, if you are camped. Where the trails merge, you travel the piney outskirts of the camp past an old picnic shelter to arrive at a loop junction (0.4 mile). The right fork travels the Genesee River side of Kisil Point Ridge; the left fork overlooks Silver Lake Outlet. At 0.9 mile the arms of the loop reunite and a spur branches to the end of Kisil Point (1.4 miles). The point view encompasses the tinsel stream of Silver Lake Outlet as it parts a thick green swath and the Genesee River Canyon, with its steep gray cliffs, eroded silt skirts, and broad floodplain. Return to the loop, taking the arm not traveled, and return to camp or car. Kisil Point Trail starts 4 miles south of the Mount Morris park entrance.

The 2.5-mile loop of the **Mary Jemison Trail** (Trail 2) unveils area history. The trail's name honors the white-woman captive who came to revere the Seneca Indians with whom she lived. The trail begins at the museum and travels to Council Grounds, where a statue of Mary Jemison, an 1800s pioneer cabin, and a tribal Council House predating the American Revolution suggest detouring. The trail then heads west, negotiating a series of confusing junctions. Follow the number "2" through mixed woods, hemlock stands, and a pine plantation to visit a couple of linear reservoirs. Evidence of beaver activity surrounds the ponds; in woods deer may cross your path. Reach the Mary Jemison Trail and Council Grounds 14.9 miles south of the Mount Morris entrance to the park.

Hike Information

Local Information

Wyoming County Tourist Promotion Agency, Inc., 30 North Main Street, Castile 14427; (800) 839-3919; www.wyomingcountyny.com

Local Events/Attractions

April through October, **Balloons Over Letchworth,** a private hot-air balloon company, offers a lofty vantage on Letchworth canyon and its waterfalls. Balloons Over Letchworth, 6773 Halvorsen Road, Portageville; (585) 493-3340; www.balloons overletchworth.com

Accommodations

Highbanks Campground in Letchworth State Park has 340 sites. Reservations: (800) 456-2267; www.reserveamerica.com. The completely restored Glen Iris Inn also offers accommodation and serves meals, (585) 493-2622; www.glenirisinn.com

22 Letchworth Trail

Across the Genesee River Gorge from developed Letchworth State Park, this linear foot trail explores the wilder eastern rim. It travels in mixed woods and snares occasional river overlooks and grand waterfall views. The Genesee River Gorge is punctuated by three major waterfalls and plummeting sandstone-shale cliffs. Wildlife sightings add surprise. The trail follows sections of a historic canal and rail corridor and makes up part of the Finger Lakes Trail (FLT).

Start: At the northern trailhead

Distance: 24.8 miles drop-off/pick-up or shuttle hike, including the vista side spurs

Approximate hiking time: 14 to 16 hours (1 to 2 days)

Difficulty: Moderate due to distance and terrain

Elevation change: The trail travels between 800 and 1,200 feet in elevation, with the high point found above the falls.

Trail surface: Earthen and grassy paths, closed road, canal greenway

Seasons: Best for hiking, spring through fall

Other trail users: Mountain bikers, horse riders, hunters, snowmobilers, snowshoers, cross-country skiers

Canine compatibility: Leashed dogs permitted (clean up after animal)

Land status: State park

Nearest town: Mount Morris

Fees and permits: No fees

Schedule: Daylight hours (Exception: There is a single lean-to in the park along the FLT where camping is allowed, but you must first secure a free permit from the state park office to do so. The state park prohibits camping anywhere else along this trail.)

Maps: Letchworth State Park map; Finger Lakes Trail Conference (FLTC) maps, The Letchworth Trail Sheets L1 and L2 (purchase online: www.fingerlakestrail.org)

Trail contacts: Letchworth State Park, 1 Letchworth State Park, Castille 14427; (585) 493-3600; http://nysparks.state.ny.us/parks

Special considerations: The park allows spring turkey hunting and deer hunting during season, October to December; wearing orange is recommended for hiker safety during deer season. Keep to the trails and keep well back of cliffs because of undermining and unstable, crumbling edges. Although ravines occur at regular intervals, they flow only intermittently and their steep, crumbling banks can deny access. Carry ample water.

Finding the trailhead: For the northern trailhead, from the Highway 36–Highway 408 junction in Mount Morris, go southwest on Highway 408 (Chapel Street) toward Nunda. In 1.8 miles turn right for Mount Morris Dam. In another 1.7 miles turn left to reach the dam overlook, parking area, and trailhead 0.1 mile ahead. *DeLorme: New York Atlas & Gazetteer:* Page 57 C5.

Find the southern terminus in Portageville at the northeast corner of the Highway 436 bridge, with off-road parking for a handful of vehicles. Because of the limited parking here, a drop-off and pick-up arrangement is better for this hike. *DeLorme: New York Atlas & Gazetteer:* Page 57 D4.

The Hike

A north-to-south hike between Mount Morris Dam and Portageville travels the undeveloped eastern rim of the Genesee River Gorge, rolling through mixed forest, pine plantation, and meadow scrub. Ravines punctuate and dictate the line of travel. Although few in number, river vistas are prized, especially at the trail's south end, where rim overlooks applaud two of the three river falls. Solitude abounds, and wildlife sightings can be rich and varied, with turkey, raccoon, fox, grouse, deer, beaver, frog, and skunk.

Part of the greater Finger Lakes Trail (FLT), the Letchworth Trail is well marked with yellow paint blazes, FLT markers, and trail registers. The blue spurs heading left (east) lead to access points off River Road and opportunities to shorten the hike. The blue spurs to the right (west) lead to river overlooks. Numbers indicate Letchworth State Park trails.

A view of the dam starts off travel. Vultures often roost atop the structure, while cliffs and the broad green floodplain complete the scene. Ahead, at the picnic area overlook, the view brings together the peninsular ridge of Hogback, a pinched river bend, the developed west rim of Letchworth State Park, and the distant rural countryside.

Beneath the mixed-tree bower, poison ivy, Virginia creeper, waterleaf, and witch hazel frame the path. When distanced from the edge, the trail becomes more rolling, traversing the rim plateau. The ravines seasonally carry water and show small cascades; a few ravines show the remains of old structures.

Fog can claim the canyon, alternately masking and unmasking the cliff's ragged spires, ribs, and points. Where the trail edges a couple of fields, be careful of the trailing wire from old fences. Where Trail 16 meets and leaves the trail, you travel a tight, moist corridor of mixed woods and shrubs to enter a plantation of spiny-armed pines. Crows may raise a noisy filibuster.

On the side route to Fiddler's Elbow Viewpoint, you travel a deciduous flat and low ridge to the open vista. After emerging from a deep, steep-forked ravine on the FLT, you find the next vista detour. Here you travel the spine of a thin wooded ridge between the forked ravine on the right and a bowled ravine on the left, reaching a gorge viewpoint at the tip. The river far below shows a split flow and textured tapestry.

South on the FLT, you encounter some stately trees, including—if winds and time allow it to persevere—a gnarly old oak with eighteen major arm branchings. Past a small log shelter and another road access, the ravines shape steeper climbs and descents. Afterward, you cross the overgrown road to the abandoned hamlet of Saint Helena.

◀ *Genesee River canyon, Letchworth State Park*

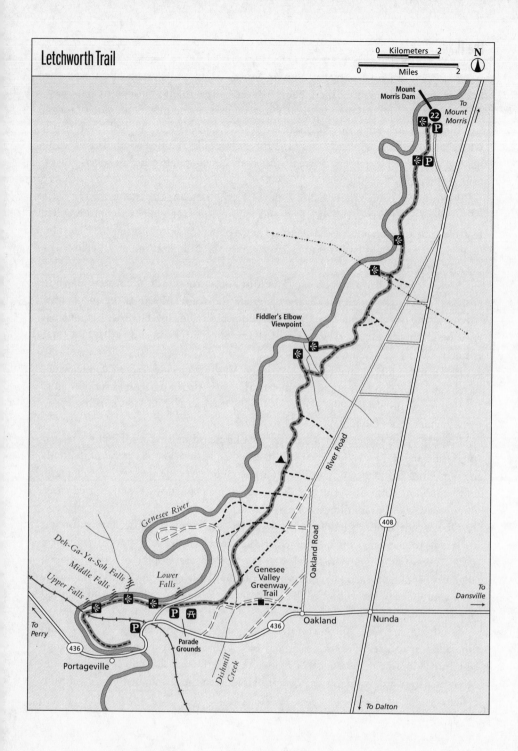

Letchworth Trail

Mount
Morris Dam

To
Mount
Morris

22
P

P

Fiddler's Elbow
Viewpoint

River Road

408

To
Dansville

Genesee River

Deh-Ga-Ya-Soh Falls

Middle Falls

Upper Falls

Lower
Falls

Oakland Road

Genesee
Valley
Greenway
Trail

Oakland

Nunda

To
Perry

P

P

436

Parade
Grounds

436

Dishmill Creek

Portageville

To Dalton

The FLT briefly jogs left with Trail 9 and then splits off to cross over Trail 9, entering a dark hemlock stand. At beaver-remodeled Dishmill Creek, the trail follows a closed stretch of River Road before continuing south along the Genesee Valley Greenway Trail. Here the tracked path paints a black stripe down the grassy lane of what once was the Pennsylvania Railroad. Alongside stretches the ditch of the 1862–1878 Genesee Valley Canal. Birch, basswood, beech, maple, and tulip trees weave a lush green tunnel, but mosquitos can speed your steps.

Beyond Parade Grounds Picnic Area, follow the greenway to the river's rim and flat rock vantages. Spy 400-foot cliffs both upstream and directly across the river. Deep in the canyon, the broad Genesee River flows over outcrop. Ahead you gather superb impressions, including a cross-canyon look at the 200-foot waterfall on Deh-Ga-Ya-Soh Creek and views of the 107-foot Middle Falls and the 70-foot horseshoe surge of Upper Falls with High Bridge (the railroad bridge). The FLT then rolls south to end in Portageville.

Miles and Directions

0.0 Start from the northern trailhead; hike the rim trail south.

0.9 Reach parking and the Hogsback overlook (view hairpin turn on the river).

3.1 Detour right on a 50-foot spur to a vista atop a loose mud-shale slope; stay back from the edge.

4.6 Keep right where a spur leads left to River Road.

5.6 Reach a powerline corridor; hike the corridor to the right 0.4 mile to add a river vista.

6.4 Return to Letchworth Trail/FLT; turn right (south).

7.7 Meet Trail 16, which heads left to River Road; continue southbound on FLT.

9.3 Reach a junction; detour right to Fiddler's Elbow Viewpoint (9.7). Backtrack to the trail.

10.1 Continue south on FLT.

11.7 Detour right, passing between ravines to the next gorge viewpoint (12.1); backtrack to trail.

12.5 Resume south on FLT.

14.7 Cross State Park Trail 22. **Note:** To the right is River Road in 0.4 mile.

16.1 Reach a small log shelter (permit required for overnight use).

17.3 Cross the old Saint Helena Road.

19.0 The FLT briefly jogs left on the woods road of Trail 9, before veering away on its own.

19.9 Turn right onto the closed section of River Road (Trail 8), crossing culvert of Dishmill Creek.

20.9 Leave River Road, rounding the gate to the right to follow Genesee Valley Greenway Trail (Trail 7).

22.7 Cross the park road below Parade Grounds Picnic Area to follow the greenway to the river's rim.

23.2 Find overlooks of Middle and Upper Falls.

24.0 Find an Upper Falls view.

24.8 End at the Highway 436 bridge in Portageville.

Hike Information

Local Information

Livingston County Chamber of Commerce, 4635 Millenium Drive, Geneseo 14454; (585) 243-2222 or (800) 538-7365; www.fingerlakeswest.com

Local Events/Attractions

In Geneseo the **1941 Historical Aircraft Group Museum** restores, preserves, displays, and celebrates World War II and Korean War aircraft and recognizes U.S. military personnel for their contributions. The museum presents a calendar of fly-in events, including the Geneseo Air Show in mid-July. The 1941 Historical Aircraft Group Museum, 3489 Big Tree Lane, Geneseo 14454; (585) 243-2100; www.1941hag.org

Accommodations

Highbanks Campground in Letchworth State Park (across Genesee Gorge) has 340 sites. Reservations: (800) 456-2267; www.reserveamerica.com. The park's completely restored Glen Iris Inn also offers accommodation and serves meals, (585) 493-2622; www.glenirisinn.com.

Organizations

The **Finger Lakes Trail Conference** maintains and maps the trail. FLTC, 6111 Visitor Center Road, Mount Morris 14510-9527; (585) 658-9320; www.fingerlakestrail .org

Honorable Mentions

Niagara Frontier

K Alabama Swamps Trails

At the site of ancient Lake Tonawanda, the vast marshes north of Alabama represent a critical wildlife habitat and an exciting natural area. Together Iroquois National Wildlife Refuge (NWR) and the adjoining New York State wildlife management areas open the gate to 20,000 acres of prime wetland, maintained in a fairly wild and protected state. Nesting eagles find favor with the habitat. Spring migrations swell the bird counts, and a cacophony of honks and calls fills the air.

Five easy walks between 0.5 mile and 5 miles long introduce the wild lands. In Iroquois NWR, they are the 1.2-mile Kanyoo Trail to an observation tower, the 5-mile out-and-back Feeder Road trail between ponds, the 3-mile out-and-back Onondaga Nature Trail along Onondaga Marsh and woodland, and the 2-mile marsh boardwalk and dike loop of the Swallow Hollow Trail. The nature paths at Oak Orchard Environmental Education Center shape the fifth hike; they explore North Marsh and its open-water shore. Onondaga Nature Trail is closed to hiking during shotgun deer season, and you may choose to avoid Feeder Road during its two months of hunting season. Contact the NWR for dates. Side dikes off Feeder Road are closed during nesting season, March 1 to July 15; heed all notices.

From the junction of Highway 63 and Highway 77 in Alabama, go north on Highway 63 for 0.8 mile and turn left (west) onto Casey Road to reach the refuge headquarters in 0.6 mile. Continue west on Casey Road another 0.8 mile and turn northwest onto Highway 77 (Lewiston Road) to reach the marked trailhead for Kanyoo Trail on the right in 0.9 mile. Gated Feeder Road lies east off Highway 77, 300 feet farther north. *DeLorme: New York Atlas & Gazetteer:* Page 70 D1.

For the other three trails, from the junction of Casey Road and Highway 63 (east of the headquarters), go north on Highway 63 for 0.1 mile and turn right (east) onto Roberts Road. In 1.1 miles turn north on dirt Sour Springs Road to reach Onondaga Nature Trail on the right in 0.8 mile. For Swallow Hollow Trail and the Oak Orchard nature trails, stay east on Roberts Road, go 1.5 miles past its intersection with Sour Springs Road and turn north onto Knowlesville Road. Find Swallow Hollow Trail on the left in 1.8 miles; Oak Orchard on the right, 0.1 mile farther north. *DeLorme: New York Atlas & Gazetteer:* Page 70 D2.

Contact Iroquois NWR, 1101 Casey Road, Basom 14013; (585) 948-5445; http://iroquoisnwr.fws.gov or Oak Orchard Environmental Education Center, New York State Department of Environmental Conservation, Region 8, 6274 East Avon–Lima Road, Avon 14414; (585) 226-2466; www.dec.ny.gov.

Tifft Nature Preserve

Near the Lake Erie shore, this 264-acre urban sanctuary marks a success story in land reclamation. Its low grassland hills (formerly a small landfill), wetland woods, thickets, ponds, and a 75-acre freshwater cattail marsh support a thriving bird population while offering a peaceful retreat from Buffalo's city pace. Five miles of trail and three boardwalks tour the preserve. The individual nature trails range from a fraction of a mile to 1.3 miles in length, visit viewing blinds, and tour mounds, wetlands, Berm Pond, Warbler Walk, and Heritage Boardwalk. An entrance fee is charged; trails are open dawn to dusk.

From Highway 5 in south Buffalo, take the Tifft Street/Fuhrmann Boulevard exit. Westbound traffic will head 0.5 mile south from the exit, turn left under the freeway, and again turn left onto a one-way road, merging with the traffic exiting from Highway 5 East. Go 0.5 mile north on the one-way road to reach the preserve parking lot on the right (east). Locate the trailheads near the visitor center cabin or 0.1 mile east of the cabin, where the service road crosses a bridge over the southeast arm of Lake Kirsty. *DeLorme: New York Atlas & Gazetteer:* Page 55 B5. Tifft Nature Preserve, 1200 Fuhrmann Boulevard, Buffalo 14203; (716) 896-5200 or (866) 291-6660; http:// www.sciencebuff.org.

Chautauqua–Allegheny Region

Historically, the Seneca Nation of the Iroquois Confederacy occupied this southwest corner of New York. Edged by Lake Erie, the region was key to trade and an important front to control and defend. The Seneca Nation fulfilled the role of western gatekeepers and had a respected form of government that reportedly served as a rudimentary model for the Founding Fathers in forging our nation's government.

The geography of the region includes the long flat summits and V-shaped valleys of the Allegheny Plateau, the Upper Genesee River, Chautauqua Lake, and the Chautauqua Creek Gorge. Unlike the rest of the state, the Allegheny Plateau was untouched by ice age glaciers.

Hardwood forest fern floor, Allegany State Park

Allegany State Park encompasses 65,000 acres of the Allegheny landscape, making it the largest park in the state system. Two developed lake areas, Red House and Quaker, form the two-chambered heart of this vast park playground.

The region puts forth a soothing landscape of mixed hardwood-conifer forests, boulder caves, wildflower meadows, and relaxing waters—the ideal escape for the frazzled and the harried. The understated beauty of this natural backdrop neatly pairs with the famed Chautauqua Institute, a cultural center for music, art, lecture, and contemplation, known the world over.

Chautauqua County is the largest Concord grape growing region in the world. Grape arbors, vineyards, and wineries figure prominently in the rural countryside. Amish communities, farmstands, Victorian villages, and historic sites and figures contribute to the charm of the lightly populated region. Four seasons give the land a changing face, inviting frequent returns.

In Chautauqua County, a pair of long-distance trails, the Earl Cardot Eastside Overland Trail and the Fred J. Cusimano Westside Overland Trail, string through New York State Department of Environmental Conservation forest parcels and along private land, for see-the-country travel. Abandoned railbeds, nature trails, and state park paths to summits, stony realms, hushed forests, and inviting shores engage hiker, snowshoer, and cross-country skier.

23 Fred J. Cusimano Westside Overland Trail

Between Sherman and Panama, this long–distance linear trail strings 24 miles through a series of state forests in Chautauqua County, traversing agricultural easements in between. Changing forest, meadow and pond habitats, and rural and forest views flavor the way. Multiple trailheads allow you to vary the hike's length. Established shelters allow for overnight stays and stargazing, suggesting you stretch out your Westside sojourn.

Start: At the northern trailhead

Distance: 19.2 miles point-to-point

Approximate hiking time: 1 to 2 days

Difficulty: Strenuous, when hiking the full 19 miles of the selected hike

Elevation change: This rolling trail travels between 1,500 and 1,850 feet in elevation.

Trail surface: Earthen path, mowed track, woods road, rural and forest roads

Seasons: Best for hiking, spring through fall

Other trail users: Mountain bikers, snowshoers, cross-country skiers, hunters (on public lands in fall)

Canine compatibility: Dogs permitted (as a courtesy, leash animals when crossing private lands)

Land status: State forest, county, and private land

Nearest town: Panama for minimal services; otherwise, Chautauqua

Fees and permits: No fees or permits required

Schedule: No time restrictions, but occasional temporary closures because of logging

Maps: Fred J. Cusimano Westside Overland Trail map (online: www.tourchautauqua.com [go to outdoors] or www.co.chautauqua.ny.us/ parks/parksframe.htm). The map is necessary to locate trailheads and useful to carry because it has incremental mileages.

Trail contacts: Chautauqua County Parks Department, 2105 South Maple Avenue, Ashville 14710; (716) 763-8928; www.co .chautauqua.ny.us/parks/parksframe.htm

Special considerations: Be alert for arrows and blazes showing the changes in direction. Some sections are overgrown or subject to mud. Respect easements through and along private lands, which are open to hikers only. There is no camping within 150 feet of road, trail, or water and none on private land. Any overnight forest stay longer than three nights at one site requires a New York Department of Environmental Conservation (DEC) permit. Contact the DEC Region 9 suboffice in Falconer. The designated camp shelters offer basic amenities, including latrines and working wells. All DEC rules apply for fire building and wood collecting. Trailheads are well signed and the trail generally well blazed. Wearing orange during the fall hunting season is a wise precaution. The trail is closed to all-terrain vehicles (ATVs) and horses.

Finding the trailhead: For the northern terminus, from Interstate 86 take exit 6 at Sherman and go north 0.4 mile on Highway 76, turning right (east) onto Highway 430. Proceed 7.3 miles and turn left onto Hannum Road. Follow Hannum Road for 3.1 miles to find the trailhead at road's end (last 0.8 mile on dirt). *DeLorme: New York Atlas & Gazetteer:* Page 39 C6.

For the hike's southern terminus, from the junction of Highway 474 and County Road 33 in the village of Panama (5.6 miles south of I-86), go 1.8 miles west on Highway 474. Trailhead parking is north off Highway 474. *DeLorme: New York Atlas & Gazetteer:* Page 39 D7.

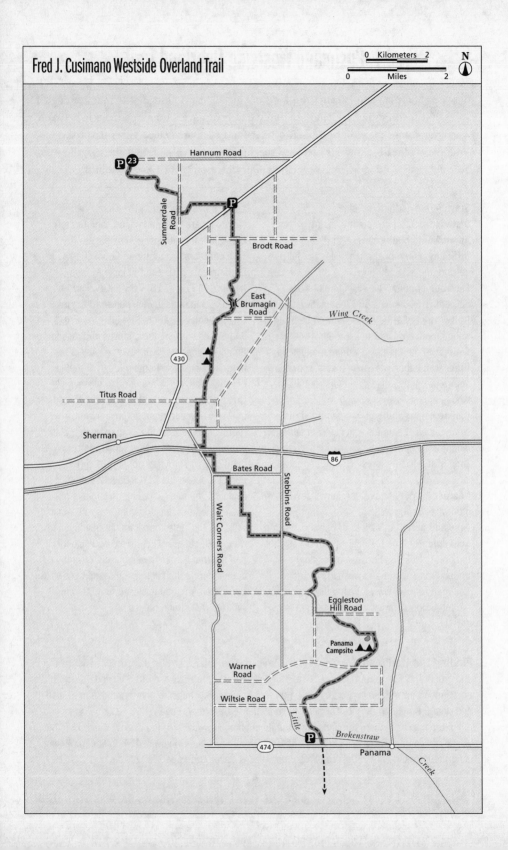

Fred J. Cusimano Westside Overland Trail

0 Kilometers 2

0 Miles 2

N

Hannum Road

P 23

Summerdale Road

P

Brodt Road

East Brumagin Road

Wing Creek

430

Titus Road

Sherman

Bates Road

86

Stebbins Road

Wait Corners Road

Eggleston Hill Road

Panama Campsite

Warner Road

Wiltsie Road

Little

Brokenstraw

474

P

Panama

Creek

The Hike

Southbound, you pass through second-growth woods of maple, black locust, ash, and hop hornbeam. Travel is rolling. A closed road and drainage crossings precede travel on Summerdale Road. Where foot trail resumes, private land stretches left.

Cross Highway 430 and enter Mount Pleasant State Forest. Beyond a meadow break, oaks appear in the upper canopy. Ferns, wild raspberry, horsetail reed, and poison ivy contribute to the tangle. Where the trail traverses a bog, planted spiny-armed spruce and hardwoods face off.

After crossing Brodt Road, a dense spruce grove swallows or abuts the trail. Mud exceeds the logs' reach at a bog crossing. The trail bears right where a grassy track merges on the left. Big maple or beech attract note. The trail then drops down to a footbridge crossing. After crossing a gravel road and a couple more creek bridges, the trail jogs right on East Brumagin Road before resuming south on woods road.

Mixed forest leads to a pair of three-sided log shelters, available first come, first served. Follow the dirt road away from the shelters. The trail rolls from red pine plantation to field. To the left is an artificial pond visited by geese and ringed by grass and shrubs. Cross a gas well track and pass abandoned apple trees to leave state forest, and briefly follow dirt Titus Road. Southbound travel resumes along private land.

You will follow a section of fence and plank boardwalk and skirt a wet meadow and shrub corridor, returning to woods. The route traces straight lines at fences. Be alert for the blazes indicating turns, especially where the trail is overgrown. I-86 becomes a part of the terrain. After skirting a field, the trail crosses under the interstate on Wait Corners Road. On the east side of Wait Corners Road, continue again on private land. Field segments hold the hike's vistas and offer different wildlife viewing. Turkey, owl, and hawk may capture attention.

The trail follows Bates Road (used by area Amish) east to resume its way south at the top of the hill. The hilltop trail then draws a seam between rolling fields. Views are rural: hay bales, fields, silos, barns, and huddles of black-and-white dairy cows. Blue-capped fence posts act as guides; step stiles ease fence crossings.

From Stebbins Road, you enter Edward J. Whalen Memorial State Forest and red pine plantation on mowed path with a mild incline. Cross a cable corridor, beginning a gentle descent between spruce plantation and maple hardwood forest. Footbridges span the deeper hollows. After following truck trail, you cross a ramped footbridge over a tinsel flow shadowed by hemlocks. Mature American beech trees, threatened elsewhere in the East, add to viewing.

After a climb, you follow sun-drenched dirt Eggleston Hill Road left and keep left at the junction. The hike then resumes south, entering the towering makeup of North Harmony State Forest. Avoid routes left.

At a cattail-edged bass pond, you follow the trail along the east shore to the Adirondack-style shelters of Panama Campsite. These look out on the pond, meadow, and reflected forest. Tamaracks rise above camp. When leaving, you pass east of the shelters. A sharp climb then leads to the crossing of a two-track. Afterward the trail parallels Warner Road to the right before crossing over it to resume south. Now travel the southern half of North Harmony Forest to Snake Forest Road (a truck trail). Trace it briefly left before resuming right on a foot trail.

The crossing of Wiltsie Road marks the last interruption until Highway 474, the chosen ending. You travel a meadow swath, pass spiny hemlock, and view big birches near the footbridge over a headwaters of Little Brokenstraw Creek. Because mountain bikers favor the Highway 474 access, be alert hiking out.

Miles and Directions

0.0 Start from the northern trailhead (Trailhead A, the Hannum Road trail parking). Round the boulder barricade and ascend south on blue-blazed trail into Chautauqua State Forest. **Note:** Hiking north leads to Chautauqua Gorge.

1.0 Reach Summerdale Road; follow it right (south).

Panama Campsite shelter along Fred J. Cusimano Westside Overland Trail, North Harmony State Forest

1.5	Resume on trail, heading left (east).
3.0	Cross Highway 430 to enter Mount Pleasant State Forest at a large trailhead parking lot. **Option or Bailout:** This site offers an alternative start or a place to shorten the hike.
3.8	Cross Brodt Road, a single-lane dirt country road.
5.8	Follow East Brumagin Road right for 0.3 mile and then resume south on old woods road.
6.5	Reach shelters; follow the dirt road beyond the shelters to the right for 0.1 mile to resume south.
7.4	Head right 0.2 mile on dirt Titus Road to resume hiking south along private property.
8.4	Follow a county road left to pick up the southbound trail next to a fenceline.
9.3	At the foot of a field, turn right (west), crossing over a fence step-stile to follow Wait Corners Road south under I-86. Resume the trail as it continues on the east side of Wait Corners Road.
10.0	Follow Bates Road east 0.5 mile to continue south on the trail at the top of the hill.
12.6	Angle left across Stebbins Road to enter Edward J. Whalen Memorial State Forest.
13.6	Follow a truck road right 0.8 mile to pick up the southbound trail. Be alert for blazes.
14.8	Follow Eggleston Hill Road left 0.3 mile to a road junction and again turn left per arrows.
15.5	Enter North Harmony State Forest.
16.4	Reach the Panama Campsite shelters; on leaving, pass east of the shelters.
17.0	Cross Warner Road.
18.4	Cross Wiltsie Road.
19.2	End at the Highway 474 trailhead (west of Panama). **Option:** You may continue south on the Westside Overland Trail, crossing the highway and edging private land. Carry the brochure and watch for blazings. You'll end at Town Line Road (24 miles).

Hike Information

Local Information

Chautauqua County Visitors Bureau, P.O. Box 1441, Chautauqua 14722; (866) 908–4569; www.tourchautauqua.com

Local Events/Attractions

The internationally known **Chautauqua Institution** is celebrated for its lecture and concert series, its restful grounds, its National Historic Landmark architecture, and its atmosphere for betterment of learning and spiritual renewal. Chautauqua Institution, 1 Ames Avenue, Chautauqua 14722; (800) 836–ARTS; www.ciweb.org

24 Allegany State Park, Red House Headquarters– Eastwood Meadows Loop

The biggest park in the state system, this "wilderness playground" in southwestern New York brings together even-height ridges, V-shaped valleys, man-made lakes, second-growth forests, and block-fractured boulder realms. Two recreation areas, Red House and Quaker, make up the park. No single trail could showcase the full offering, but the Red House Headquarters–Eastwood Meadows Loop Hike offers a good peek at it and travels a stretch of trail common to three long-distance trails: North Country, Conservation, and Finger Lakes. Likely, you'll want to add one or more of the optional trails because this is a great park worthy of your time.

Start: At the Red House Administration Building

Distance: 10.9 miles out-and-back on lasso-shaped trail

Approximate hiking time: 6 to 7.5 hours

Difficulty: Moderate due to terrain

Elevation change: This hike has about an 800-foot elevation change.

Trail surface: Earthen path

Seasons: Best for hiking, spring through fall

Other trail users: Snowshoers

Canine compatibility: Leashed dogs permitted (proof of shots required), but no pets in buildings, bathhouses, or along cross-country ski trails

Land status: State park

Nearest town: Salamanca

Fees and permits: Park admission fee

Schedule: Park open 24 hours, daylight hours for trails (Exception: Trail camping is allowed at the designated lean-tos along the North Country Trail but only after you have first contacted park police about your plans and your hiking group and have police approval; 716-354-9111. There is no other trail camping in the park.)

Maps: Allegany State Park Guide Map (available at the park); Finger Lakes Trail Conference map, Sheet M1/CT1 (purchase online: www .fingerlakestrail.org)

Trail contacts: Allegany State Park, 2373 ASP Route 1, Suite 3, Salamanca 14779; (716) 354-9121; http://nysparks.state.ny.us/parks

Special considerations: When exploring 65,000-acre Allegany State Park, keep to trails and carry maps, so as not to get lost. Never push beyond your wilderness aptitude. Because hunting occurs anywhere in the park except at the lakes areas, rangers advise you to wear orange during deer hunting season, October into December. On Sunday the park closes to hunting, again allowing worry-free hiking.

Finding the trailhead: For the Red House Recreation Area: From the Southern Tier Expressway (Interstate 86) west of Salamanca, take exit 19, reaching the entrance station in 0.7 mile. The trails radiate from the lake area, off ASP Routes 1, 2, and 2A. The featured hike starts at the Red House Administration Building on ASP 1. *DeLorme: New York Atlas & Gazetteer:* Page 41 D6.

For the Quaker Recreation Area: From I-86 west of Salamanca, take exit 18 and go 4 miles south on Highway 280 to the entrance station. Find trails off ASP Routes 3 and 1. *DeLorme: New York Atlas & Gazetteer:* Page 41 D5.

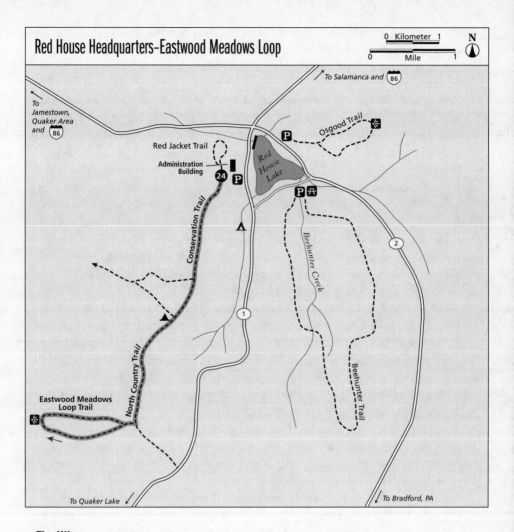

Red House Headquarters-Eastwood Meadows Loop

0 Kilometer 1

0 Mile 1

N

To Salamanca and 86

To Jamestown, Quaker Area and 86

Osgood Trail

Red Jacket Trail

Administration Building

24

P

P

Red House Lake

P

Conservation Trail

Beehunter Creek

2

1

Beehunter Trail

North Country Trail

Eastwood Meadows Loop Trail

To Quaker Lake

To Bradford, PA

The Hike

The described lasso-shaped hike starts south from the Red House Administration Building to Eastwood Meadows Loop. It begins on a blue park trail and then continues south along the shared long-distance route of the park's big three, the North Country Trail (NCT), the Finger Lakes Trail (FLT), and the Conservation Trail (CT), before adding the loop.

As an alternative, this hike can be fashioned into a 4.6-mile shuttle hike (without the meadow loop) or 7.3-mile shuttle hike (with the meadow loop) by spotting a vehicle at the North Country or close-by Eastwood Meadows Trailhead. Both parking areas are on ASP 1, about 4 miles south of the park campground.

From the back of the administration building, you ascend left past an old foundation toward a trail sign in the power line corridor. The sign indicates CONSERVATION

HIKING TRAILS, 2.3 MILES. You continue your ascent in uneven spurts following the blue state park trail among hardwoods and meadow clearings. Briefly, noise from the campground rides upslope but quickly vanishes. Mossy rock slabs contribute to the forest character.

A side trail that connects to the long-distance trails in the Beck Hollow Area arrives on the right; keep south on the blue trail. It ascends through an area of large upturned roots then levels, passing among midaged hardwoods, groves of hemlock, and pockets of young beech and shrubs, eventually coming to a drainage crossing.

Where you come upon a North Country Trail bivouac area and meet up with the shared white-blazed route of the NCT, FLT, and CT, you follow the white blazes left (south), continuing toward Eastwood Meadows Loop. A sagging, unsafe lean-to also shares the general neighborhood; for safety avoid it. An idyllic stroll unrolls before you. The modest gradient and trouble-free path allows your glance to sweep the surroundings. A midstory of mountain elder, red-berried in fall, alternates with the spatially open forest. Later, where a hemlock-hardwood forest enfolds the route, ferns embroider the trail's sides and snags open up the cathedral.

After a lengthy walk, you reach a trail junction. Take the trail on the right to add Eastwood Meadows Loop. Upon meeting a grassy woods road, you turn right to reach the actual loop and there head left for a clockwise tour. The forest sameness is soothing to the eyes and soul. Big-toothed aspen whisper in the canopy. By proceeding forward 100 feet where the loop swings right to begin its return, you'll find a limited opening and a view that stretches west across meadow clearing and the Bay State Brook drainage to spotlight an Allegany ridge.

The loop's return then descends through a similar forest with a shrubby understory of nettles and brambles. Although not exactly a gauntlet, at times you must evade the prickly overhang. Black cherry trees stand as giants in the woods. Close the loop and return to the white-blazed trail.

Backtrack the big three to the bivouac area and return via the blue state park trail to the Red House Administration Building. Or, if you arranged a shuttle vehicle, continue south (right) on the white-blazed trail to the ASP 1 trail parking areas, alternately passing through stands of beech, maple, and hemlock and the shrubby meadow and fern clearings from the site's former ski runs.

Miles and Directions

0.0   Start behind the Red House Administration Building; ascend left toward the trail sign in the power line corridor.

0.1   Reach the trail sign for Conservation Hiking Trails; continue ascent on blue state park trail.

1.5   An orange connector to the long-distance trails heads right; continue forward on blue trail.

2.3   Meet the shared white-blazed long-distance route at a bivouac area; follow the white blazes left (south) toward Eastwood Meadows Loop. **Note:** Turning right (north) on the white-blazed route leads toward Beck Hollow and the Beck Hollow trail shelter.

4.1 Reach a junction; turn right and keep right at a grassy woods road for Eastwood Meadows Loop. **Note:** If you continue south on the white-blazed trio, you'll reach trail parking on ASP 1 in 0.5 mile (a shuttle hike option).

4.4 Reach the loop junction; turn left (clockwise).

5.5 Locate a vista, where the loop swings right for the return leg.

6.5 Close the loop; return to the 4.1-mile junction.

6.8 Back at the junction; backtrack north to the administration building. **Note:** If you arranged for a shuttle vehicle, bear right, coming out at the ASP 1 trail parking lots in 0.5 mile.

8.6 Return to the bivouac area junction; follow the blue state park trail right.

10.9 End back at the Red House Administration Building.

Options

Red House Hiking Options

The 0.7-mile loop of the **Red Jacket Trail** begins on the west side of the Red House Administration Building. The trail's rustic stone stairs, bridge, and path lead uphill to a marked trail junction beneath a power line; go right, coming to the loop junction. The hike's split-level loop contours a maple, black cherry, and hemlock treed slope above Red House Lake. The understory displays half a dozen fern varieties; pines claim the lower slope. Deer browse near the trail at first and last light. Rustic benches offer open and leaf-filtered glimpses at Red House Lake, its outlet, the park bikeway, and a round-topped hill. Midway, a recessed stone wall and a tree-masked rusted steel tower hint at the ski jump that once stood here.

The 2.7-mile **Osgood Trail** travels the round-topped hill at the northeast end of Red House Lake. It starts off McIntosh Trail, east of the ASP 1–ASP 2 junction. Chipmunks, songbirds, woodpeckers, and deer play cards of surprise. You pass through the fruit tree corridor into the hemlock-pine woods, ascending to the loop junction. Continue uphill; the unmarked trail to the right closes the loop. Where the trail contours above the McIntosh drainage, flat rock slabs punctuate the forest. At the hill's meadow crown, a break in the tree rim funnels views west. On descent, the trail passes through an attractive meadow plateau drained by springs. Be watchful where the trail traverses mossy slabs. A well-worn false trail heads straight downhill as the primary trail curves right, bringing the loop and hike to a close.

South of Red House Lake, the 6.5-mile **Beehunter Trail** travels the ridges drained by Beehunter Creek to form a loop. The trail ascends steadily and steeply, attaining the ridge spine for a more comfortable tour. Thick grasses spread beneath an open forest of oak, maple, ash, and hemlock. To the east, filtered views span the Beehunter Creek drainage to a sunbathed ridge. In places, mossy, slick rocks compose footing. Cross 15-foot-wide Beehunter Creek; wading may be necessary if the water is high. Parklike forest, red-berried elder in August, and a fern-draped split rock characterize the ridge ascent and descent. Beyond a hemlock grove, you'll follow a woods road across a service road and field to a trailhead sign. There a dirt road leads you back to the bike trail and the last Beehunter Creek crossing. End at the picnic area.

Quaker Hiking Options

This area's representative sampling travels ridges, tops peaks, explores a boulder realm, and visits a natural spring.

The 5-mile out-and-back **Mount Tuscarora Trail** starts south of the Quaker entrance station; there is road-shoulder parking only. Its foot trail ascends through dark hemlock-hardwood forest, passing parallel to a drainage. With a burst of climb, you top and trace the ridge. Indian pipe, baneberry, huckleberry, witch hazel, striped maple, beech, and small oaks frame travel. Claim the first summit (elevation 2,064 feet) at 2.25 miles and the upper plateau (elevation 2,144 feet) at 2.5 miles. Here stands an abandoned fire tower, missing its lower flight of stairs and several of its landings. The tower now serves only as a landmark, and trees enfold the site. Although the ridge trail continues to Coon Run Road, backtrack as you came. (**Note:** The park's Summit Fire Tower on South Mountain above Red House Lake has been restored and opened; contact the Allegany State Park Historical Society for information: www.asphs.org.)

The 2.5-mile **Three Sisters Trail** travels a loop visiting only one sister, West Sister, and begins west of the rental office (west of the ASP 1–ASP 3 junction). Pass into a pine-hardwood forest with a shrubby understory, skirt a pine-hemlock stand, and cross under a power line to cross a footbridge. The trail traverses both grassy meadow and open forest—a virtual sauna on sunny, humid days. Pockets of bee balm, a red member of the mint family, adorn the drainage. The steady ascent can be rocky, with rustic corduroys aiding passage at soggy reaches. The forest fills out and the trail tops and follows the ridge left to summit West Sister (1.4 miles), but finds no views. On your descent, beware—the grassy footpath can be slippery when wet. Cross a natural spring on a rock slab and pass under the power line to meet and descend Ranger Trail (a road) near cabins 1, 2, and 4. Just before you reach ASP 3, a footpath heads left, bringing the hike to its end.

For the 3-mile out-and-back **Bear Caves–Mount Seneca Trail,** the preferred access is the eastern one (1.4 miles east of the ASP 1–ASP 3 junction). The trail heads north off ASP 3. Bring flashlights to look into the boulder caves, and come prepared for some stooping and squeezing in the small rooms and passages less than 200 feet long. Naturalist-led tours will help you locate the openings. This trail ascends the steep bouldery slope on a wide, worn path, reaching an entire community of the massive boxy boulders and outcrops. Crossbedding, balanced rocks, eroded nooks, fissures, and overhangs plus the adorning mosses, lichens, and ferns capture attention. At the base of the rocky realm, follow the primary trail to the right; a secondary trail rounds to the left. You traverse the woodsy top of the rocks. Where the trail is again at the base of the rocks, you tour in familiar Allegany forest. The crossing of Slide Hollow may require wading during high water. The trail contours, then turns sharply right for a steep assault on Mount Seneca. Clintonia, trillium, and mayflower decorate the floor. You emerge at the summit (1.5 miles), viewing the wooded ridge of Mount Onondaga to the northeast and the immediate peak to the east. Although the trail continues, return as you came.

The 0.5-mile out-and-back **Bear Springs Trail** begins on the west side of ASP 1, 2.2 miles north of the ASP 1–ASP 3 junction. Enter a woods of maple, black cherry, and hemlock to the left of the sign. The trail slowly descends. The spatially open forest shows a lush fern floor and a profusion of woods flora not seen elsewhere in the park. Oxalis, mayflower, trillium, and whorled pogonia and other orchids contribute to the array. Soon after crossing a drainage, the trail reaches the 6-foot-high stonework grotto protecting the springs. Although the trail continues, traveling field and hardwood forest, return as you came.

Hike Information

Local Information
Cattaraugus County Tourism, 303 Court Street, Little Valley 14755; (800) 331-0543; www.enchantedmountains.info

Local Events/Attractions
Just north of Randolph, you can explore the backroads and hillsides that are home to an **Old Order Amish community.** While touring this lovely countryside, you can glimpse their simple life and purchase quilts, furniture, and baked goods at their shops and roadside stands, but never on Sunday. Contact Cattaraugus County Tourism.

Accommodations
Allegany State Park campgrounds are open year-round and have a total of 424 campsites, 375 cabins, and 7 rental cottages. Reservations: (800) 456-2267; www.reserveamerica.com

Honorable Mention

Chautauqua–Allegheny Region

M Deer Lick Nature Sanctuary

Southeast of Gowanda, this 400-acre National Natural Landmark wins you over with familiarity versus drama. Quiet hardwood forests, dark hemlock stands, lush meadows, and gentle creeks are the hallmarks of this sanctuary owned by The Nature Conservancy (TNC). Bordered to the north by the South Branch Cattaraugus Creek and New York State's Zoar Valley Multiple Use Area, the sanctuary completes the puzzle of unbroken open space that forms a vital natural wildlife corridor. A relaxed 5-mile day hike strings together the four color-coded trails of this sanctuary, but any of the trails will do. Pets, smoking, and picnicking are prohibited at the preserve, which is open daylight hours only.

From central Gowanda, go south on Highway 62 for 0.5 mile and turn left (east) onto Hill Street. In 0.4 mile turn right onto Broadway Road and in another 0.6 mile turn left onto Point Peter Road. Stay on Point Peter Road for 2.3 miles and turn left to enter the sanctuary (0.5 mile past the Point Peter Road–Forty Road fork). Find a small parking area, trail register, and pit toilets near the trail's start. *DeLorme: New York Atlas & Gazetteer:* Page 41 A4. Contact The Nature Conservancy, Central and Western New York Office, 1048 University Avenue, Rochester 14607; (585) 546-8030; www.nature.org.

Finger Lakes Region

This region at the saddle of New York enjoys a signature landscape. Its long, thin, glacier-gouged north-south trending lakes look as if Mother Nature raked her fingers down the state's middle. Dramatic east-west tributary gorges, with spirited falls, tumbling cascades, and imposing cliffs contribute to the region's singularity. Rolling woods and grasslands, low steep ridges and hills, vital wetlands, and diked ponds complete the discovery.

Ice age glaciers fashioned the region's unusual flat-bottomed, deep trench lakes and molded the landscape around them. A gently rolling, bumpy terrain of drumlins sits to their north, while an impassable deposit of piled rock debris (a moraine, spe-

Painted turtle, Beaver Lake Nature Center

cifically the Valley Heads Moraine) rises to the south. Because of this moraine, the drainage from the Finger Lakes flows north into Lake Ontario. Waters south of the moraine flow to the Susquehanna River. In a race to join the trench lakes, tributary waters catapult over hanging valleys left behind by the retreating glaciers.

At the Seneca-Cayuga county border northeast of Seneca Falls, Montezuma National Wildlife Refuge occupies a remnant ancient lake formed when the glaciers melted. Today these wetlands serve a diverse domestic and migratory bird population. During the building of the Erie Canal, Montezuma was a place of heartache. Mosquitos here carried a form of malaria that claimed the lives of many Irish workers. Displaced Irish made up much of the canal project workforce.

The well-drained rocky deposits at the south ends of the Finger Lakes are ideally suited to wine grapes, so, as you might expect, wine-country touring is popular here. Apple orchards thrive in the north—one of the tastier Great Lake effects.

This region holds claim to New York's tallest waterfall (Taughannock Falls), the lone national forest in the state (Finger Lakes National Forest), the birth of the Women's Rights Movement, and the founding of the Church of Jesus Christ of Latter-day Saints at Hill Cumorah. The region is traversed by the Erie Canal and the long-distance Finger Lakes Trail, which unites the area's natural splendors. You'll encounter the history of early New York at the site of a Sapony Indian village and while strolling lands awarded in payment to soldiers of the Revolutionary War.

25 Beaver Lake Nature Center

At this 650-acre Onondaga County Park, northwest of Syracuse, 9 miles of superbly groomed nature trails and boardwalks explore lake, marsh, meadow, and woods habitats. Thirty thousand spring-migrating Canada geese and 10,000 fall migrants swell the resident bird and animal populations. The trails serve all levels of ability, and repeat tours bring new appreciation—just ask the park's "100 milers" who regularly walk the eight trails. The Lake Loop, featured here, is the shining core. The site's interpretive panels, benches, observation platforms, blind, and high-powered binoculars enhance discovery.

Start: At the visitor center, Lake Loop trailhead
Distance: 3-mile loop
Approximate hiking time: 1.5 to 2 hours
Difficulty: Easy
Elevation change: The trail is virtually flat.
Trail surface: Boardwalk and woodchip path
Seasons: Best for hiking, spring through fall
Other trail users: Cross-country skiers (The Lake Loop is exclusive to cross-country skiers in winter; adjacent trails serve snowshoers. In winter, snowshoes are available for rent.)
Canine compatibility: Dogs not permitted
Land status: County Park
Nearest town: Baldwinsville

Fees and permits: Vehicle entrance fee
Schedule: Year-round, grounds: 7:30 a.m. to posted closing time (varies with season); building opens 8:00 a.m.
Maps: Beaver Lake Nature Center flier (available online and at the site)
Trail contacts: Beaver Lake Nature Center, 8477 East Mud Lake Road, Baldwinsville 13027; (315) 638-2519; www.onondaga countyparks.com/parks/beaver
Special considerations: Seasonally, this site can be buggy, so carry repellent. There can also be seasonal flooding on the Lake Loop.

Finding the trailhead: From New York State Thruway Interstate 90, take exit 39, go north on Interstate 690/Highway 690 for 5.8 miles, and take the second Baldwinsville exit as indicated for the nature center. Go west on Highway 370 for 2 miles, then turn right on East Mud Lake Road, following the signs. The nature center is on the left in 0.7 mile. The Lake Loop starts to the right of the visitor center; the other named trails start to the center's left. Scenic carved signs identify each trail. *DeLorme: New York Atlas & Gazetteer*: Page 74 C3.

The Hike

A woods walk characterizes the early distance of the Lake Loop, which seldom hints at the centrally located 206-acre glacial lake—the site's namesake, Beaver Lake. The wide woodchip path travels among spruce-pine woodland, towering tulip and beech trees, and a congestion of young, spindly maples. Virginia creeper, poison ivy, and fern contribute to the understory. Where Lake Loop crosses the other park trails, signs indicate the junctions.

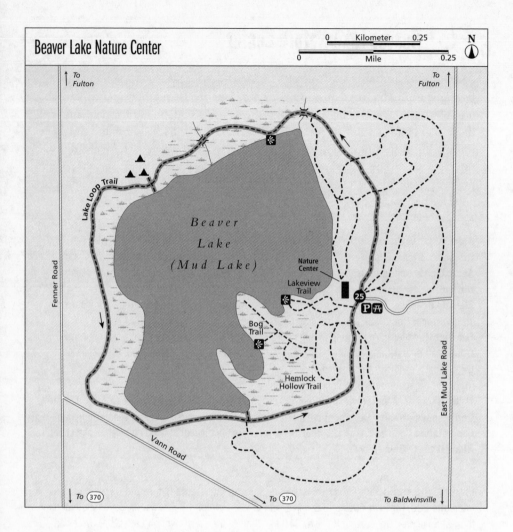

Where boardwalk carries you across the lake outlet, white water lilies decorate the flow in summer, and turtles sometimes sun on logs. Highbush blueberry, alder, nettles, dodder, ferns, and cattails rise among the wetland tangle. Ahead, an elevated bench overlooks Beaver Lake, and later, duckweed coats a small inlet drainage where cardinal flowers may decorate a log.

Wide foot trail replaces the boardwalk, and soon after, side trails branch right to three lean-tos and left to a canoe landing site. Canoes are a popular way to explore the lake. Periodically, the county offers guided canoe trips, and canoe rentals are available. In the wet ash-maple woodland, poison ivy abounds. Back on boardwalk, you pass a small catfish water with rimming cattail, loosestrife, and arrowhead.

The trail then passes through pine plantation and meadow, skirting below the Vann Road lake overlook. As the Lake Loop continues, a spur accesses the parallel loop of the Three Meadows Trail. Hemlock hollows and transition woods now alternately claim attention on the loop. Travel is again removed from the Beaver Lake shore. A small wetland pond sits trailside. En route to the visitor center, you pass the Hemlock Hollow, Bog, and Lakeview trailheads, which suggest side trips.

Miles and Directions

0.0 Start from the visitor center trailhead; head right, following the Lake Loop counterclockwise.

0.5 Cross the boardwalk over the lake outlet.

1.2 Reach the shelters and canoe landing.

2.5 Pass the spur to Three Meadows Trail.

3.0 Return to the visitor center.

Options

The final leg of the Lake Loop provides access to both the Hemlock Hollow Trail and the Lakeview Loop, which suggest options to extend the hike. Because the Hemlock Hollow Trail is the lone access to the Bog Trail, likely you'll choose to combine these two walks.

The **Hemlock Hollow Trail** swings a 0.4-mile loop through a dark hemlock woods with oak, birch, beech, and interspersing witch hazel. Midway, the 0.6-mile ladle-shaped **Bog Trail** branches west, traveling boardwalk and trail along a former island, now a marshy Beaver Lake peninsula. By keeping right at the two initial Bog Trail junctions (the ladle loop), you first explore the length of the peninsula (the handle). Spurs off the "handle" lead to a bog-pond overlook, a one-story lake observation platform, and a couple of lakeshore accesses. At the lake platform, high-powered binoculars pull cross-lake herons into close scrutiny. On your return take the boardwalk (ladle) loop, capping your bog visit with marsh study. Sweet gale, arrowhead, cranberry, loosestrife, and carnivorous pitcher plant are among the finds here.

The wheelchair-accessible 0.3-mile **Lakeview Loop** draws a figure-eight through similar deep woods, with plaques explaining the intricate habitat interactions. A beautiful big oak marks the second loop junction. Off the second loop, spurs lead to two lake vistas. At the larger viewing stop, you find benches and telescopes, including one telescope low enough for comfortable use from a wheelchair. An osprey snatching a fish from the lake, the growing wake of a beaver, or some 30,000 migrant geese waiting for the spring thaw in Canada can dazzle onlookers. Late March to early May marks the peak time for viewing Canada geese. In fall a smaller contingent of geese stops over on the lake.

Hike Information

Local Information

Syracuse Convention and Visitors Bureau, 572 South Salina Street, Syracuse 13202; (315) 470-1910; www.visitsyracuse.org

Local Events/Attractions

The **Onondaga Lake Park** complex in northwest Syracuse includes a carousel, skate park, dog park, walking trails, and boating, as well as the Salt Museum (salt was an early Syracuse industry), and the re-created Sainte Marie among the Iroquois French Mission that stood on this lakeshore (1656–1658). At the latter, volunteers in period dress introduce life skills of the seventeenth century. The museum here explains the cultures of the Haudenosaunee (Iroquois), the French, and the meeting of the two. Onondaga Lake Park, 106 Lake Drive, Liverpool 13068; (315) 453-6768; www.onondagacountyparks.com

26 Interloken National Recreation Trail

Northeast of Watkins Glen, the gentle ridges and open flats of New York State's one and only national forest were once inhabited by Iroquois Indians and later partitioned into military parcels issued in payment to veterans of the Revolutionary War. Through a farmer's relief act in the Great Depression, the lands returned to government hands and today serve recreational users. This linear multiuse national recreation trail (NRT) strings north to south through the national forest, exploring natural and planted forest stands, open meadows, shrubby transitional lands, and pond habitats. The diversity supports fish, birds, and mammals.

Start: At the northern trailhead
Distance: 12-mile shuttle
Approximate hiking time: 6.5 to 8 hours
Difficulty: Moderate
Elevation change: The trail has a 550-foot elevation change, with its low elevation of 1,300 feet in the south, its high elevation of 1,850 feet on Hector Backbone.
Trail surface: Earthen path, grassy tracks, and boardwalk crossings
Seasons: Best for hiking, spring through fall
Other trail users: Hunters, cross-country skiers (This is primarily a foot/cross-country ski trail, but limited marked stretches may be shared with horse riders and mountain bikers.)
Canine compatibility: Leashed dogs permitted (cleanup requested)
Land status: National forest
Nearest town: Watkins Glen
Fees and permits: No fees or permits required
Schedule: No time restrictions, but there is a 14-day limit in the forest for camping

Maps: Finger Lakes National Forest recreation map (available at the district office or online: www.fs.fed.us/r9/forests/greenmountain/htm/fingerlakes/f_rec.htm)
Trail contacts: Finger Lakes National Forest, Hector Ranger District, 5218 Highway 414, Hector 14841; (607) 546-4470; www.fs.fed.us/r9/forests/greenmountain/htm/fingerlakes/f_home.htm
Special considerations: Where the trail is shared-use, you need to be alert for horse riders and yield the right-of-way to them. There is no camping within 50 feet of the trail, and you should wear fluorescent orange during hunting season, late September into December. You may encounter occasional blowdowns on the trail, and despite such improvements as boardwalks and gravel, muddy patches still exist. The forest service is always on the lookout for volunteers to help maintain this trail. Metal stakes, wooden signs, and orange markings variously indicate the trail.

Finding the trailhead: From the Highway 227–Highway 96 junction in Trumansburg, go north on Highway 96 for 1.5 miles and turn left onto County Road 143, proceeding 4.8 miles. Turn right onto County Road 146 for 1 mile and then go left onto Parmenter/Butcher Hill Road for 0.6 mile. The northern trailhead is on the left. *DeLorme: New York Atlas & Gazetteer:* Page 59 D7.

For the southern trailhead, at the County Road 5–Highway 79 intersection in Burdett, go 0.9 mile east on Highway 79 and turn left onto Logan Road (County Road 4) for 1.1 miles. Turn right onto Wyckoff Road. In 0.5 mile head right on Burnt Hill Road for 0.4 mile; the trailhead is on the left. *DeLorme: New York Atlas & Gazetteer:* Page 45 A7.

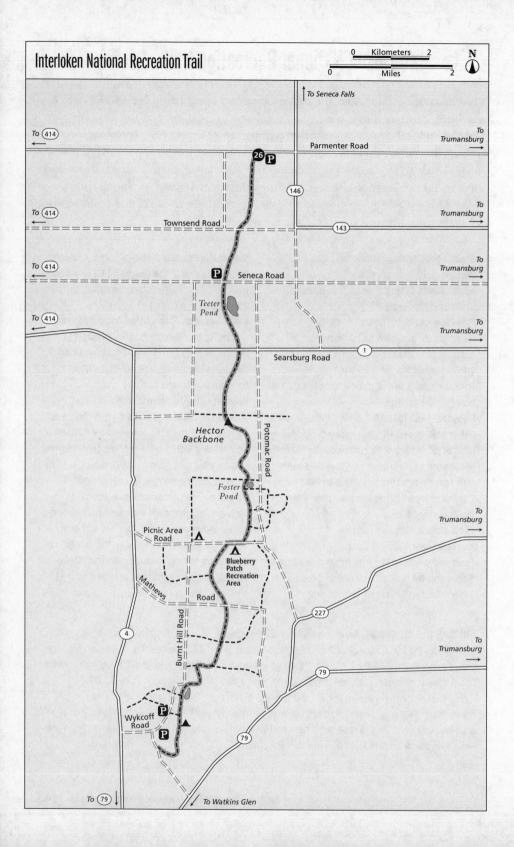

Interloken National Recreation Trail

The Hike

Southbound, the national recreation trail (NRT) enters a mature mixed woods with a lush understory. An aspen-shrub complex, a woodlot of young maples and pines, and an open meadow variously enfold travel. Cross Townsend Road and later a 10-foot-wide drainage that may require wading in high water. Veer left for a mild ascent to pass through a gate.

You next wade through knee-high grasses, descending to and crossing Seneca Road. Bypass the No-Tan-Takto Horse Trail and traverse an aspen-shrub complex, reaching Teeter Pond. This expansive marsh and open water attracts wildlife and anglers after warm-water fish species. Snags, shrub islands, and reflections of the cloud-filled sky can add to its welcome. Pass to the right of the pond.

A full mixed forest carries the tour to the next gate at the corner of a large pasture. Follow the diagonal-staked course of the NRT across Teeter Grassland. The trail again parts deep grasses sprinkled with clover, daisy, and buttercup. A row of maples guides you out the gate to Searsburg Road. Attend to all gates because cattle grazing is used as part of forest management.

Upon crossing Searsburg Road, a mowed swath enters the woods for a gentle climb, but muddy passages can weigh down boots. A leafy abundance stretches from the lower story to the canopy. An occasional bright azalea patch seasonally steals the stage. Warblers can enliven the woods.

At a signed junction with the Backbone Trail, continue straight for the NRT, traversing a pine plantation with accents of fairy slipper. Back in an oak-maple woodland, you'll skirt a private property on the right; keep to the trail. A thinned forest of big trees and boardwalks precede the shrubby outskirts of Foster Pond.

While touring the pond outskirts, keep to the tracked path straight ahead. The Backbone Trail (northbound) heads left, and in 200 feet its southbound counterpart journeys right. Afterward, the Interloken NRT rounds the south shore of Foster

NATIONAL RECREATION TRAILS

The National Trail System Act of 1968 authorized the creation of a national trail system, including outstanding-caliber recreational, scenic, and historical trails. Although the creation of National Scenic Trails and National Historic Trails requires an act of Congress, National Recreation Trails (NRTs) may be designated by the Secretaries of Interior and Agriculture. These public trails travel federal, state, county, and municipal lands through rural, urban, and natural wilds. NRTs can serve multiple users and have significant recreational, historical, scenic, and natural qualities that commend them. More than 1,000 national recreation trails now exist, and they can be found in all fifty states, with new trails added annually. The trails range from a fraction of a mile to a whopping 485 miles in length.

Pond. Keep alert for where the NRT then turns right. This is the first of three junctions where side trails branch east to Potomac Road. Thick vegetation encloses the trail before you return to woods.

Next, follow Picnic Area Road right (west) to pick up the southbound NRT past Blueberry Patch Recreation Area. You enter an oak-conifer transition habitat with tall shrubs. At back-to-back junctions, you will proceed straight. Pass from a younger woods of maple and big-toothed aspen to a more mature, mixed complex, coming to a gate and another stretch through pasture. As the footpath angles uphill to the left, a microwave tower may be visible to the east. Ridges and farmland sweep west. Despite the tall grasses that overhang it, the path is more passable than it first appears.

From Mathews Road return to woods, soon passing among snags and 8-foot-tall shrubs. After you cross the overgrown corridor of Burnt Hill Trail, the NRT enters a rolling meander through planted and natural woods. The NRT briefly merges with the Gorge Trail. After an area of mature oaks and more conifer plantations, you travel the levee of a wildlife pond at a corner on Burnt Hill Road. The scummy crescent can percolate with frogs, but watch out for poison ivy.

Continue straight past South Slope Trail and, upon meeting the Finger Lakes Trail (FLT), bear left. A lean-to sits in the nearby grassy clearing. Proceed forward, following the FLT/Interloken Trail. With a rolling descent, you traverse a shrubby bog, skirting a frog pond, passing through a gap in a stone wall, and traveling along boardwalk to end at the southern terminus.

Miles and Directions

0.0 Start from the northern trailhead; hike the NRT south.

1.2 Cross Townsend Road.

2.1 Cross Seneca Road.

2.2 Proceed forward past the No-Tan-Takto Trail.

2.5 Reach Teeter Pond; pass along the west shore.

3.3 Cross Searsburg Road.

4.4 Meet the Backbone Trail; continue straight on the NRT.

5.7 Again meet the Backbone Trail and continue straight on the NRT.

5.8 Reach Foster Pond; travel east along its south shore.

6.1 Reach a junction; follow the NRT to the right. **Note:** The path straight ahead comes out at Potomac Road. (This is the first of three junctions where side trails branch east to Potomac Road.)

6.9 Reach Picnic Area Road; follow the road right (west) 0.2 mile to resume southbound on the NRT (here, a foot trail on the left).

7.4 Reach the first of back-to-back junctions; proceed straight at each. **Note:** At the second junction, the Ravine Trail heads right.

8.4 Cross Mathews Road.

9.1 Cross the overgrown Burnt Hill Trail.

Teeter Grassland along Interloken National Recreation Trail, Finger Lakes National Forest

9.6 Follow the Gorge Trail right for 0.1 mile and then proceed straight, where the Gorge Trail turns right.

10.2 Travel the levee of a wildlife pond.

10.5 Continue straight past South Slope Trail.

11.0 Meet the main Finger Lakes Trail (FLT); bear left.

12.0 End at the southern trailhead.

Hike Information

Local Information

Seneca County Tourism, One Di Pronio Drive, Waterloo 13165; (800) 732-1848; www.visitsenecany.net, or **Schuyler County Chamber of Commerce,** 100 North Franklin Street, Highway 14, Watkins Glen 14891; (607) 535-4300 or (800) 607-4552; www.schuylerny.com

Local Events/Attractions

Women's Rights National Historical Park (NHP) in Seneca Falls follows the history of the Women's Rights Movement through museum exhibits, video, and guided tours. In 1848 Elizabeth Cady Stanton, along with four other women, invited the public to the first Women's Rights Convention here in Seneca Falls. Her home is among those toured. Women's Rights NHP, 136 Fall Street, Seneca Falls 13148; (315) 568-2991; www.nps.gov/wori

Accommodations

Blueberry Patch Campground, open year-round but operated as walk-in only in winter, has nine fee sites available first come, first served.

Organizations

Finger Lakes Trail Conference helps maintain and map the trail. FLTC, 6111 Visitor Center Road, Mount Morris 14510-9527; (585) 658-9320; www.fingerlakestrail .org

27 Taughannock Falls State Park

The Finger Lakes Region boasts several prized east–west gorges with companion gorge and waterfall trails, but each pens a unique signature. Taughannock Falls autographs this park with a flourish. Cradled in an amphitheater of 400-foot cliffs and spilling 215 feet from a hanging canyon, the waterfall conjures images of Yosemite National Park in California and ranks as one of the tallest waterfalls east of the Mississippi River. The park's hiking trail duo neatly combines, so you can admire the falls canyon from gorge belly and canyon rim.

Start: At the Taughannock Falls trailhead

Distance: 5 miles combining the out-and-back interior trail with the rim loop

Approximate hiking time: 2.5 to 3.5 hours

Difficulty: Easy

Elevation change: The Gorge Trail segment has a 100-foot elevation change, the rim loop about a 550-foot elevation change.

Trail surface: Paved or surfaced walk and earthen path

Seasons: Best for hiking, spring through fall

Other trail users: None

Canine compatibility: Leashed dogs permitted, cleanup required. (Because the interior trail can buzz with people, you'll have a better walk with your dog along the rim loop.)

Land status: State park

Nearest town: Ithaca

Fees and permits: Park entrance fee

Schedule: Year-round, dawn to dusk; North and South Rim Trails closed in winter

Maps: State park brochure (obtain at the park)

Trail contacts: Taughannock Falls State Park, 2221 Taughannock Park Road, Trumansburg 14886; (607) 387-6739; http://nysparks .state.ny.us/parks

Special considerations: There is no swimming in Taughannock Creek, and mountain bikes are prohibited. Stay on trails because of the danger of falling rocks. Icy conditions in winter or spring can result in temporary closures of the normally year-round Gorge Trail. The park allows bow hunting for deer in season, October to early December, but it's generally conducted away from trails. Pack in, pack out.

Finding the trailhead: From the junction of Highway 13/34 and Highway 89/96/79 (the corner of State and Meadow Streets) in Ithaca, head north on Highway 89 for 9.1 miles. Turn left (west) to enter the trailhead parking lot; trails leave from the southwest corner of the parking area. *DeLorme: New York Atlas & Gazetteer:* Page 60 D2.

The Hike

The park trails start from a site once occupied by Taughannock Indian camps and a cabin that sheltered a soldier during the Revolutionary War. The interior trail and Falls Overlook on the north rim tender the best views of Taughannock Falls, but the rim loop grants perspectives on the canyon and its exciting creek.

First exploring the canyon interior, you hike the Gorge Trail (an interpretive trail with a paved walk) west upstream to the waterfall viewpoint.

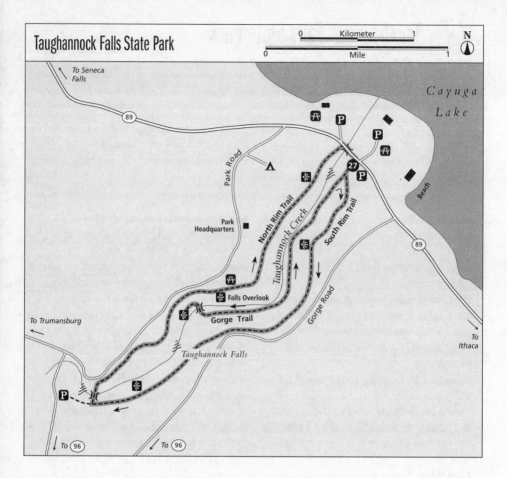

Taughannock Falls State Park

Before reaching the falls, an impressive 15-foot-high ledge spans the 75- to 100-foot width of Taughannock Creek. At the ledge's northern corner, the water spills at an angle, its chutes carving deep channels into the sedimentary ledge. The uniformly flat bedrock was planed long ago by torrents of melting ice and rock. Hemlock, basswood, maple, and oak overhang the path.

Upstream a lower ledge spans the creek, and the steep wooded slopes yield to skyward-stretching cliffs. Swallows, hawks, and cardinals dwell in the canyon as do great-horned owls, whose appetites spelled an end to a peregrine release program here in the 1970s.

The sandstone-shale cliffs become more prominent, steep, eroding, and jointed, with boxy overhangs and tenuously held trees. Sycamores join the ranks. Across the bridge the waterfall amphitheater humbles onlookers. With multiple streamers and wisping spray, the 215-foot vertical falls plunges to an awaiting, 30 feet deep, pool. Spray-nurtured greenery adorns the canted base of the 400-foot cliffs. You couldn't ask for a more lovely or authoritative stop sign.

You then backtrack downstream to add the rim loop. Back at the trailhead, next to the trail information hut, you'll see where the South Rim Trail veers left; take it for clockwise travel.

Ascend the stairs of the South Rim Trail, top the rim, and turn right. A mixed deciduous-hemlock forest provides shade. Deer encounters are possible. After a half mile, an open up-canyon view replaces the teasing canyon glimpses so far granted by the rim trail. This view spotlights the upper reaches of Taughannock Falls.

After the rim terrain pushes you out onto Gorge Road to round a steep side drainage, the trail and lightly used road remain closely paired. At a U-shaped scouring of the rim, a dizzying look down applauds the canyon bottom. You next travel a broad wooded plateau and round a deep rim gash. Cedar, birch, willow, berried shrub, tiger lily, daisy, and harebell adorn the trail corridor.

You cross the hiker bridge over Taughannock Creek before reaching a road bridge and the park boundary. Upstream a 100-foot falls spills at a hairpin turn of the now-pinched gorge. Downstream the prominent tree-capped rim, jutting points, vertical cliffs, and an ancient plunge pool washed by the slow-moving stream compose the scene. Following the North Rim Trail, you pass through a small field, bearing right to follow the mowed shoulder of the park road, before returning to foot trail, now in a narrow hemlock-hardwood corridor near a wire-mesh fence.

At Falls Overlook, you gain a bird's-eye view of the rock amphitheater and starring waterfall. This vantage presents the upstream water flowing up to and over the abrupt ledge of the hanging valley, as well as the full length of the 215-foot drop. Taughannock House, a luxury hotel that operated here from the 1860s until the turn of the twentieth century, formerly claimed this view.

Descend past a picnic area and the campground. Views span downstream, taking in the broad creek bottom, wooded canyon, Cayuga Lake, and its east ridge. Stone stairs lead to Highway 89, at the north side of the Taughannock Creek bridge. Turn right, cross the bridge, and return to parking.

Miles and Directions

0.0 Start from the Taughannock Falls trailhead at the southwest corner of trail parking; hike the Gorge Trail west upstream, staying inside the gorge.

0.7 Cross the footbridge of Taughannock Creek, reaching the Taughannock Falls viewpoint; backtrack downstream to the South Rim Trail's start.

1.5 Follow South Rim Trail uphill and turn right on the rim.

3.3 Cross the Taughannock Creek bridge to the North Rim Trail. Follow the North Rim Trail downstream.

4.0 Reach Falls Overlook; continue downstream.

4.7 Meet Highway 89; turn right and cross the road bridge over Taughannock Creek.

5.0 End at trailhead parking.

Hike Information

Local Information

Seneca County Tourism, One Di Pronio Drive, Waterloo 13165; (800) 732-1848; www.visitsenecany.net or **Ithaca/Tompkins County Convention and Visitors Bureau,** 904 East Shore Drive, Ithaca 14850; (607) 272-1313 or (800) 28-ITHACA; www.visitithaca.com

Local Events/Attractions

This area is noted for its **farmstands, U-picks, cideries, and wineries.** Contact the Ithaca/Tompkins County Convention and Visitors Bureau. The Cayuga Wine Trail links a dozen wineries on the west side of Cayuga Lake, north of the park. Circling the lake, the Wine Trail gathers a handful more. Cayuga Wine Trail, P.O. Box 123, Fayette 13065; (607) 869-4281 or (800) 684-5217; www.cayugawinetrail .com

Accommodations

Taughannock Falls State Park campground, open late March to mid-October, has eighty-four sites, some with cabins. Reservations: (800) 456-2267; www.reserveamerica .com

Taughannock Falls, Taughannock Falls State Park

28 Onondaga Trail

Southeast of Syracuse, this blue-blazed trail, an extension of the Finger Lakes Trail (FLT) and part of the North Country National Scenic Trail, rolls from rim to drainage, touring hemlock glen and hardwood forest between Spruce Pond and Chickadee Hollow Road. It then surrenders to roadway travel all the way to Cuyler before resuming as foot trail passing through state forests to meet the main FLT. This hike features the northern Onondaga stretch to Chickadee Hollow Truck Road. En route you pass a hang-gliding site, gather vistas, and visit hollows, but mostly you enjoy a pleasant forest sojourn.

Start: At the northern (Spruce Pond) trailhead
Distance: 15.6 miles out-and-back
Approximate hiking time: 9 to 11 hours
Difficulty: Strenuous
Elevation change: The trail has a 750-foot elevation change, with the high point on Morgan Hill.
Trail surface: Earthen path, doubletrack, and woods road
Seasons: Best for hiking, spring through fall
Other trail users: Hang gliders, hunters, snowshoers, cross-country skiers
Canine compatibility: Dogs permitted but must be controlled at owner's side by leash or voice command
Land status: Department of Environmental Conservation (DEC) and private land
Nearest town: Truxton
Fees and permits: No fees or permits required

Schedule: No time restrictions
Maps: Finger Lakes Trail Conference map, The Onondaga Trail, Sheet 01 (purchase online: www.fingerlakestrail.org)
Trail contacts: New York State DEC, Region 7, 1285 Fisher Avenue, Cortland 13045; (607) 753-3095; www.dec.ny.gov
Special considerations: This trail travels both public and private lands, so keep to the trail, obeying posted notices. In Labrador Hollow Unique Area, there is no camping and no fires, and that goes for private land, too. When following the woods roads, you need to keep a sharp eye out for the continuations of the foot trail. A long lapse between markers may indicate the need to backtrack and find the trail. Hang gliders must secure a special permit from the DEC.

Finding the trailhead: From Interstate 81 take exit 14 for Tully and go east on Highway 80 for 4.5 miles, passing through Tully and merging with Highway 91 North. At 4.5 miles turn south on gravel Herlihy Road, go 1.9 miles, and continue straight at the junction to reach the Spruce Pond Fishing Access in another 0.1 mile; there is parking for ten vehicles. *DeLorme: New York Atlas & Gazetteer:* Page 61 B6.

The Hike

Southbound, you cross the earthen levee of square-shaped Spruce Pond to strike up a slope of beeches and maples, following blue blazes. A dark spruce plantation,

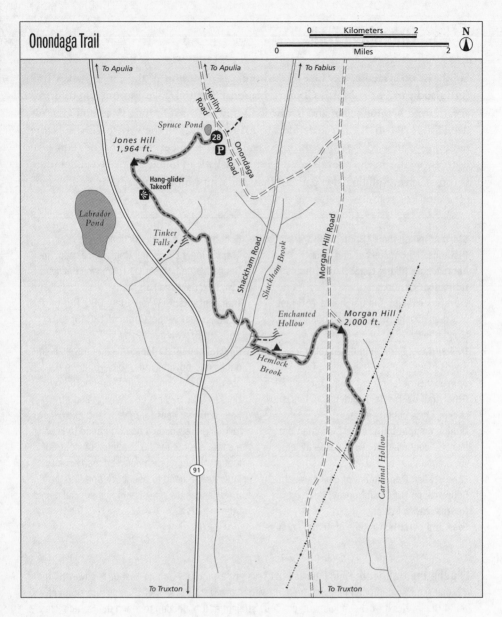

aspen-ash woods, and an aisle of seasonally fragrant azalea in turn claim the way. Atop Jones Hill you first travel private land that has been logged before entering Labrador Hollow—a unique area. As the trail passes above the steep western slope, faint side paths spur to the rim for seasonal views. Keeping to the trail, you traverse the meadow gap of Hang Glider Leap, the official hang-glider takeoff. Here the view opens to the steep-sided north-south valley of oval Labrador Pond.

Next you follow the doubletrack south, descending the rim. Here, keep an eye out for the return to foot trail, which heads left into leafy forest. The tour again flip-flops between road and trail; keep left, still descending. A sharp descent leads to the gulf rim of Tinker Falls Creek. The severity of the slope restricts views of the 50-foot falls, which weeps from an overhang. Although tracked paths descend suicidally toward the falls, they are both unofficial and irresponsible, damaging terrain and risking injury. Do not approach the dangerous, sloughing edge or in any way attempt cross-country travel to improve your view. But taking a few steps to your right affords a relatively safe look into the cliff bowl and gorge. If you truly want to see the falls, a 0.3-mile DEC spur ascends along the creek from Highway 91 to a base-of-the-falls view.

Proceed ahead, crossing Tinker Falls Creek just upstream from the overhang, and make a steep angular ascent to a woods road. Be careful at the creek crossing, though; the rocks are mossy and the drop precipitous. Follow the road grade left a few steps to pick up the foot trail on the right. The hike again alternates between foot trail and woods road as it ascends away from the drainage. Cross the nose of a ridge and descend through plantations of spruce and tamarack to cross Shackham Road.

You next ford Shackham Brook. Vandals delivered the fatal blow to the old footbridge that was here, necessitating its removal. Fording is usually no problem, except during spring runoff. Soon after, you will cross Enchanted Hollow. A side excursion up either side of this hollow finds pretty cascades. The Onondaga continues forward to contour a hemlock-spruce slope, pursuing Shackham Brook upstream. The trail then hooks left to travel parallel to and upstream along the aptly named Hemlock Brook. Past an 8-foot mossy waterfall and camp flat, you reach a lean-to overlooking the steep-sided drainage. Hemlock Brook is the prettiest spot on the trail, so you might choose to snack or picnic here before moving on. After the crossing of Hemlock Brook, the trail climbs sharply away.

Back on a woods road, watch for the foot trail to descend left. After the trail dips through a steep side drainage, cross Morgan Hill Road. Side trails branch left to the Morgan Hill bivouac area. Continue to seek out the blue Onondaga Trail markers. Truck trails and snowmobile routes interweave the area. Woodpecker, grouse, and deer may surprise.

The hike passes through tree plantation and mixed woods, with a few big-diameter trees, to meet Chickadee Hollow Road, a lightly used truck trail. Although the Onondaga Trail continues to the right on this road, for this hike turn back, returning the way you came.

Miles and Directions

0.0 Start from the northern (Spruce Pond) trailhead; cross the earthen levee and strike uphill.

1.3 Enter Jones Hill–Labrador Hollow Unique Area.

1.5 Reach the hang-glider site; follow the doubletrack descending south.

1.7 Look for and follow the foot trail heading left off the doubletrack.

2.5 Reach the gulf rim of Tinker Falls Creek; keep to the trail, crossing Tinker Falls Creek upstream from the overhang.

4.0 Cross Shackham Road.

4.3   Reach Enchanted Hollow. **Side trip:** Upon crossing the hollow, you can detour upstream along the marked woods road, finding hollow views and a stepped cascade in 0.1 mile.

5.0   Reach the lean-to at Hemlock Brook. Descend to and cross Hemlock Brook on flat stones and then take the foot trail as it angles sharply uphill.

5.8   Reach Morgan Hill Road; angle across the road, picking up the trail as it ascends.

7.1   Cross an open utility corridor.

7.8   Reach Chickadee Hollow Road, a lightly used truck trail, and turn around, backtracking to Spruce Pond and the trailhead. **Option:** The Onondaga Trail continues to Cuyler and beyond to state forests and the main FLT, but much of it is now on variously used roads. Because past hikers misused the right-of-way across private land, by letting dogs run loose and straying themselves from the trail, the former trail has been closed to all. If you choose to continue, follow the Onondaga Trail as it heads right on Chickadee Hollow Road, left on Morgan Hill Road, left on Highway 13, left on West Keeney Road and right on Tripoli Road to Cuyler, where the hike again returns to trail past the cemetery, heading southward. (Carry and follow the FLT Onondaga Trail Sheet O1 map.)

15.6 End at the Spruce Pond trailhead.

Forest with maple along Onondaga Trail, Morgan Hill State Forest

Hike Information

Local Information

Syracuse Convention and Visitors Bureau, 572 South Salina Street, Syracuse 13202; (315) 470-1910; www.visitsyracuse.org or **Cortland County Convention and Visitors Bureau,** 37 Church Street, Cortland 13045; (607) 753-8463 or (800) 859-2227; www.cortlandtourism.com

Local Events/Attractions

Cortland County is agricultural and its agribusiness trail map takes you on a country drive that is both tasty and educational. You can visit research facilities, farmstands, Christmas tree farms, stables, cideries, dairies, nature centers, and more. The Cortland County Ag Trail map is available online at www.cortlandtourism.com, or you can contact Cortland County Convention and Visitors Bureau.

Organizations

Finger Lakes Trail Conference helps maintain and map the trail. FLTC, 6111 Visitor Center Road, Mount Morris 14510-9527; (585) 658-9320; www.fingerlakestrail .org

▶ Poison Ivy, Oak, and Sumac

These skin irritants can be found most anywhere in North America and come in the form of a bush or a vine, having leaflets in groups of three, five, seven, or nine. The oil they secrete can cause an allergic reaction in the form of blisters, usually about twelve hours after exposure. The itchy rash can last from ten days to several weeks. The best defense is to wear clothing that covers the arms, legs and torso or apply nonprescription lotions that can be washed off with soap and water.

If you think you were in contact with the plants, wash with soap and water to remove any lingering oil from your skin.

Should you contract a rash from any of these plants, use an antihistamine to reduce the itching and apply a topical lotion to dry up the area. If the rash spreads, consult your doctor.

29 Watkins Glen State Park

This park presents one of the premier gorge and waterfall settings in the Finger Lakes Region, and in the nation. Charged with excitement, the hike brings together majestic 200-foot cliffs and the nineteen waterfalls, turbulent chutes, and deep plunge pools that punctuate a 545-foot drop on Glen Creek. A loop fashioned by the Gorge and Indian Trails presents the canyon spectacle. Scenic bridges, tunnels, and twisting staircases make the trail an attraction as well.

Start: At the concession area (lower) trailhead
Distance: 2.8-mile lollipop
Approximate hiking time: 2 to 2.5 hours
Difficulty: Moderate due to the 832 stairsteps and possibility of slippery wet footing
Elevation change: The hike has about a 500-foot elevation change.
Trail surface: Stone steps and natural surface
Seasons: Best for hiking, spring through fall
Other trail users: None
Canine compatibility: Dogs not permitted on Gorge Trail
Land status: State park
Nearest town: Watkins Glen
Fees and permits: Entrance parking fee
Schedule: Park, year-round; Gorge Trail, mid-May through early November; sunrise to sunset

Maps: State park brochure (obtain at the park)
Trail contacts: Watkins Glen State Park, P.O. Box 304, Watkins Glen 14891; (607) 535-4511; http://nysparks.state.ny.us/parks
Special considerations: The parking lot can fill at peak times. A fee shuttle bus runs between the lower concession and upper entrance for those who have time for just one-way travel or who prefer to descend rather than ascend the trail's 832 steps. Purchase tickets at the bus. Watch your footing because natural springs and the mist from the waterfalls can dampen the walks and steps, making them dangerous. Icy conditions close down the trail. Outside the gorge, the park allows the bow hunting of deer in season.

Finding the trailhead: In Watkins Glen find the park entrance west off Franklin Avenue/Highway 14, south of Fourth Street. *DeLorme: New York Atlas & Gazetteer:* Page 45 A7.

The Hike

The bustle at the park entry echoes the site's roots as a private resort in the late 1800s. Off-hour, off-season, and rainy-day visits allow for a quieter, unhurried communion with the grandeur of the gorge. Be sure to bring your camera because snapshots come as fast as blinks.

For an upstream hike, you start at the west end of the parking lot. The stone arch of Sentry Bridge together with the bulging canyon walls shape a keyhole view of a

Cavern Cascade, Watkins Glen State Park

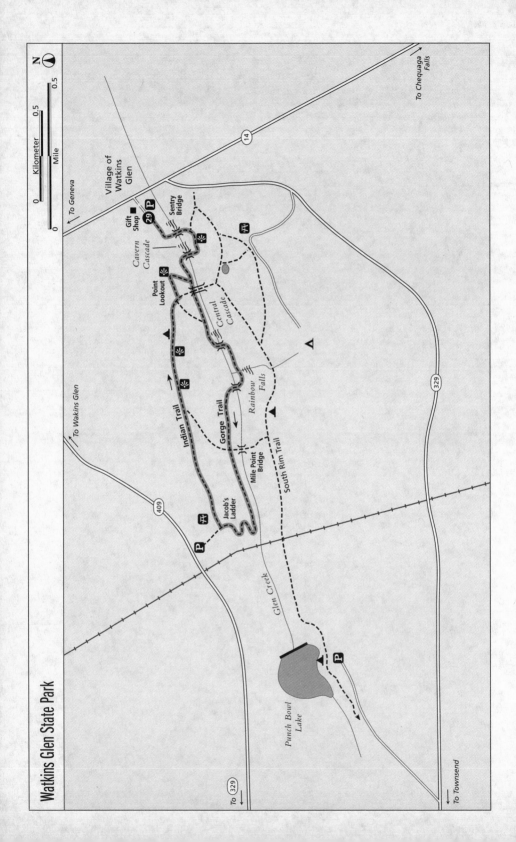

Watkins Glen State Park

waterfall recessed in the shadows, the first in a line-up of great waterfall views. Ascend the first of three tunnels bored into the rock, emerging at Sentry Bridge, which presents an up-canyon view of the pinched gorge, distant views of Watkins Glen village, and close looks at the jointed, layered rock. The Gorge Trail crisscrosses Glen Creek four times but bypasses both High and Mile Point Bridges.

Across Sentry Bridge, look for the Finger Lakes Trail (FLT) to head left; it travels along the south rim. You remain in the gorge, continuing up Watkins Glen. As the Gorge Trail ascends the stairs to Cavern Cascade, look down to a heart-shaped plunge pool. Now pass behind the droplet curtain for a unique perspective. Ahead stretches the Spiral Tunnel staircase, which opens to a view of the site's suspension bridge (High Bridge). Keep to the gorge, passing under the bridge.

As the canyon walls cup and divide, each bend holds an aura of mystery. A leafy bower claims the Narrows, while a dry, concave bowing of the gorge characterizes the Cathedral. A tiered upstream cascade feeds the 60-foot plunge of Central Cascade, the tallest waterfall in the park. Rainbow Falls showers over the south rim. Beyond it, you come to a bridge and Spiral Gorge, a dark, more brooding passage.

The trail returns to the glaring light at Mile Point Bridge. You continue west along the north wall, bypassing both the bridge and a trail to the right. In the calm above the lower-canyon storm, you'll ascend the stairs dubbed "Jacob's Ladder." The ladder staircase leads both to Indian Trail (the loop's return) and the upper entrance. Look for the Indian Trail to head right just past a midway bench on Jacob's Ladder.

A low rock wall or mesh fence edges Indian Trail as it travels the north rim and slope. Evergreens, dogwood, oak, maple, beech, sassafras, and black cherry contribute to a forest roster that now conceals Glen Creek. The spur from Mile Point Bridge arrives on your right, and before long you again overlook Rainbow Falls.

Staying along the rim, you find a Central Cascade overlook, which provides a totally new perspective. The trail then skirts a cemetery and descends sharply past a lean-to to reach the suspension bridge. Lovers Lane arrives on the right; continue straight ahead (east) to Point Lookout and the park entrance. A detour out onto the bridge, however, provides a grand look 85 feet down to the creek and out the canyon. At Point Lookout, you obtain a fine cross-gorge view. Descend the stairs, meeting the Gorge Trail at Spiral Tunnel. Here you retrace the start of the hike back to the trailhead.

Miles and Directions

0.0 Start from the lower (concession area) trailhead; hike upstream.

0.1 Cross Sentry Bridge, meeting the FLT. Continue upstream on the Gorge Trail.

0.3 Reach Spiral Tunnel and the loop junction; remain on the Gorge Trail.

0.7 View Rainbow Falls.

1.0 Pass Mile Point Bridge, staying on the north side of the gorge.

1.5 Ascend Jacob's Ladder to the midway bench and there follow Indian Trail as it heads right (downstream).

1.8 Pass the spur to Mile Point Bridge.

2.0 Overlook Rainbow Falls.

2.3 Reach the suspension bridge and a junction; continue straight. **Note:** A detour onto the bridge offers a plunging view to the creek as well as looks out the canyon.

2.4 Reach Point Lookout.

2.5 Close the loop at Spiral Tunnel; backtrack to the lower trailhead.

2.8 End at the concession area.

Options

Another hiking option while at the park is the **FLT.** The park's section of the FLT travels the wooded south rim 3.5 miles out and back to an upstream artificial lake. It shares the first 0.1 mile with the Gorge Trail. After crossing Sentry Bridge, you veer left on the FLT, ascend some one hundred steps to the south rim, and turn right on the service road. Spurs branch to the south entrance, campground, and gorge; keep to the white-blazed FLT. Much of the way, appreciation of the gorge is audio rather than visual. You pass beneath a scenic railroad bridge and view a ragged vertical outcrop. The trail then rounds the nose of a hemlock-shaded point and descends in spurts to Punch Bowl Lake. You overlook the dam and its vertical falls and then dip to where beaver gnawings dot the lakeshore. Bullfrogs, cedar waxwings, and red-winged blackbirds animate the site. Marsh grasses claim the upper lake, while cattail peninsulas extend into the open water. This hike's return is as you came, but the FLT does continue upstream.

Hike Information

Local Information

Schuyler County Chamber of Commerce, 100 North Franklin Street, Highway 14, Watkins Glen 14891; (607) 535-4300 or (800) 607-4552; www.schuylerny.com

Local Events/Attractions

Watkins Glen International celebrates car racing with everything from NASCAR to vintage motorsport racing. From May through October you, too, can take three paced laps around the course. For schedules, fees, and details, contact Watkins Glen International, 2 North Franklin Street, Watkins Glen 14891; (607) 535-2338; www .theglen.com

Accommodations

Watkins Glen State Park campground, open early May to mid–October, has 285 sites. Reservations: (800) 456-2267 or www.reserveamerica.com

30 Buttermilk Falls State Park

Buttermilk Falls caps a dramatic 500-foot free fall on Buttermilk Creek that occurs over a distance of 0.75 mile. Cascades, rapids, bedrock slides, emerald pools, platy cliffs, and a 40-foot rock spire help write the canyon drama. The upper glen holds a more soothing woods–water union. Easy interlocking park trails explore the Buttermilk Creek gorge, its upstream glen, and Treman Lake.

Start: At the lower gorge trailhead, in the park's main area

Distance: 5.2-mile barbell-shaped hike

Approximate hiking time: 3 to 3.5 hours

Difficulty: Easy

Elevation change: The hike has a 650-foot elevation change: 500 feet on the lower Gorge–Rim Trail loop, and 150 feet on the upper Bear Trail–Treman Lake Loop.

Trail surface: Earthen and paved path

Seasons: Best for hiking, spring through fall

Other trail users: None

Canine compatibility: Leashed dogs permitted but not in bathing areas (You must present proof of pet's rabies inoculation upon entering park.)

Land status: State park

Nearest town: Ithaca

Fees and permits: Park entrance fee

Schedule: Year-round, gorge trails close early November; daylight hours

Maps: State park brochure (obtain at the park)

Trail contacts: Buttermilk Falls State Park, c/o Robert H. Treman State Park, 105 Enfield Falls Road, Ithaca 14850; (607) 273-5761 (summer) or (607) 273-3440; http://nysparks .state.ny.us/parks

Special considerations: Insect repellent is needed in park's meadow areas.

Finding the trailhead: From the junction of Highway 79 and Highway 13/34 (the corner of Seneca and Meadow Streets) in southwest Ithaca, go south on Highway 13/34 for 1.8 miles and turn left to enter the main area of Buttermilk Falls State Park. *DeLorme: New York Atlas & Gazetteer.* Page 46 A2.

For the upper area, continue 0.1 mile farther south on Highway 13/34 and turn left (east) onto Sandbank Road. Go 2.2 miles and turn left onto West King Road. In 1.2 miles turn right onto the park road to reach the upper day-use area in 0.8 mile. *DeLorme: New York Atlas & Gazetteer.* Page 46 A2.

The Hike

This get-to-know Buttermilk Creek hike stitches together four of the park trails: Gorge, Rim, Bear, and Treman Lake, showcasing waterfalls, creek, and lake. Some ten falls greet you along this hike.

Starting near the swimming hole below Buttermilk Falls, you cross the dam to ascend the Gorge Trail, which travels the west wall. Broad Buttermilk Falls sheets over a magnificent canted cliff sloping to the artificial pool. Crossbeds accent the light-colored rock, and small ledges fold the racing waters into cascades. A steep stairway ascends alongside the falls, isolating aspects of the watery spectacle.

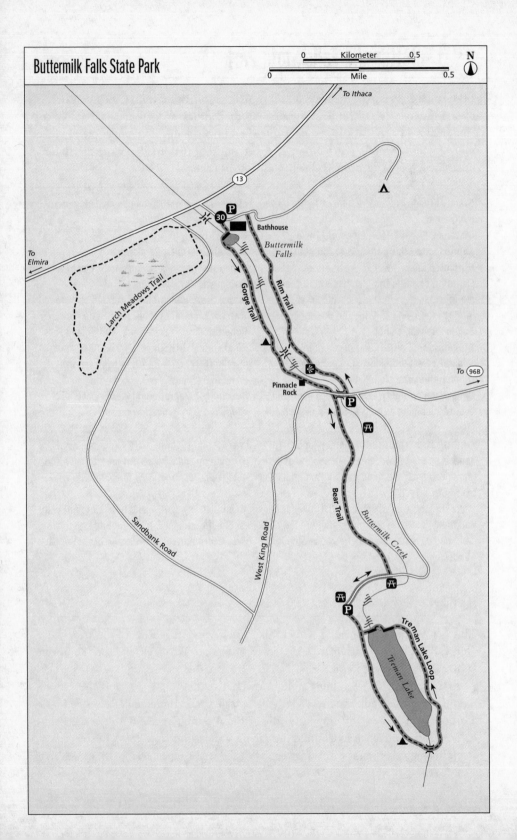

Buttermilk Falls State Park

0 | Kilometer | 0.5
0 | Mile | 0.5

N

To Ithaca

13

P

30

Bathhouse

Buttermilk Falls

Rim Trail

Gorge Trail

To Elmira

Larch Meadows Trail

Pinnacle Rock

To 96B

P

Bear Trail

Buttermilk Creek

Sandbank Road

West King Road

P

Treman Lake Loop

Treman Lake

Beech, hemlock, and a burst of understory greenery complement the canyon water. Upstream a three-tier, three-dimensional falls graces the creek. One level spills through a grotto where the gorge walls pinch together.

Cascades, historic plunge pools, eroded cliff scallops, and hemlock coves build on the canyon's fascination. The trail affords perspectives from below, alongside, and atop the cascades. You will spy a lean-to uphill to the right before arriving at a crescent footbridge over Buttermilk Creek. It leads to the Rim Trail on the east wall, allowing you to shorten the hike. Stay along the west wall.

A ribbony side falls washes over the cliff as a split-level hourglass falls punctuates Buttermilk Creek. Next find Pinnacle Rock, a 40-foot chiseled gray spire isolated from the cliff. Delicate ferns decorate the erosion-resistant ledges. Maple, ash, and basswood shade the way to West King Road.

You now cross West King Road and follow the Bear Trail, which continues upstream on the west shore. This trail travels the broad wooded glen, passing some 40 feet from the stream. Hemlock, basswood, maple, oak, and beech shade a plush, green understory. Side trails descend to the bank, while skunk cabbages claim the moist slopes. Where the trail emerges at a picnic area, you can either continue upstream along the creek or follow the road to the site's comfort station, where the Treman Lake Loop starts.

For counterclockwise travel, stay along the west shore, bypassing the dam and spillway feeding to the picnic area falls to travel forest. Cross-lake views find an attractive cliff scallop and cove. Geese often occupy a small island. You cross a side-drainage footbridge to round the marshy head of Treman Lake, bypassing an orange-blazed trail near a second lean-to. Afterward cross the scenic stone bridge over Buttermilk Creek to travel the east shore. Steps top a couple of knolls for overlooks of the lake's cattail waters and the dam's curvature. From the shore, you might see sunfish guarding their cleared nests or the nose of a snapping turtle. Beware of poison ivy along the shore and trail. Cross the stone dam and outcrop to complete the loop. Now backtrack the trail to the comfort station and then to West King Road.

Back at West King Road, you now cross the bridge to the east shore and hike the Rim Trail downstream. Past an overlook of Pinnacle Rock, the trail gently descends. The views are few and short-lived. As the descent steepens, the trail shows a paved surface, and the corridor becomes more open. Beyond Buttermilk Falls Overlook (a filtered view), the trail descends and contours the slope above the campground road to exit at the refreshment stand.

Miles and Directions

0.0 Start from the falls swimming hole; cross the dam to the west wall and hike up-canyon on the Gorge Trail.

0.5 Reach a bridge; continue forward on the Gorge Trail. **Bailout:** You may cross this bridge to the Rim Trail and turn left (downstream) for a 1.1-mile loop.

0.6 Reach Pinnacle Rock.

0.8 Reach West King Road; follow the Bear Trail upstream along the west bank of Buttermilk Creek. **Bailout:** You can cross the West King Road bridge to reach the Rim Trail and follow it downstream for a 1.7-mile loop.

1.5 Reach a picnic area.

1.7 Reach Treman Lake Loop; hike it counterclockwise starting along the west shore.

3.4 Close the loop; backtrack downstream to West King Road.

4.3 Reach West King Road; cross the bridge and follow the Rim Trail left downstream.

4.9 Reach Buttermilk Falls Overlook.

5.2 End near the refreshment stand.

Options

▶ **Until 1779 and the Revolutionary War, the park's Larch Meadows held a Sapony Indian village of log cabins. In that year, advance word of the approaching Sullivan Campaign forced the tribe to flee. Although flight spared their lives, the arriving troops torched all the cabins, ending an era.**

The park's **Larch Meadows Trail,** a 1-mile interpretive loop, examines a unique marsh. You start next to the ballfield restroom, 0.1 mile south of the main entrance, off Sandbank Road. A fine brochure (available at the entrance station) explains this habitat, part of ancient Cayuga Lake. You hike along the southern edge of the ballfield and bear left before the end of the field on a wide mowed swath. Although short, the trail traverses a variety of habitats: mixed woods, skunk cabbage wetland, willow stands, clusters of spreading black walnut, and waist-high ferns, grasses, and wildflowers. Past a 4-foot-diameter sycamore, the trail meets and briefly follows a service road to the right. The trail then resumes to the right, returning to the ballfield.

Hike Information

Local Information

Ithaca/Tompkins County Convention and Visitors Bureau, 904 East Shore Drive, Ithaca 14850; (607) 272-1313 or (800) 28-ITHACA; www.visitithaca.com

Local Events/Attractions

The **Art Trail** takes you on a tour of forty-six artist studios in the Ithaca area. The media is varied: clay, paint, fiber, film, computer-generation, wood, and more; www.arttrail.com

Accommodations

Buttermilk Falls State Park campground, open mid-May to mid-October, has fifty-two sites. Reservations: (800) 456-2267 or www.reserveamerica.com

◀ *Buttermilk Falls, Buttermilk Falls State Park*

31 Robert H. Treman State Park

Tied up in the attractive woodland package of glacier-scoured Enfield Glen, this park unites a narrowed gorge; platy cliffs; the stepped waters, cascades, and waterfalls of Enfield Creek, including the 115-foot Lucifer Falls; a historic mill; and the stunningly beautiful and awesome stone constructions of the Civilian Conservation Corps. The park is named for the benefactor who presented the lands to New York State in 1920, Ithaca merchant and parks commissioner Robert H. Treman. The park's Gorge and South Rim Trails together shape a fine discovery loop.

Start: At the lower gorge trailhead, near park headquarters
Distance: 4.2-mile loop
Approximate hiking time: 2.5 to 3.5 hours
Difficulty: Moderate
Elevation change: There is a 400-foot elevation change between the park's lower and upper sections. A decided climb leads from the lower parking lot into the canyon proper, and stone steps and the Cliff Staircase add to the workout.
Trail surface: Earthen and paved path and stone stairs
Seasons: Best for hiking, spring through fall
Other trail users: None
Canine compatibility: Leashed dogs permitted but not in bathing area (You must present proof of your pet's rabies inoculation upon entering park.)
Land status: State park
Nearest town: Ithaca
Fees and permits: Park entrance fee
Schedule: Year-round, all gorge trails close early November; daylight hours
Maps: State park brochure (obtain at the park)
Trail contacts: Robert H. Treman State Park, 105 Enfield Falls Road, Ithaca 14850; (607) 273-3440; http://nysparks.state.ny.us/parks
Special considerations: Be careful during wet conditions, when leaves and walks can be slippery.

Finding the trailhead: From the junction of Highway 13 and Highway 327, 5 miles south of Ithaca, turn west on Highway 327 and proceed 0.1 mile to enter the lower park on the left. An upper entrance sits farther west off Highway 327; follow signs. *DeLorme: New York Atlas & Gazetteer:* Page 46 A2.

The Hike

From the lower trailhead, the Gorge Trail jump-starts the heart with a cardiovascular workout taking you up slope and up canyon on a steep set of stairs. The trail rolls, staying mainly in woods, keeping Enfield Creek a secret save for a distant whisper. Beech, birch, oak, and hemlock fashion the overhead shade.

After a half mile you overlook the creek, which presents different personas depending on season and water year. Here it sheets over bedrock shelves, spilling in glistening slides and stepped cascades. The water's movement over time has shaped

The Old Mill (1847) interior, Robert H. Treman State Park

smooth contours and ledge breaks. The creek's steep banks keep it pristine despite the trail's popularity.

The trail takes you to and from the waterway before settling in alongside the creek at a mile. Platy shale cliffs and the bending creek define the trail's course. Cliffs draw eyes skyward with their bulges, incised breakages, and precarious-hanging trees.

Beyond the junction with the Red Pine Trail, you'll overlook a waterfall that spans the width of the creek. The water plunges over the initial ledge, strikes the sloped base rock, and glides into a pool, where the splashpoint draws a line of white bubbles.

Hiking past an Enfield Creek bridge, you come to Lucifer Falls, the tallest of the Enfield waterfalls and a showstopper, gracefully dropping and curving over yellow-ish cliffs in a magnificent high-walled amphitheater of platy shale and steep flowing greenery. The trail's stairway, balcony, and railing built by the Civilian Conservation Corps (CCC) seamlessly blend into the character of the natural cliff—a remarkable engineering and architectural feat. The masterful work of the CCC is as much recommendation of this gulf as the waterfalls and cliffs.

Ahead, an upper falls sits snugged in a corner. You then cross Enfield Creek at the next bridge, following the left bank overlooking a skinny channel marked by potholes and waterfalls. This is a younger gorge, where a natural reroute of Enfield Creek has cut a new course through bedrock. The lower gorge scours out a historic trench that filled with glacial debris at the end of the last ice age. Views from the bridge stretch out the lower canyon.

Where the South Rim Trail (the loop's return) heads left, cross the stone bridge over Fish Kill Creek to reach the upper developed park, historic mill, and a waterfall on Fish Kill Creek. The gristmill, on the national and state historic registers, serves as

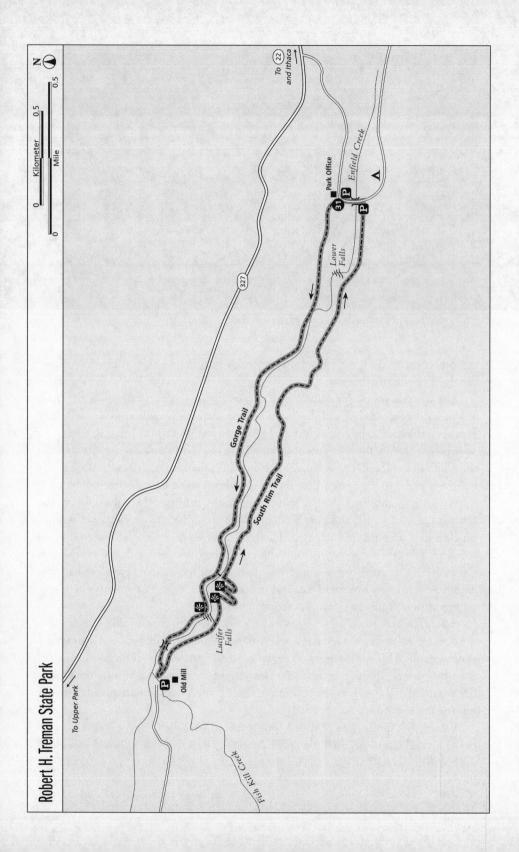

Robert H. Treman State Park

To Upper Park

Fish Kill Creek

Old Mill

P

Lucifer Falls

South Rim Trail

Gorge Trail

327

Lower Falls

Park Office

31

P

P

Enfield Creek

To 22
and Ithaca

N

Kilometer
0   0.5

Mile
0   0.5

a museum and houses a restroom. Exhibits are devoted to mill operation, the hamlet of Enfield Falls that preceded the park, and the history of the CCC.

Following the South Rim Trail back down canyon, you ascend the slope, turning left on a service road and then left on the crescent spur to an Enfield Creek overlook. This is one of two dramatic canyon overviews that present the steep shale canyon, the stylish stone stairways, and the tiny hikers tracing the paths below. The second overlook adds Lucifer Falls. More splendid CCC construction follows as you descend the Cliff Staircase. Uphill travelers repeat a common complaint, "More stairs!"

At the base of the stairs, the South Rim Trail turns right and soon returns back upslope but it never actually traces the rim. Tulip trees enter the mix, and knocking woodpeckers announce their presence. Moisture can bring out red efts. Continue on the wide grade for wooded glen travel. After the trail enters its descent, watch for the rim trail to fork left, leaving the primary contouring grade. You will overlook the Lower Falls summer swimming area before emerging at the cabin area. Angle left through the cabin area to the park road. To return to headquarters parking, take the pedestrian bridge where Enfield Creek flows over the park road.

Miles and Directions

0.0 Start from the lower gorge trailhead, near park headquarters; ascend the rock stairway.

1.4 Reach the Red Pine Trail junction; continue forward to the upper gorge.

1.5 Reach an Enfield Creek bridge; continue forward to the upper gorge. **Bailout:** You can cross here, turning left on the South Rim Trail for a 3.2-mile loop, but you will miss viewing Lucifer Falls and the Old Mill.

1.6 Reach Lucifer Falls Overlook.

1.8 Cross a bridge over Enfield Creek and follow the left bank upstream.

1.9 Reach South Rim Trail (on your left). Delay your loop return, instead crossing the bridge over Fish Kill Creek to reach the upper park and mill museum.

2.0 Reach the Old Mill; backtrack downstream over the Fish Kill Creek bridge and follow the South Rim Trail (now a right).

2.2 Arrive at a service road; turn left.

2.3 Follow the crescent spur left to an Enfield Creek overlook.

2.4 Overlook Lucifer Falls; descend the Cliff Staircase.

2.5 Reach a junction; turn right, continuing on the South Rim Trail. **Note:** Straight leads to the bridge over Enfield Creek first mentioned at 1.5 miles and the Gorge Trail.

3.5 The trail begins to descend.

3.7 Turn left at the fork.

3.9 Overlook the Lower Falls Swim Area.

4.0 Emerge at the cabin area trailhead; angle left toward the park road.

4.1 Cross the pedestrian bridge where Enfield Creek flows over the roadway.

4.2 End the loop back at headquarters parking.

Hike Information

Local Information
Ithaca/Tompkins County Convention and Visitors Bureau, 904 East Shore Drive, Ithaca 14850; (607) 272-1313 or (800) 28-ITHACA; www.visitithaca.com

Local Events/Attractions
Adjacent to the Cornell University campus, **Cornell Plantations** celebrates growing things and the changing of the seasons within its 50 acres of botanical gardens, vast natural areas, and a 150-acre arboretum. The Plantations is open daily free of charge from sunrise to sunset; peak season is May through mid-October. Cornell Plantations, One Plantations Road, Ithaca 14850; (607) 255-2400; www.plantations.cornell.edu

Accommodations
Robert H. Treman State Park campground, open mid-May through November, has eighty-six campsites (cabin sites are only available through early November). Reservations: (800) 456-2267 or www.reserveamerica.com

A PARK WITH A PAST

Before this land became Robert H. Treman State Park, it housed the thriving mill community of Enfield Falls in the early 1800s. Although few clues remain today, the hamlet existed for fifty years and had as many as fifteen permanent structures: homes and outbuildings, shops, and businesses. The first gristmill was built in 1817 by Isaac Rumsey. After fire claimed that mill in the 1830s, Jared Treman (Robert's grandfather) built the current mill. The glen's attractive cliff, woods, and falling water attractions have long been an area lure and helped fill the rooms and stable of the hamlet's Enfield Falls Hotel. Youngsters collected a charge of 10 cents to see the waterfalls. The hotel was also the hamlet's social center, hosting dances. Within the Old Mill today, exhibits and historic maps further flesh out the story of this park predecessor.

During the Great Depression, the Civilian Conservation Corps, Company 1265 had an established camp in what is now the upper park. The men, mostly from urban centers and as many as one hundred in number, lived first in tents and then in more durable wooden barracks and structures. The corps completed critical construction jobs here and in neighboring parks in the Finger Lakes Region. You'll witness their legacy in the quality masonry along trails and at campgrounds. They were key in this park's recovery from the flood of 1935. If you look closely at the park's cliff walls, you may spy the workers' carved initials or names, "CCC," or "1265"—a proud and fragile thread to the past.

Honorable Mentions

Finger Lakes Region

N Howland Island Unit, Northern Montezuma Wildlife Management Area

In Cayuga County, north of Cayuga Lake and about 25 miles west of Syracuse, the Barge Canal and Seneca River isolate this 3,100-acre interior island, where eighteen dikes create an extensive network of ponds that attract waterfowl. Low, rolling hills (drumlins deposited by glacial action 10,000 years ago), planted floodplain, unkempt fields, and hardwood stands complete the island mosaic. The habitats sustain 200 bird species, as well as deer, fox, various small mammals, turtle, frog, fish, and newt. The site's management roads and dikes lay out easy strolls. But high water can make the entire unit inaccessible because a Seneca River culvert crossing or fording is required to enter the complex. Once at the island, you hike the management road 1.5 miles to the ponds area (just past the Quonset hut). You arrive at Brooder Pond where dikes lay out loop options. Bring insect repellent and mosquito netting for more enjoyable visits. You may choose to avoid the area during hunting season. Heed waterfowl nesting closures April through May.

From Interstate 90 take exit 40 at Weedsport. From the toll booth, go south on Highway 34; in 0.2 mile turn west onto Highway 31. Passing through the village of Port Byron, reach Savannah in 13.5 miles and there turn north onto Highway 89. Go 0.3 mile and, at the north edge of town, turn east onto County Road 274 (Savannah–Spring Lake Road). Proceed 2.3 miles and turn right onto Carncross Road to reach trail parking where the road dead-ends at the Seneca River culvert in 0.6 mile. There is parking for a handful of vehicles. *DeLorme: New York Atlas & Gazetteer.* Page 74 D1. Contact New York State Department of Environmental Conservation, Region 7, 1285 Fisher Avenue, Cortland 13045; (607) 753-3095; www.dec.ny.gov.

O High Tor Wildlife Management Area

South of Canandaigua Lake, three separate land parcels compose High Tor Wildlife Management Area (WMA). In the southernmost and largest of the three (3,400 acres), service road, mowed tracks, and foot trail explore wetland, gully, field, and woods. The closed management road running straight through the WMA is the most logical path; it begins off Bassett Road. Side tracks off the management road add visits to area ponds. The Bristol Hills Branch of the Finger Lakes Trail (FLT) also traverses the WMA; look for its orange blazes.

Sightings of yellow warbler, muskrat, hawk, and ruffed grouse, as well as white-tailed deer bounding through the tall grass, can halt your steps. Swallowtail, monarch, and admiral butterflies seasonally flutter about your ankles and the wildflowers that spangle the road shoulders. Hiking the management road is ideal for being alone with your thoughts or sharing an outing with your dog (which must be leashed or under voice control because this is a wildlife area). The WMA is open daylight hours only. Carry drinking water.

From the junction of Highway 53 and Highway 21 in Naples, go south on Highway 53 for 0.8 mile and turn left (east) toward Italy Valley on County Road 21. In 1.9 miles turn left onto Bassett Road. Find trailhead parking 0.3 mile ahead on the left. *DeLorme: New York Atlas & Gazetteer*: Page 58 D3. Contact New York State Department of Environmental Conservation, Region 8, 6274 East Avon–Lima Road, Avon 14414; (585) 226-2466; www.dec.ny.gov.

Central–
Leatherstocking
Region

Squeezed by the Adirondacks, the Catskills, and the Finger Lakes country, this region represents the central bridging piece in the state puzzle and celebrates the countryside made famous by James Fenimore Cooper. It sits at the boundary of the Appalachian Plateau and Lake Ontario Lowlands. Here you will find shining "glimmerglass" lakes, forested ridges, swamps, fields, caverns, and caves. State parks, wetlands, and forests encompass these open spaces for discovery. Beyond the natural areas, tranquil pastoral settings claim the backroads. Syracuse is the primary town in the north, Binghamton in the south.

Ancient tribal routes crisscrossed this region before canal, rail, highway, and modern trails. This is the traditional land of the Onondaga Nation (the people of the hills), one of the Six Nations of the Haudenosaunee (Iroquois). The Onondagas were "the keepers of the council fire." Between 1788 and 1822, the Onondaga Nation had lost nearly all of its land through dealings with white governments. Today, this Nation's territory covers 7,300 acres south of Syracuse near Nedro.

While traveling across territory lands, you might see a spirited game of lacrosse; this is a traditional Native American game that has caught fire at eastern United States schools. Other traditional games here are Snowsnake (where hand-fashioned sticks are thrown down a snow track), and Longball (which involves a V-shaped boundary, leather ball, bat, and running).

Salt attracted the Onondaga people and later the white settlers to the Syracuse area. Covering this area about 400 million years ago, an ancient sea (not unlike the Middle East's Dead Sea or Utah's Great Salt Lake) evaporated, depositing the salt. Early treaties revolved around the ownership of salt, and the valued preservative and flavoring became the driving force behind early Syracuse industry. The resource was fully exploited once the Erie Canal was built, bringing with it ready-made markets. For more of this salty tale, you'll have to visit the Salt Museum on the grounds of Onondaga Lake County Park in northwest Syracuse.

In the central region, a section of the original Erie Canal channels you through the past and welcomes travel on foot or by bicycle. The Syracuse Erie Canal Museum together with several fine smaller museums set the stage for travel. While touring this region, you may stumble upon such historic names as William Seward (of Seward's Folly, the purchase of Alaska fame) and Harriet Tubman (escaped slave and Underground Railroad hero), in addition to James Fenimore Cooper, who penned *The Last of the Mohicans*.

Lock 21, Old Erie Canal State Historic Park

32 Old Erie Canal Heritage Trail

Between DeWitt and Rome, east of Syracuse, this linear New York state park salutes a 36-mile vestige of the historic 363-mile Erie Canal, which linked the Hudson River to the Great Lakes. One of the great engineering feats of its day, the canal opened the West to transportation and commerce—a boon to nineteenth-century New York State. Barge-towing mules plodded the towpath from 1825 to 1918. Today the towpath is a multiuse national recreation trail that strings past parks, museums, and historic structures.

Start: At the western (Ryder Park) trailhead
Distance: 36 miles point-to-point between DeWitt and Rome, including 2.2 miles on road between Durhamville and Highway 31, or 22.4 miles from DeWitt to Durhamville to limit road travel
Approximate hiking time: Anywhere from a few hours to a couple of days
Difficulty: Easy
Elevation change: The flat trail travels at an elevation of 425 feet.
Trail surface: Stone dust or earthen towpath, with brief road links
Seasons: Best for hiking, spring through fall
Other trail users: Cyclists, horse riders, joggers, anglers, snowmobilers, snowshoers, cross-country skiers
Canine compatibility: Leashed dogs permitted (Keep your canine closely reined because this is a shared-use trail and dogs pose a risk to riders. Bring drinking water for your dog.)
Land status: State park and private Erie Canal Village
Nearest town: DeWitt or Rome

Fees and permits: No fees or permits for trail; admission charges for trailside museums and Erie Canal Village
Schedule: Open year-round, dawn to dusk
Maps: State park flier (write or call to obtain from park office)
Trail contacts: Old Erie Canal State Historic Park, RD 2, Andrus Road, Kirkville 13082; (315) 687-7821; http://nysparks.state.ny.us/parks
Special considerations: A 2.2-mile road interruption occurs between Durhamville and State Bridge (at Highway 46 and Highway 31), and a handful of shorter road links occur elsewhere on the trail. On the towpath's western end, footbridges at Cedar Bay and Poolsbrook Picnic Areas, at Green Lakes State Park, and at the Fayetteville side canal allow for passage between the north and south shore attractions. Road bridges serve the eastern end. You will find restrooms and drinking water at Cedar Bay and Poolsbrook Picnic Areas and at Green Lakes State Park and in communities along the canalway.

Finding the trailhead: From Interstate 481 in East Syracuse, take exit 3E for Highway 5/Highway 92 and go east toward Fayetteville. In 0.8 mile, where Highway 5 and Highway 92 split, go left (north) on Lyndon Road for 0.8 mile, bearing left onto Kinne Road. Go 0.4 mile and turn right onto Butternut Drive to find Ryder Park and the western trail terminus on the right in 0.1 mile. *DeLorme: New York Atlas & Gazetteer:* Page 75 D6.

Find the eastern terminus west of Rome, off Highway 46. *DeLorme: New York Atlas & Gazetteer:* Page 76 C4. Durhamville, the preferred ending for hikers, is on Highway 46 north of Oneida. *DeLorme: New York Atlas & Gazetteer:* Page 76 D2.

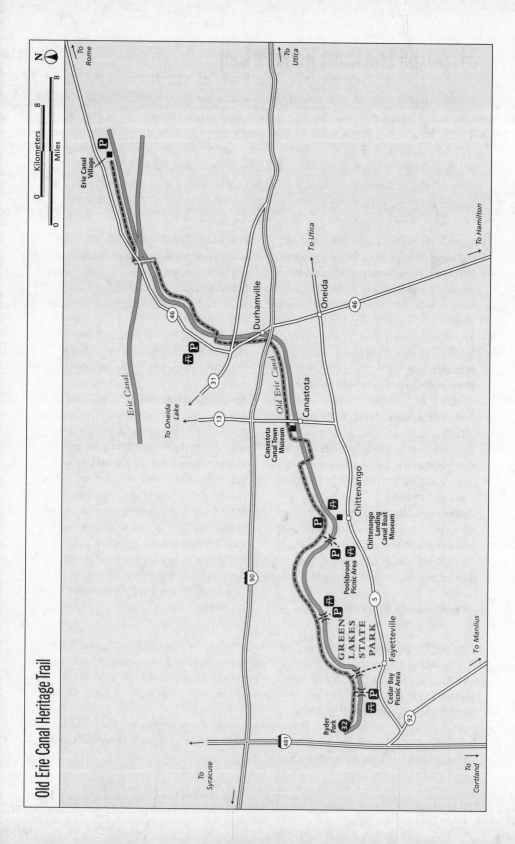

Old Erie Canal Heritage Trail

N

Kilometers
0   8
Miles
0   8

To Rome
To Utica
To Utica
To Hamilton
To Syracuse
To Cortland
To Manlius

Erie Canal Village

46
Erie Canal

Durhamville

31
To Oneida Lake

Oneida
46

13
Canastota

Old Erie Canal

Canastota Canal Town Museum

Chittenango

Chittenango Landing Canal Boat Museum

Poolsbrook Picnic Area

GREEN LAKES STATE PARK

Fayetteville

Cedar Bay Picnic Area

Ryder Park

90

5

92

481

32

The Hike

Virginia creeper, poison ivy, and wild grape entangle the towpath's diverse tree border of maple, box elder, elm, ash, and more. The corridor remains largely undeveloped, with a few encroaching houses near towns. Parallel roadways can add noise, but mostly the hike brings relaxation, hugging the canal straightaways and gentle bends. Corridor inhabitants, such as woodchucks, painted and snapping turtles, rough-winged swallows (which nest in the unmortared stonework), warblers, bluegills, and carp, can lend comedy and surprise. Eastbound, you initially have mileage markers and cross-road labels, but later such aids wane.

At Butternut Creek, you can overlook the cut stones of a lateral aqueduct. Where the route crosses under the rustic steel footbridge to Cedar Bay Picnic Area, you pass the Canal Center. The center, operated by the Erie Canal Museum in Syracuse, is generally closed, but the grounds hold an old tow hoist and watering basin from canal days, as well as a memorial to Moses DeWitt (1766–1794), early settler, militia major, and judge.

The tour slips into character with areas of intermittent to full shade and uninterrupted canal viewing. Where the Erie Canal widens into a pond beyond Burdick Road, a side canal paired with its own towpath trail arrives from Fayetteville. A footbridge stitches this spur to the national recreation trail.

After Manlius Center, the route opens up and the setting is rural. The footbridge to Green Lakes State Park may suggest a side trip. At Kirkville Road, a couple of picnic tables and a small lawn suggest a stop. When the canal widens to a pond, cross-canal views stretch to scenic Poolsbrook Picnic Area, with its benches, tables, shade willows, and apple trees; the park access comes later where a footbridge spans the again-narrowed canal.

At Lakeport Road you can cross the road bridge to the Chittenango Landing Canal Boat Museum (open daily 10:00 a.m. to 4:00 p.m. July and August; irregular hours other times). It has indoor and outdoor exhibits, including historic dry-dock bays being rebuilt in their original stone, replica sawmill and blacksmith buildings, a mule-drawn steamboat, and fine pictorial history.

The towpath narrows at Canaseraga Road, touring hayfields and cornfields. The trail then flip-flops between northern and southern towpaths between West Shore Railroad and Bebee Bridge Road. You'll parallel State Street into Canastota and at Buck Street follow Canal Street east 0.25 mile before resuming on towpath. On Canal Street, you'll find canal artifacts and photos in the Canastota Canal Town Museum, housed in a circa-1874 building on the National Register of Historic Places.

At North Court Road, you angle left across the road to resume northern towpath travel at the edge of a cornfield. Canal Street maintains a parallel course. By Cobb Street, leafy trees lace over the route for scenic strolling.

After the detour to the Interstate 90 overpass, towpath travel continues to Durhamville. For hiking, it's best to end at Durhamville, because a breach in the towpath here requires you to walk 2.2 miles on road. If you choose, though, you can restart towpath travel on the north side of Highway 31 at State Bridge. Stretched before you is another 11.4 miles of trail, taking you through the rural countryside, first on the southern towpath, then on road to the northern towpath at Lock 21. Eastbound from the lock, you initially walk beside the modern New York State Barge Canal before resuming along the heritage canal.

October through April you can end at the privately owned Erie Canal Village off Highway 46, a re-created canal-era community. But May through September, when the village towpath is used for mule-drawn canal boat tours, you must end at Fort Bull Road, 1 mile sooner.

Miles and Directions

0.0   Start from the western (Ryder Park) trailhead; hike the northern towpath east.

0.8   Cross under the footbridge to Cedar Bay Picnic Area.

1.6   Cross Burdick Road.

3.0   Reach Manlius Center.

4.6   Reach the footbridge to Green Lakes State Park; continue east on towpath. **Side trip:** From the footbridge crossing, a 0.2-mile service road ascends to the Highway 290 cross-ing to the park. Restrooms are found at the park office; the park's two deep lakes require a longer detour.

6.1   Cross Kirkville Road.

7.3   Cross Poolsbrook Road, later coming to the footbridge crossing to Poolsbrook Picnic Area; the hike continues east.

8.6   Reach the White Bridge Road trailhead with limited parking. **Option:** This site offers an alternative start or place to spot a shuttle vehicle.

11.0   Reach Chittenango Landing Canal Boat Museum.

12.5   Cross Canaseraga Road.

14.9   At West Shore Railroad, cross from the northern towpath to the south shore; continue east.

15.7   Reach Bebee Bridge Road; turn left (north), cross the road bridge to the northern towpath, and continue east.

16.4   Reach Canastota; follow Canal Street east. **Note:** Here you pass the Canastota Canal Town Museum.

19.5   The towpath halts at North Court Road; angle across the road to pick up the northern towpath at the edge of a field.

22.0   Cross the I-90 overpass; follow the towpath east to Durhamville.

22.4   Reach Durhamville and a breach in towpath travel. **Option:** End here or continue north along Canal Road to Highway 31 at State Bridge.

24.6   Towpath resumes on the north side of Highway 31 at State Bridge; continue east.

31.0   Follow arrows along Lock Road to Lock 21; cross to the north shore and resume east.

35.0   Reach Fort Bull Road, the hike's end (May through September).

36.0   Reach Erie Canal Village, the hike's end (October through April).

Towpath trail, Old Erie Canal State Historic Park

Hike Information

Local Information

Syracuse Convention and Visitors Bureau, 572 South Salina Street, Syracuse 13202; (315) 470-1910; www.visitsyracuse.org or **Madison County Tourism,** P.O. Box 1029, Brooks Hall, First Floor, U.S. Highway 20, Morrisville 13408; (315) 684-7320 or (800) 684-7320; www.madisontourism.com

Local Events/Attractions

The **Canastota Canal Town Museum,** open May through October, occupies an original canal-era building and holds canal and town memorabilia. Canastota Canal Town Museum, 122 Canal Street, Canastota 13032; (315) 697-3451 or (315) 697-5002. **Chittenango Landing Canal Boat Museum** is an active archaeological project beside the historic canal. Here a boat bay has been excavated and a canal boat is being reconstructed as it would have been built in the nineteenth century. Museum exhibits and historic structures complete the offering. Chittenango Landing Canal Boat Museum, 7010 Lakeport Road, Chittenango 13037; (315) 687-3801; www .chittenangolandingcanalboatmuseum.com

Accommodations

Green Lakes State Park campground, closed in winter, has 139 sites. Reservations: (800) 456-2267 or www.reserveamerica.com

Organizations

Parks & Trails New York helps promote, expand, and protect trails, parks, and open spaces statewide and prints and sells a cycling guide to the Erie Canal. Parks & Trails New York, 29 Elk Street, Albany 12207; (518) 434-1583; www.ptny.org

CLINTON'S FOLLY

The Erie Canal linked the Hudson River to Lake Erie. In the beginning, Governor DeWitt Clinton's canal met with a wall of skepticism. But by its completion in 1825, "Clinton's Folly" was hailed as the engineering marvel of the day. The finished canal stretched 363 miles long and incorporated eighty-three locks to smooth out an elevation gain of 568 feet. Eighteen aqueducts spanned the side waters. The Erie Canal brought construction jobs, a new working class of canallers, and ultimately prosperity. Its acclaim spread across the big pond, and before long, grand tours of the Erie Canal became a must-see New World attraction for visiting Europeans, right along with Niagara Falls. The Erie Canal legacy continues to grow, as it contributes top-notch recreation to leisure boaters, cyclists, and pedestrians. Two segments, the 70-mile Erie Heritage Canal in western New York and the 36-mile Old Erie Canal at the center of the state, offer snapshots of the corridor's engineering, natural and cultural offering, and history.

33 Beaver Creek Swamp Loop

In southeast Madison County, this loop in Beaver Creek State Forest travels the wooded and meadow outskirts of Beaver Creek Swamp. The well-marked circuit is part of the extensive 130-mile Brookfield Trail System serving foot, horse, and snowmobile travelers. Although the rolling trail rarely comes in contact with its centerpiece, Beaver Creek Swamp, the enfolding hemlock-hardwood forest, conifer plantations, spring and summer wildflowers, and wildlife endorse travel. Only horseflies can jar the otherwise tranquil spell.

Start: At the southern Fairground Road trail-head

Distance: 9.5-mile loop

Approximate hiking time: 5.5 to 6.5 hours

Difficulty: Moderate due to terrain

Elevation change: The trail has a 200-foot elevation change.

Trail surface: Gravel and earthen trail, mowed track, woods road, and brief truck-trail segments

Seasons: Best for hiking, spring through fall

Other trail users: Horse riders, hunters, snowmobilers, snowshoers, cross-country skiers

Canine compatibility: Leashed dogs permitted

Land status: Department of Environmental Conservation (DEC)

Nearest town: Waterville/Sangerfield area

Fees and permits: No fees or permits required

Schedule: No time restrictions

Maps: Brookfield Trail System DEC brochure (available at trailhead and at DEC office)

Trail contacts: New York State DEC, Region 7, 2715 Highway 80, Sherburne 13460; (607) 674-4017; www.dec.ny.gov

Special considerations: The hike incorporates two short truck-trail segments that are open to vehicles, maximum speed 25 miles per hour. Timbering can occur as part of forest management. Because travel can be hot, carry plenty of water. A bandanna for the head and insect repellent can bring some tranquility during bug season.

Finding the trailhead: From the junction of Fairground Road and Main Street (Skaneateles Turnpike) in Brookfield (east of Hamilton), go north on Fairground Road for 1 mile to find trailhead parking on the left. When arriving from U.S. Highway 20, turn south on Bliven Road between Bridgewater and Sangerfield, coming to a Y junction in 1.4 miles. Bear left on Fairground Road and continue 3 miles to find the trailhead on the right, with parking for five vehicles. *DeLorme: New York Atlas & Gazetteer:* Page 63 B5.

The Hike

You'll hike the gravel track west from the parking lot for a clockwise tour. Yellow DEC markers indicate the hiker/horse trail; in places old orange snowmobile markers will also be seen. Scarlet tanager, woodchuck, and rabbit may number among the early wildlife sightings. Birch, alder, and shrubs frame the open trail. Keep to the gravel path, crossing the horse bridge over Beaver Creek, where high railings protect horse and rider.

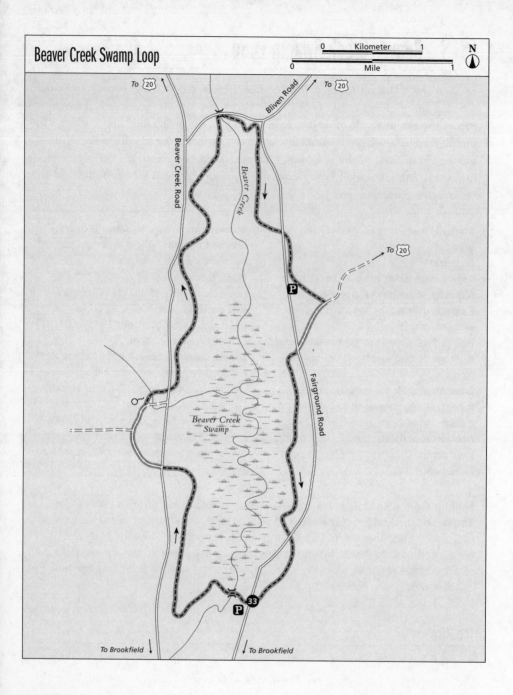

Beaver Creek Swamp Loop

Kilometer
0 1

Mile
0 1

N

To 20

Bliven Road

To 20

Beaver Creek Road

Beaver Creek

To 20

P

Fairground Road

Beaver Creek
Swamp

P 33

To Brookfield

To Brookfield

Be sure to pause on the bridge, because it serves up the best view of Beaver Creek Swamp. Far-stretching views north and a more restricted view south present the attractive marsh. Dark-flowing Beaver Creek meanders through the broad swamp bottom, framed in turn by bog grass, wetland shrubs, and trees. Lilies and other aquatics decorate the shallow edge, and dragonflies buzz the surface.

A mowed swath continues the tour, with a scenic row of maple and black cherry trees toward the swamp, a tidy pine plantation to the left. Rock walls sometimes border the route, while wild strawberries offer tasty bites in June.

At the initial junction turn right to traverse a low hemlock-clad ridge for a cool, shady passage. Oxalis and mayflower decorate the floor. Descending the ridge, cross a small drainage dotted with false hellebore. An aspen stand and spruce plantation now vary the walk. Within the long grassy meadows dotted by pine and aspen, keep an eye out for turkeys.

Occasional engine sounds precede the crossing of Beaver Creek Road and the start of a truck-trail segment. You travel the semishaded dirt road uphill, hiking past a connector to the greater Brookfield Trail System on the left. Before long, the loop turns left, entering the woods and passing a small rock-lined pond built for fire protection in the1930s. Descend and cross a side brook below the rock ruins of an old dam, where you'll follow the levee to the right (downstream) along a ditch.

Crossing back over Beaver Creek Road, you follow the Glenn Bacon Trail, a mowed swath touring an open meadow corridor with full-skirted spruce, woody shrubs, hawkweed, daisy, buttercup, and floral stalks. Before long, the trail ascends sharply and steadily through mixed forest then levels to traverse another long meadow, coming to a tribute to Glenn Bacon, a horseman who advanced the recreational opportunities in this area. A bench and picnic table overlook Beaver Creek Swamp and the wooded east ridge—a textured tapestry of mottled wetland, shrubs, leafy trees, and sharp plantation outlines.

Stay on the mowed track, alternately touring open field and spruce corridor. The trail rolls as it approaches Bliven Road for a road-bridge crossing of Beaver Creek. A few rural homes come into view. On the opposite shore, the trail passes between meadow and plantation. In the mixed woods ahead, a regal 4- to 5-foot-diameter white pine presides trailside, wind, time, and saw allowing. Soon the trail crosses Fairground Road, touring in meadow and tamarack and traveling past the primary trailhead for equestrian users.

Keep to the east side of Fairground Road, ascending a grassy doubletrack in a cedar-hardwood forest. Where the trail tops out, you meet a truck trail. Turn right on it, descending to and angling left across Fairground Road. You then descend via foot trail, passing through meadow and crossing over drainages. Past the tamarack seed orchard and spruce corridor, you again cross Fairground Road for a brief swing along the wooded east slope before coming out on Fairground Road across from the trail parking.

Miles and Directions

0.0 Start from the southern Fairground Road trailhead; hike the gravel path west for clockwise travel.

0.8 Reach a junction; head right.

2.2 Cross Beaver Creek Road; follow a truck trail, still ascending.

2.4 Continue forward, past a connector to the greater Brookfield Trail System on the left.

2.7 Turn left, entering the woods, bypassing a small rock-lined pond.

3.1 Cross Beaver Creek Road to follow the Glenn Bacon Trail.

5.2 Cross the Bliven Road bridge over Beaver Creek.

6.1 Reach the first crossing of Fairground Road.

6.4 Pass a parking area for equestrian users; continue along the east side of Fairground Road, ascending via grassy two tracks.

6.9 Meet a truck trail; turn right on it, descending to Fairground Road.

7.5 Cross Fairground Road; descend via footpath.

9.0 Again cross Fairground Road to travel the wooded east slope.

9.5 Emerge at Fairground Road opposite the trailhead; cross the road, closing the loop.

Beaver Creek in Brookfield Swamp, Beaver Creek State Forest

Hike Information

Local Information

Madison County Tourism, P.O. Box 1029, Brooks Hall, First Floor, US 20, Morrisville 13408; (315) 684-7320 or (800) 684-7320; www.madisontourism.com

Local Events/Attractions

Talons! A Bird of Prey Experience, offers you a chance to observe and even work with trained birds of prey and falconers. Join a hawk walk; reservations and fee required. Talons! A Bird of Prey Experience, 89 N Main Street, Earlville 13332; (315) 415-1686; www.talonsbirdsofprey.com.

The National Baseball Hall of Fame and Museum holds the golden story of baseball. 25 Main Street, Cooperstown 13326; (800) HALL-OF-FAME; www.baseballhalloffame.org

▶ Trail Etiquette

Zero impact. Always leave an area just like you found it—if not better than you found it. Avoid camping in fragile, alpine meadows and along the banks of streams and lakes. Use a camp stove versus building a wood fire. Pack up all of your trash and extra food. Bury human waste at least 100 feet from water sources under 6 to 8 inches of topsoil. Don't bathe with soap in a lake or stream—use prepackaged moistened towels to wipe off sweat and dirt, or bathe in the water without soap.

Stay on the trail. It's true, a path anywhere leads nowhere new, but paths serve an important purpose: They limit impact on natural areas. Straying from a designated trail may seem innocent but it can cause damage to sensitive areas—damage that may take years to recover, if it can recover at all. Even simple shortcuts can be destructive. So, please, stay on the trail.

Honorable Mentions

Central–Leatherstocking Region

P Glimmerglass State Park

In the heart of James Fenimore Cooper country, the wooded flank of Mount Welling-ton and the field, shrub, and woodland habitats of this state park compose the under-stated setting of Hyde Bay on Otsego Lake—the liquid jewel of the area. Because of the lake's sparkle, Cooper dubbed it "Glimmerglass" in his popular tales about a frontier hero, "the Leatherstocking." In this soothing backdrop, you can enjoy short outings and subtle discoveries.

Historic Hyde Hall marks the launch for a pleasant 3.5-mile hike that combines two loops: the short Otsego Lake loop on service road that serves up filtered lake views, and the longer blazed loop up Mount Wellington. On the latter, you travel the forested slope of evergreens and restless deciduous trees to the upper reaches of Mount Wellington, where you obtain a restricted overlook of the lake and park. Deer sometimes share the view. The route then descends through forest and fern habitat to the mansion area. There you follow the road between the twin gate cottages and beneath the domed arch of Tin Top, crossing the grounds to close the loop. Hyde Hall, a dignified stone-block manor formerly owned by Lieutenant George Clarke (a New York State governor from 1736 to 1744), is open for guided tours summer weekends. Other trails in the park visit beaver pond, woodland, and field.

From U.S. Highway 20 in East Springfield, turn south on County Road 31, fol-lowing the signs to Glimmerglass State Park. In 3.9 miles turn right (west) to enter the park. From Cooperstown go 8 miles north on CR 31 to reach the turn for the park entrance. *DeLorme: New York Atlas & Gazetteer*: Page 64 B2. An admission is charged. Contact Glimmerglass State Park, 1527 CR 31, Cooperstown 13326; (607) 547-8662; http://nysparks.state.ny.us/parks.

Q Bowman Lake State Park

A quiet wooded setting, gentle terrain, and thirty-five-acre Bowman Lake are the hallmarks of this state park northwest of Oxford and west of Norwich. Bordered by 11,000 acres of state forest land, the park contributes to a broad, open space for wild-life and a tranquil arena for hikers. The long-distance Finger Lakes Trail (FLT) passes through the park and offers a 5.5-mile hike out and back to Berry Hill Fire Tower. The park's Nature Trail rolls out an easy 1.3-mile lake loop.

From the northernmost beach parking, the FLT strings north through woods and tidy pine plantation, tracing brooks and crossing quiet gravel roads, before following

Tower Road 0.6 mile to the fire tower. A rustic cabin shares the grassy hilltop with the six-story tower on the National Historic Lookout Register. The tower holds law enforcement radios and is closed to the public. The south-central New York neighborhood reveals low ridges, rolling fields, and wooded hills.

The red-marked Nature Trail starts at the nature center and heads north through the mixed forest of the developed park for a counterclockwise tour, thrice crossing park roads. Expect rocks, roots, and soggy drainages. Midway you reach a cattail shore, later finding a length-of-the-lake view. After contouring the wooded west slope, you pass closer to shore to cross the levee dam. You then skirt the picnic area to end at the nature center.

From the junction of Highway 12 and Highway 220 at the village green in Oxford, go 6 miles west on Highway 220 and turn right (north) onto Steere Road. In 1.4 miles find the park entrance on the left. *DeLorme: New York Atlas & Gazetteer.* Page 62 D2. An admission fee is charged. Contact Bowman Lake State Park, 745 Bliven Sherman Road, Oxford 13830; (607) 334-2718; http://nysparks.state.ny.us/parks.

Capital-Saratoga Region

Five major rivers—the Hudson, Mohawk, Sacandaga, Schoharie, and Hoosick—thread through this east-central New York region, with the capital complex at its core. This strategic watery hub was homeland to the Mohawk Nation and strongly contested over time. The fertile river lands were conducive to farming and water-powered industry, and the water routes were links to the fur harvest and trade in the Great Lakes area. The Dutch were the first whites to settle here in 1624. Control of this area was key both in the French and Indian Wars and in the American Revolution.

But despite the natural water routes here, transportation was difficult until the arrival of the Erie Canal in 1825. It solved the problems of differences in elevation and troubling widths and flows with a series of locks, aqueducts, and other architectural features. Almost all western commerce flowed through Albany, seated at the eastern end of the canal. Now bills and legislation flow through the city, and much of the industry of yore has faded from the landscape.

In addition to government, tourism helps feed the Capital–Saratoga economy of today, with battlefields and the history and bustle of the nineteenth century central to travel themes. Mineral springs, performing arts, and artists' colonies likewise attract tourists to this area. Museums, historic homes, and colonial cemeteries help capture the history. Harkening to the region's Dutch roots, Albany has hosted the annual tulip festival for more than half a century now.

Hiking in the Capital–Saratoga Region, you can retrace the march of the British in 1777; explore Helderberg Escarpment; visit field, forest, and wetland habitats; and venture to and along the Taconic Crest. Vistas sweep across the Mohawk and Hudson Valleys and toward the Adirondacks and drift across state borders to Massachusetts and Vermont. The region offers quiet nature strolls and vigorous hikes, with a range of walks in between, including urban walks.

◀ *Oak trunk with lichen in forest, Taconic Crest Trail*

34 Wilkinson National Recreation Trail

The two Battles of Saratoga fought in the fall of 1777 marked the turning point in the American Revolutionary War. Colonist victories over the British in this key area along the Hudson River convinced the French that the Colonists could prevail. When France responded by declaring war on Great Britain, the tide turned toward American independence. This national recreation trail (NRT), an interpretive loop through fields and woods, retraces the British march and visits sites where fortifications stood and key battles raged.

Start: At the visitor center trailhead
Distance: 4.8 miles out-and-back, including Breymann's Redoubt detour and Freeman Loop
Approximate hiking time: 2.5 to 3.5 hours
Difficulty: Easy
Elevation change: The trail has about a 200-foot elevation change.
Trail surface: Mowed, earthen, and paved path
Seasons: Best for hiking, spring through fall
Other trail users: Snowshoers, cross-country skiers
Canine compatibility: Leashed dogs permitted on trails, no dogs in buildings
Land status: National park
Nearest town: Stillwater
Fees and permits: User fees charged for the hiking trail and the auto tour during fee season, May through October
Schedule: Grounds, sunrise to sunset; visitor center, 9:00 a.m. to 5:00 p.m. daily except major holidays; trail and auto tour road, early April through November
Maps: Saratoga Park brochure (available online or obtain at visitor center); Wilkinson Trail brochure (obtain at visitor center)
Trail contacts: Saratoga National Historic Park, 648 Highway 32, Stillwater 12170; (518) 664-9821, extension 224 for information desk; www.nps.gov/sara
Special considerations: Well-signed with station posts and arrow markings, the NRT occasionally crosses a horse trail and slips across the auto-tour route four times. Because ticks do occur here, take the necessary precautions and check yourself and your pet for ticks. In spring, trails can be slippery. Carry drinking water for you and your pet.

Finding the trailhead: From Troy go 17.5 miles north on U.S. Highway 4 and turn left (west) to reach the Saratoga National Historic Park access road. Go 2.3 miles to the visitor center. From New York State Thruway Interstate 87 south of Saratoga Springs, take exit 12 and follow the well-marked route to the park. It travels Highway 67 east, U.S. Highway 9 north, Highway 9P east, Highway 423 east, and Highway 32 north to enter the park in 12 miles; be alert for the frequent turns. *DeLorme: New York Atlas & Gazetteer*: Page 81 D5.

The Hike

Exit the back door of the visitor center and turn right, following the trimmed grass and cinder path past cannons and memorials to reach both the trail kiosk and the initial junction, interpretive station A. Bear left for the trail. The wide mowed track passes through a shrubby transition habitat; woods of planted pine, maple, oak, aspen,

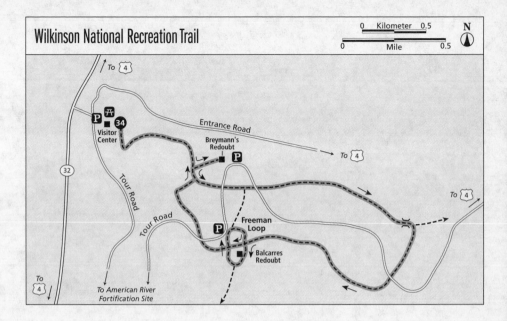

Wilkinson National Recreation Trail

and fruit trees; and rolling untamed fields of thigh-high grasses and wildflowers. Islands of trees spot the fields. The National Park Service (NPS) purposely manages the property to communicate the look of the land during the campaign of 1777. Only a few neighborhood rooftops break the spell.

Downy woodpeckers telegraph their locations in the woods while songbirds spread cheer in the field. White-tailed deer may cross your path. Before long, a spur to the left leads to Auto Tour Stop 7, Breymann's Redoubt. Here you converge on a paved walk to find interpretive boards, a pair of cannons, and posts outlining the site of the German breastwork. The crude log barrier 200 yards long and 7 feet high was intended to protect the British right flank. Although imposing, the Colonists overwhelmed the site, driving off the Crown forces on October 7, 1777. From the redoubt you bear right on a paved lane to the Boot Monument, a tribute to Benedict Arnold, who received a leg wound while distinguishing himself in the fray.

You then return to the Wilkinson Trail and turn left, quickly reaching the loop junction at station C; go left (clockwise). Aster, Queen Anne's lace, and goldenrod interweave the autumn fields. After crossing the tour road for the first time, you pass through a pine corridor, reaching the Liaison Trail at station D. Proceed forward, following the Wilkinson Trail through mixed woods.

The second road crossing follows. The trail now travels a wooded plateau between the Mill Creek and Great Ravine drainages. When the British marched along this route in 1777, old-growth trees 6 feet in diameter cloaked the highland. A couple of plank crossings precede the footbridge at station F. Upon crossing the bridge, bear right. This open field would have been cultivated in the eighteenth century. You again

Cannons, Saratoga National Historic Park

cross over the auto tour road, still in field, often astir with insects.

The Wilkinson Trail then dips through a ravine to tour a low ridge clad in pine. Beyond station J stretches another long open field. At the base of a rise, you cross over a horse trail before ascending to meet a paved walk. Here the Wilkinson Trail bisects the 0.6-mile Freeman Loop; go left, adding a clockwise tour of this side trail.

This circuit and its spurs visit the John Freeman Farm and Balcarres Redoubt, noting the battles of September 19 and October 7, 1777. You will discover the posts outlining a British fortification that withstood a fiery American onslaught; a monument to a fallen American captain; Bloody Knoll, named for the many casualties on October 7, 1777; and an obelisk and exquisitely crafted cannons. Interpretive panels, some with recorded messages, relate the history while lilacs recall the farm. The Liaison Trail, which you encountered earlier, also meets up at the Freeman Loop.

After completing Freeman Loop, turn right, resuming the Wilkinson Trail. You will pass through field and pine stand to make one last crossing of the tour road. At station N, you cross over a horse trail, coming to a T junction with a mowed path. Go right toward the visitor center; to the left lies Barber Wheatfield, another battle site. Close the loop at station C and bear left, returning to the visitor center.

Miles and Directions

0.0   Start from the visitor center trailhead. Exit the center's back door and turn right to reach the trail kiosk and station A in 500 feet; bear left for the Wilkinson Trail (WT).

0.6   Reach a junction; take the left spur to Auto Tour Stop 7, Breymann's Redoubt.

0.7   Reach Breymann's Redoubt and the Benedict Arnold site; backtrack to the WT.

0.8   Turn left on the WT, quickly reaching the loop junction at station C. Go left, clockwise.

1.1   Cross the "auto tour route."

1.2   Reach the Liaison Trail at station D; proceed forward on the WT. **Bailout:** Turn right on the Liaison Trail to shorten the loop by 2 miles.

2.0   Reach the junction at station F; bear right upon crossing the footbridge.

2.2   Cross the auto tour road.

3.2   Where the WT bisects Freeman Loop, head left, clockwise, on the 0.6-mile loop.

3.8   Close Freeman Loop; turn right to resume on the WT.

4.0   Cross the auto tour route.

4.1   Past station N, reach a T junction with a mowed path. Head right toward the visitor center. **Side trip:** Heading left at the T leads to Barber Wheatfield, another battle site.

4.2   Close the loop back at station C; bear left toward the visitor center.

4.8   End at the visitor center.

Hike Information

Local Information

Saratoga Convention and Tourism Bureau, 60 Railroad Place, Suite 100, Saratoga Springs 12866; (518) 584-1531; www.discoversaratoga.org

Local Events/Attractions

Saratoga Spa State Park, noted for its mineral waters and classic architecture, is a National Historic Landmark. It is home to the Saratoga Performing Arts Center, the Spa Little Theater, the National Museum of Dance, the Saratoga Automobile Museum, and a wide range of recreation opportunities. Saratoga Spa State Park, 19 Roosevelt Drive, Saratoga Springs 12866; (518) 584-2535; http://nysparks.state.ny .us/parks

35 Taconic Crest Trail

The nearly 40-mile-long Taconic Crest Trail strings from southwest Vermont through New York to Pittsfield State Forest in Massachusetts. Hiking the New York section of the trail north from Petersburg Pass (on Highway 2) to the Highway 346 trailhead at the Hoosic River showcases the trail's finest attributes. It travels hardwood forests, serves up multistate views, and visits a geologic oddity—a snow hole. The area south of Petersburg Pass has been troubled by ATV use; the DEC is working to reclaim mudholes and damaged spots.

Start: At the Petersburg Pass/Highway 2 trailhead
Distance: 8.8-mile shuttle
Approximate hiking time: 5 to 6.5 hours
Difficulty: Strenuous
Elevation change: From Petersburg Pass (elevation 2,100 feet), the trail climbs to the hike's high point at White Rock (elevation 2,500 feet). Where the hike ends at Highway 346 is the low point (500 feet).
Trail surface: Earthen path, woods road
Seasons: Best for hiking, spring through fall
Other trail users: Snowshoers, cross-country skiers
Canine compatibility: Leashed dogs permitted (Carry water for your animal and dispose of animal waste away from trails and water.)
Land status: Department of Environmental

Conservation (DEC), Williams College, and private land
Nearest town: Berlin
Fees and permits: No fees or permits required
Schedule: Daylight hours on Williams College Land; no restrictions on DEC land
Maps: Taconic Hiking Club, Taconic Crest Trail map (Write: Taconic Hiking Club, 45 Kakely Street, Albany 12209)
Trail contacts: New York State DEC, Region 4, 1130 North Westcott Road, Schenectady 12306; (518) 357-2073; www.dec.ny.gov
Special considerations: There is no camping in the Williams College Hopkins Memorial Forest or on any private land. Use care when crossing Highway 2. Be sure to leash dogs to protect research sites, wildlife, and other trail users. Bring water for you and your pet.

Finding the trailhead: From the Highway 2–Highway 22 junction at Petersburg (or Petersburgh), go 5.3 miles east on Highway 2 to reach the large, open parking lot for Petersburg Pass Scenic Area on the right. The northbound trail starts across the highway. *DeLorme: New York Atlas & Gazetteer:* Page 67 C7.

Reach the trail's northern terminus off Highway 346, 2.5 miles east of North Petersburg. The small developed trailhead is on the south side of the highway just before the Hoosic River bridge and the route's crossing into Vermont. *DeLorme: New York Atlas & Gazetteer:* Page 67 B7.

The Hike

You ascend north on a steep footpath behind the sign that says PETERSBURG to meet up with the white-blazed Taconic Crest Trail, which arrives on the right. Over-the-shoulder views present Petersburg Pass and Mount Raimer. A spur presents a western perspective of the valley below and the Adirondacks beyond.

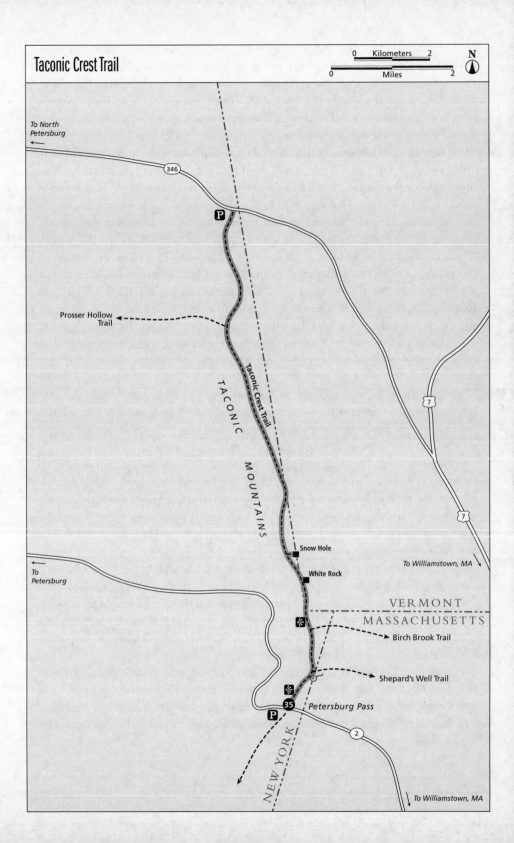

Taconic Crest Trail

Kilometers
0   2

Miles
0   2

N

To North
Petersburg

346

P

Prosser Hollow
Trail

TACONIC

Taconic Crest Trail

MOUNTAINS

Snow Hole

White Rock

To Williamstown, MA

VERMONT

MASSACHUSETTS

Birch Brook Trail

Shepard's Well Trail

To
Petersburg

35

P

Petersburg Pass

2

NEW YORK

To Williamstown, MA

In 2,600-acre Hopkins Memorial Forest, the rolling trail traverses the west flank, or Taconic crest. From full-canopy forests of birch, beech, maple, oak, and black cherry, you enter areas of low-stature trees with shrubby understories. Heralds of June-blooming azaleas can grab attention. Proceed forward past the marked Shepard's Well Trail. Candelabra-trunked trees dip low their shades of autumn. Elsewhere silver snags (victims of the pear thrip infestation of the late 1980s) draw eyes skyward.

Where the Birch Brook Trail heads right, hip-high fountains of interrupted ferns claim the trail's left side. The crest trail steadily climbs, slipping into southwest Vermont before returning to New York at White Rock, a signed landmark. This site owes its U.S. Geological Survey designation to the milky-white quartz scattered throughout the woods. Open berry fields present vistas of the rolling New York terrain.

From White Rock the trail drifts east, dipping into beech forest. At the marked Y junction, detour right for a short descent to the Snow Hole. This ground cavity shows jagged, mossy walls that meet in an ill-fitting bite. When entering the chasm, you discover another bite—that of the chill air from the snow and ice that linger into summer. The chill supports a boreal understory of hobblebush, club moss, and oxalis. Area rocks wear the names and dates from visitors from one hundred years ago, but the genuine etchings must be sorted from prankster and modern markings. A path overlooks the cavity and its cavelike end. Backtrack and resume northbound crest travel.

Where the trail flattens, puddles may require evasion. Disks have a fairly dependable spacing, so watch for them. As the trail ascends, you'll find disks marking a little-tracked crescent along the eastern slope that soon returns to the main grade. Because it extends only a limited view, you may opt to proceed forward.

After a measured descent, proceed forward at the next woods road junction. An ascent then leads you past some showy black cherry trees. A steeper descent follows, where loose rock and downward-pointed roots can steal footing. As the ridgetop narrows, you catch glimpses down the east and west flank but no open views. Where the ridge regains its height, enjoy a pretty grass-and-fern passage. The trail then dips west, returning to the crest at a junction. Keep right.

Blue DEC disks join the familiar white diamond markers. At the Prosser Hollow Junction, yellow disks lead left (west) to Prosser Hollow trailhead. You continue north, tracing the crest on woods road. Where you descend into a big horseshoe bend, keep alert for the multiple markers showing where you abandon the woods road to follow a lightly tracked footpath through woods. This section lacks a history of foot traffic but should improve with time and boots.

The trail rolls over a huckleberry-clad hill to cross an old grade and start the biggest descent of the hike. The steepness, brushing grasses, and muddy spots that can steal footing or engulf the boot complicate travel, and insects can annoy. But superior trail markings, birdsongs, and sightings of fox, deer, grouse, and woodpecker help erase hard feelings.

Another set of multiple markers sends you left across and down the slope to where the trail crosses a gravel road. The trail later zigs right, through a meadow of knee-high vegetation with milkweed and ox-eye daisy, returning to forest, still descending. A brook crossing on stones leads to the Highway 346 trailhead.

Miles and Directions

0.0 Start from the Petersburg Pass trailhead; head north on the crest trail.

0.7 Proceed forward past the Shepard's Well Trail.

1.5 Proceed forward past the Birch Brook Trail.

2.5 Reach White Rock; continue on the crest trail, which drifts east here.

2.9 Reach a marked Y junction; detour right for a 250-foot descent to the Snow Hole. **Bailout:** The Snow Hole makes a satisfactory turnaround site for out-and-back travel.

3.0 Return to the Taconic Crest Trail; turn right (north).

3.5 Disks mark a little-tracked 0.2-mile crescent spur along the eastern edge of the slope. Because of its limited view, continue ahead on the main wide grade.

4.0 Reach a woods road junction; proceed forward, ignoring the route that angles in on the right.

4.9 Reach a junction; keep right, avoiding the unmarked woods road that heads left.

6.1 Reach Prosser Hollow Junction; proceed north on the crest trail to Highway 346. **Option:** The yellow disks to the left lead west to the Prosser Hollow trailhead for an alternative 7.5-mile shuttle. (Study area maps for how to get to this trailhead to spot a shuttle vehicle.)

6.6 Reach a junction; continue forward (northbound), ignoring a trail angling back to the right.

6.9 Leave the woods road as it descends into a big horseshoe bend, following markers and foot trail left into woods.

7.5 Reach a set of multiple markers; head left across and down the slope to cross a gravel road.

8.0 Trail zigs right, passing through a transitioning meadow of knee-high vegetation.

8.2 Reenter forest, still descending as the crest drops to the Hoosic River Valley.

8.8 Cross a brook to end at the Highway 346 trailhead.

Hike Information

Local Information
Travel Hudson Valley, (800) 232-4782; www.travelhudsonvalley.org

Local Events/Attractions
Bennington Battlefield State Historic Park and the visitor center at Barnett Homestead in Hoosic Falls recap a moment in Revolutionary War history. On this battlefield in 1777, the militiamen from several states under the command of General Stark defeated the British who were attempting to raid the American storehouses and stables at Bennington. Bennington Battlefield State Historic Park, c/o Grafton Lakes State Park, P.O. Box 163, Grafton 12082; (518) 686-7109; http://nysparks.state.ny.us/parks

Accommodations

Cherry Plain State Park, south of Petersburg off Highway 22, is open Memorial Day to Labor Day and has twenty campsites. Reservations: (800) 456-2267; www .reserveamerica.com

Organizations

Taconic Hiking Club helps maintain the trail and trail register sheets. Taconic Hiking Club, 45 Kakely Street, Albany 12209; http://taconichikingclub.blogspot.com

Honorable Mentions

Capital–Saratoga Region

R Five Rivers Environmental Education Center

At this nationally recognized environmental education center, just west of Delmar, you can examine habitat interrelationships while touring field, forest, meadow, and pond. The center takes its name from the five major rivers flowing into the greater area: the Hudson, Mohawk, Sacandaga, Schoharie, and Hoosick. Six easy self-guided nature trails explore the center grounds. The trails range from a fragment of a mile to 2 miles long. Bird-watching, spring and summer wildflowers, and sightings of beaver, deer, turtle, and frog engage nature trail hikers. Take the necessary precautions for ticks, and carry insect repellent. The site is open year-round (weather permitting), sunrise to sunset; interpretive center: 9:00 a.m. to 4:30 p.m. Monday through Saturday and 1:00. to 5:00 p.m. Sunday (closed major holidays).

From the junction of County Road 52 (Elm Avenue) and Highway 443 (Delaware Avenue) in west Delmar, go 1.4 miles west on Highway 443 and turn right (north) on Orchard Street at a sign for the center. Go 0.4 mile and turn left on Game Farm Road, reaching the center entrance and parking lot on the right in 0.3 mile. *DeLorme: New York Atlas & Gazetteer:* Page 66 C2. Contact Five Rivers Environmental Education Center (EEC), New York State Department of Environmental Education, 56 Game Farm Road, Delmar 12054; (518) 475-0291; www.dec.ny.gov.

S John Boyd Thacher State Park

This 2,300-acre state park west of Albany boasts 6 miles of the famous Helderberg Escarpment—one of the richest fossil-bearing formations in the world—as well as Mohawk–Hudson Valley panoramas, a historic Indian trade route, echoes of Tory spies, and a Revolutionary-times paint mine. Waterfalls and mixed woods complement the limestone cliff landscape. Goshawk, rabbit, deer, and fox find habitat here. Short trails throw open the park pages: the 1-mile out-and-back Indian Ladder Trail, the 2.5-mile Escarpment Trail, and a 1-mile nature loop.

Between Indian Ladder and LaGrange Bush Picnic Areas, the park's premier Indian Ladder Trail wraps below the 100- to 200-foot-high light-colored platy cliffs of Helderberg Escarpment. Here the Mohawk Schoharie built a shortcut to the valley, placing a sturdy notched trunk against the cliff for descending and scaling. Today stonework steps pull that duty. The cliffs command eyes skyward with bulges, overhangs, flutes, fissures, clefts, and hollows. Millions of years ago an uplift of limestone, sandstone, and shale followed by ages of weathering and erosion brought about the site's vertical fracturing. You pass the outlets to underground streams and Outlet and Minelot Falls. Numbered signs identify features.

The thin footpath of the Escarpment Trail hugs the fenced escarpment rim as it skirts the developed park. Views sweep the Mohawk–Hudson Valley and the escarpment arc. Clear days reveal the distant ragged outline of the Adirondack High Peaks and Vermont Green Mountains. Ravens, hawks, and vultures soar below the rim.

The Nature Trail (or Forest Trail) travels textured woods of maple, hickory, oak, hemlock, white pine, aspen, and paper birch. Lady's slipper, violet, clintonia, and mayflower sprinkle the forest floor.

The least-complicated approach is to take Highway 85 west from Albany (Highway 85 is exit 4 off Interstate 90) and follow it to Highway 157 (about 10 miles). Go right on Highway 157 and continue 4 miles into the park. A vehicle entrance fee is collected Memorial Day through Labor Day; gates close promptly at dusk. Plan to be off the trails accordingly. *DeLorme: New York Atlas & Gazetteer.* Page 66 C1. Contact John Boyd Thacher State Park, 1 Hailes Cave Road, Vorheesville 12186; (518) 872-1237; http://nysparks.state.ny.us/parks.

The Catskills

Claiming a big chunk of the southern heel of this boot-shaped state, this region brings together the chiseled beauty and lore of the Catskill Mountains, the blinding white cliff-and-crag realm of the Shawangunks, and the outlying wooded ridges parted by thin valleys. This is a countryside of kill and clove, the land of Rip Van Winkle and Sleepy Hollow. Naturalist John Burroughs walked its reaches and drew from its inspiration.

At the emotional and geographic heart of this region is Catskill Park, consisting of both private and public forest preserve lands set aside as "forever wild." Since its foresighted start in 1885, the park has swelled to 300,000 acres. It encompasses ninety-eight peaks topping 3,000 feet. The Catskills lift sufficiently skyward to show alpine characteristics. The peaks typically present an abrupt, broken eastern slope paired with a tamer west flank.

Artist Rock view, Catskill Park

Quarries pulled rocks from the mountains for paving and building, used both locally and in distant parts. Hemlock bark was harvested here for tanning, and the Catskills were once a key wheat and flour belt. In the nineteenth century, these mountains represented an idyllic summer retreat from the dirt, noise, congestion, and heat of the city—New York City. Popular mountain house hotels sprang up throughout the then, and still, remote hills.

The picturesque Catskills settings and grand views attracted and inspired the Hudson River School of painters and continue to draw artists today. Tourism is a thriving industry. From the slurpy goodness of maple syrup time in spring to the inviting coolness of mountaintop and hollow in summer, from autumn's fiery explosion to winter's snowy elegance, the Catskills provide nonstop wealth.

Carriageways that led to the mountain house retreats provide ideal hiking routes today. Elsewhere foot trails explore forest, field, pond, sapphire lakes, and escarpment rims. Vistas sweep the Catskills, the Mohonks, and the Hudson Valley. As if that weren't enough, this region boasts one of the finest bird-watching areas in the state, at Bashakill Wildlife Management Area.

36 North–South Lake Loop

This Catskill Mountains loop, a popular favorite, travels the escarpment and wooded outskirts of North–South Lake, snapping up cherished views and passing cultural sites. Waterfalls, azalea and mountain laurel blooms, and fall foliage complement the woodland sojourn. Although the loop rings the spectacle-shaped North–South Lake, it never approaches the lake.

Start: At the North Lake beach area trailhead

Distance: 9.3-mile loop

Approximate hiking time: 5 to 7 hours

Difficulty: Moderate

Elevation change: The rolling trail has about a 600-foot elevation change.

Trail surface: Earthen and rocky path

Seasons: Best for hiking, spring through fall

Other trail users: Horse riders (on marked shared routes only), mountain bikers (where appropriate), hunters, snowshoers, cross-country skiers

Canine compatibility: Dogs permitted but must be controlled at owner's side by leash or voice command

Land status: Department of Environmental Conservation (DEC)

Nearest town: Haines Falls

Fees and permits: Seasonal day-use fees or campground fees

Schedule: No time restrictions

Maps: Day Hikes at North–South Lake DEC brochure (available at DEC office); New York–New Jersey Trail Conference Trail Map 40, North Lake Area Catskill Trails (recommended, available at traditional and online bookstores or from the Conference: www.nynjtc.org)

Trail contacts: New York State DEC, Region 4, Stamford Office, 65561 Highway 10, Suite 1, Stamford 12167; (607) 652-7365; www.dec .ny.gov

Special considerations: Avoid the escarpment edge during icy conditions and be careful there under wet conditions. Where sections of the loop are open to joint hiker-horse usage, yield right-of-way to horse riders and control dogs.

Finding the trailhead: From New York State Thruway Interstate 87, take exit 20 at Saugerties and go north on Highway 32 to its junction with Highway 32A (6 miles from the I-87 exit). Bear left on Highway 32A, staying on it for 1.8 miles; there turn west onto Highway 23A. In 4.8 miles in Haines Falls, turn right onto County Road 18 (Haines Falls Road) for North–South Lake Campground, reaching the entrance station in 2.2 miles. Find the trailhead at the upper end of North Lake beach parking in another 1.6 miles; look for blue blazes and a sign for Artists Rock. *DeLorme: New York Atlas & Gazetteer:* Page 52 C1.

The Hike

Follow the blue trail left (north), rounding and ascending to Artists Rock, avoiding a yellow spur just ahead. Black oak, maple, pine, azalea, and mountain laurel decorate the escarpment brink. The broad sandstone ledges lay out a natural avenue. The jut of Artists Rock extends a 180-degree Hudson Valley panorama; vultures soar below the point. You ascend to the next ledge tier for a peek at North–South Lake (formerly two lakes) and then round below an immense conglomerate outcrop eroding from the cliff.

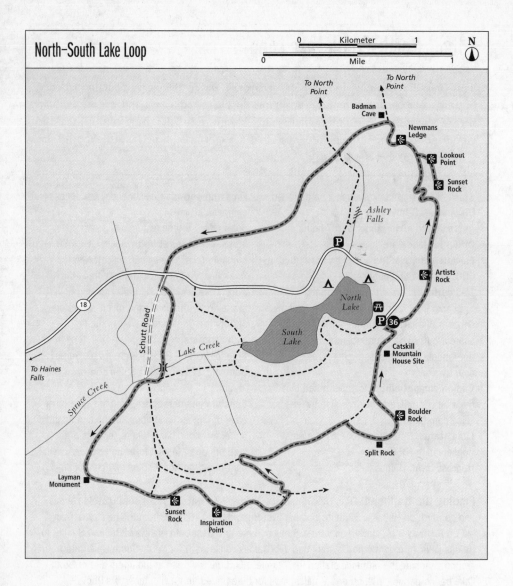

North-South Lake Loop

Kilometer 0 — 1

Mile 0 — 1

N

To North Point

To North Point

Badman Cave

Newmans Ledge

Lookout Point

Sunset Rock

Ashley Falls

P

Artists Rock

North Lake

South Lake

P 36

Catskill Mountain House Site

18

Schutt Road

Lake Creek

Spruce Creek

To Haines Falls

Boulder Rock

Split Rock

Layman Monument

Sunset Rock

Inspiration Point

At a mile, detour right to Sunset Rock for one of the finest vistas in the Catskills; the loop continues straight. This detour takes you to the escarpment edge of Lookout Point for northeast views before continuing to a series of plane-topped outcrops composing Sunset Point. Fissures a foot wide and 20 feet deep isolate the rock islands. Views sweep across North–South Lake and its wooded basin to the swaybacked ridge of High Peak and Roundtop Mountain.

Resume the counterclockwise loop toward Newmans Ledge. You ascend along a thin edge with a disturbing drop. Vistas span Rip Van Winkle Hollow to Rips Rock—this is, after all, Knickerbocker and literature's Washington Irving country. The trail then wraps and ascends to a junction below Badman Cave, shaped by an overhang and reached by a rock scramble. The loop continues straight on the yellow Rock Shelter Trail for a steady forest descent. Footing grows rocky along the brook that drains to Marys Glen.

At the trail junction near a weeping overhang, bear right, staying on the yellow trail. Spring peepers can bring noisy vitality to the glen. Where the yellow trail draws even with the top of this 10-foot waterfall, veer left for the loop. Rocks and roots trouble the descent, while maple old-timers grace the woods.

At Haines Falls Road, you angle left to walk along Schutt Road, from which you quickly turn left, following the blue Escarpment Trail. Descend along the wide lane, touring hemlock-birch forest, passing colonial rock walls, and crossing an old railroad grade.

After crossing Lake Creek, you turn right on woods road and soon after bear left on an earthen lane paralleling the creek and its scenic rockwork downstream. A forget-me-not bench separates the trail from the stream. After the trail turns away, floral shrubs fill the midstory with late-spring color and fragrance. At a rocky drainage, a rock obelisk with a boulder crown honors firefighter Frank Layman, who lost his life in the fire of 1900. Round the monument to the left and in a few steps take a sharp left back uphill to the escarpment. View the Kaaterskill drainage and the wooded ridge of High Peak and Roundtop Mountain.

You'll pass through a rock channel, for a wrapping ascent of the wooded escarpment, and proceed forward to Inspiration Point past a second Sunset Rock. Beyond Inspiration Point, the "V" of Kaaterskill Canyon opens to a Hudson Valley view. After turning right on woods road, follow the blue trail left at the upcoming junction.

Azalea, laurel, and oak frame this rocky woods-road ascent to the next junction, where the blue trail heads right on a narrowed forest lane. Ahead follow signs to the right for Boulder Rock. Past Split Rock, where massive blocks have pulled apart from the escarpment face, you'll find Boulder Rock, a naturally transported boulder that came to rest on the escarpment ledge. Bear left and meet the red trail.

Here you turn right, coming to a clearing and sign that together recall Catskill Mountain House, a grand hotel that hosted presidents and dignitaries in the nineteenth century. Round left away from the sign and ahead bear right to end back at beach parking.

Miles and Directions

0.0 Start from the upper end of North Lake beach parking; follow the blue trail left (north).

0.4 Reach Artists Rock.

1.0 Reach a junction; detour right to Sunset Rock. The loop continues forward.

1.2 Reach Sunset Rock; backtrack to the loop and turn right (1.4).

2.2 Reach Badman Cave and the Rock Shelter Trail; follow the yellow Rock Shelter Trail straight ahead for a steady descent.

2.8 At a junction near a weeping waterfall, bear right, staying on the yellow trail. **Option:**

The red trail here descends to Ashley (or Marys Glen) Falls, a beaver meadow, and the campground.

4.1 Meet Haines Falls Road; angle left to reach and briefly walk Schutt Road.

4.2 Follow the blue Escarpment Trail, turning left off Schutt Road.

4.7 Cross the Lake Creek footbridge, coming to a junction. Turn right on woods road, and soon after bear left on earthen lane paralleling Lake Creek downstream.

5.4 At the Frank Layman firefighter monument, round the obelisk to the left and in a few steps take a sharp left uphill.

5.8 Reach the escarpment; continue following the blue Escarpment Trail.

6.2 Reach Inspiration Point.

7.0 Turn right on a woods road, reaching a junction. There turn left, still on the blue trail.

7.5 Reach a junction with a red trail; continue following the blue Escarpment Trail to the right.

8.2 Follow the Escarpment Trail heading right to Boulder Rock. **Option:** The red trail bypasses Boulder Rock.

8.4 Reach Boulder Rock and bear left.

8.5 Meet the red trail and turn right, continuing on the Escarpment Trail.

9.0 Reach the Catskill Mountain House site; round to the left away from the sign.

9.1 Bear right.

9.3 End at the parking area back at North Lake beach.

Hike Information

Local Information
Greene County Tourism Promotion Office (Catskills), P.O. Box 527, Catskill 12414; (518) 943-3223 or (800) 355-CATS (2287); www.greenetourism.com

Local Events/Attractions
Together, the **Thomas Cole National Historic Site** and **Hudson River School Art Trail** introduce nineteenth-century artist Thomas Cole and his creative contemporaries and direct you to the sites that inspired their great landscape paintings. The Thomas Cole National Historic Site, 218 Spring Street, Catskill 12414; (518) 943-7465; www.thomascole.org

Accommodations
North–South Lake Campground, open early May through late October, has 219 sites. DEC office: (518) 357-2234; campground phone: (518) 589-5058

Organizations
New York–New Jersey Trail Conference helps maintain, mark, and map trails. NY–NJ Trail Conference, 156 Ramapo Valley Road (U.S. Highway 202), Mahwah, NJ 07430; (201) 512-9348; fax: (201) 512-9012; info@nynjtc.org; www.nynjtc.org

◄ *North–South Lake from Sunset Rock, Catskill State Park*

37 Indian Head Mountain Loop

West of Saugerties, this loop rewards with a classic Catskill setting, vistas, and challenge. Central to this hike are the 500-foot cliffs of Indian Head. Wildflowers, fall foliage, and wildlife sightings lend to the attraction. Above the 3,000-foot elevation, a rare spruce-fir complex claims part of the journey.

Start: At the Prediger Road trailhead
Distance: 6.9-mile loop
Approximate hiking time: 4 to 5 hours
Difficulty: Strenuous
Elevation change: The trail travels between 1,890 and 3,573 feet in elevation, with the high point found at Indian Head summit.
Trail surface: Earthen or rocky path, rocky woods road
Seasons: Best for hiking, spring through fall
Other trail users: Hunters, skilled snowshoers
Canine compatibility: Dogs permitted but must be controlled at owner's side by leash or voice command (Keep your animal leashed when crossing private land.)
Land status: Department of Environmental Conservation (DEC) land, private land at start

Nearest town: Tannersville
Fees and permits: No fees or permits required
Schedule: No time restrictions
Maps: New York–New Jersey Trail Conference Trail Map 41, Northeastern Catskill Trails (available at traditional and online bookstores or from the Conference: www.nynjtc.org)
Trail contacts: New York State DEC, Region 4, Stamford Office, 65561 Highway 10, Suite 1, Stamford 12167; (607) 652-7365; www.dec .ny.gov
Special considerations: Both the parking and the start of the trail occur on private land. Respect all posted notices to preserve the access privilege. Use caution on rocky climbs and descents. There is no camping and no campfires above the 3,500-foot elevation.

Finding the trailhead: From the junction of Highway 23A and County Road 16 in Tannersville, head south on CR 16 (Depot Street) for 5.5 miles; the road name changes several times. Turn right onto Prediger Road. Go 0.5 mile, finding trail parking along the right shoulder only. Do not clog the road or block the private residence either by parking on the left or too close to the trailhead. Leave enough space between parked vehicles for returning hikers to pull out safely. *DeLorme: New York Atlas & Gazetteer*: Page 52 C1. (See hike's Options for an alternative start.)

The Hike

From Prediger Road follow the red markers of the Devils Path away from the old cabin, passing through a stile and crossing a footbridge to enter a hemlock-deciduous woodland. Travel is on woods road with a modest incline. At the upcoming loop junction, proceed forward on the red trail toward the Devils Kitchen lean-to and Indian Head summit; the loop's return is via the blue Jimmy Dolan Notch Trail on your right.

Soon the old road tapers to trail width. Big maples and birch compose the canopy above the boulder-studded forest floor. Porcupine, deer, red eft, mouse, and toad can

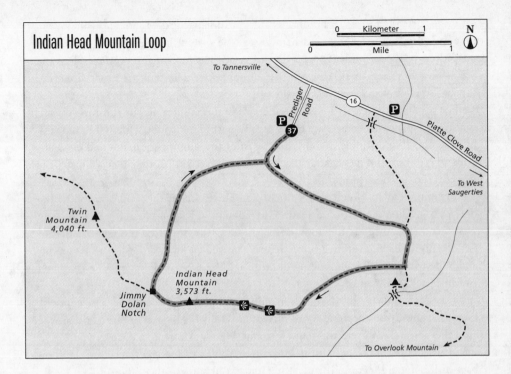

Indian Head Mountain Loop

0   Kilometer   1

0   Mile   1

N

To Tannersville

Prediger Road

16

Platte Clove Road

To West Saugerties

Twin Mountain 4,040 ft.

Indian Head Mountain 3,573 ft.

Jimmy Dolan Notch

To Overlook Mountain

divert attention. After crossing a thin creek, you turn right on a woods road (the Long Path). At the signed junction ahead, continue following the red markers, turning right to climb toward Indian Head Mountain and destinations west.

The trail, at times rootbound and rock-studded, crosses muddy drainages. A hemlock–deciduous forest houses the way. Some of the birch trees here display impressive root systems. Steep spurts interrupt the trail's otherwise comfortable ascent. Mossy rocks and ledges contribute to the mountain visuals.

After a sharp climb, you obtain an outcrop ledge overlooking the steep wooded slope for an exciting view of Roundtop Mountain, High Peak, Plattekill Mountain, Platte Clove, and the Hudson River Valley beyond the clove. Autumn blends colorful leaves with evergreen boughs.

As the thin trail contours the slope, it next extends views toward Overlook Mountain. Tackling the rocky climb ahead may require the use of hands. A corridor of spruce and fir precedes an opening extending views toward Overlook, Slide, and Plateau Mountains; Ashokan Reservoir; Cooper Lake; Mount Tobias; and postcard-pretty serial peaks.

The so-called Tax Day Storm, April 15–16, 2007, brought ice followed by heavy snow that snapped the tops of conifers and several large hardwoods above the 3,000-foot elevation. It changed the look of the forest, but biologists say it will benefit warbler and thrush populations.

Cross a small saddle for the final assault on Indian Head Mountain, which again requires some high-stepping and hand assists. Be careful here, especially under wet conditions or when burdened by a heavy pack. Vistas can suggest breathers. Past the 3,500-foot elevation mark, you top the summit ridge. The trail then rolls along the top, crossing log walks over marshy sites.

For this hike, the views are gathered en route to the summit. The summit's reward is its fragile spruce-fir complex, a rarity for this part of the country, limited to the very high reaches. No camping is allowed here. After the summit stroll, the trail descends with a bold start, and it is again rugged. Glimpses of Twin Mountain accompany the descent. Birch is now the primary tree.

At Jimmy Dolan Notch, you'll find a trail junction. For the loop, you follow the blue trail heading right toward Platte Clove Road (CR 16). The red trail continues west to other Catskill destinations. Before heading down off the mountain, a detour left (south) to the edge of the Notch offers a farewell view toward Ashokan Reservoir and Slide Mountain Ridge looking out through the natural "V" shaped by Twin and Indian Head Mountains.

The descent from the Notch remains steep, rocky, and at times sun exposed. Gradually the woods become more mixed and the trees bigger. Entering a drainage area, the descent eases and the trail arcs right. Hemlocks create a deeper woods. On woods road, the trail then contours the slope. You cross the creek to close the loop back at the initial junction. Turn left, retracing your steps to the trailhead.

Miles and Directions

0.0 Start from the Prediger Road trailhead; follow the red markers.

0.5 Reach the loop junction; proceed straight ahead on the red trail.

1.2 Cross over a thin creek.

1.8 Turn right on a woods road (the Long Path).

1.9 Reach a signed junction; follow the red trail to the right. **Note:** The blue markers straight ahead lead to Overlook Mountain.

3.2 Reach a vista outcrop ledge.

3.7 Reach a manicured view.

4.0 Cross a small saddle en route to Indian Head Mountain.

4.3 Reach the summit of Indian Head Mountain.

4.7 Descend from the summit.

4.9 Reach Jimmy Dolan Notch and a junction; follow the blue trail right toward Platte Clove Highway (CR 16). **Option:** The red trail continues west to other Catskill mountains.

6.4 Cross a creek to close the loop; backtrack left to the trailhead.

6.9 End at the Prediger Road trailhead.

Trillium on Indian Head Mountain, Indian Head Wilderness Area, Catskill Park ▶

Options

As an alternative, dry-weather start to this trail, reducing pressure on the Prediger Road trailhead, try taking the **Long Path** through Platte Clove Preserve. Look for the Long Path to descend south off Platte Clove Road (CR 16), 0.7 mile east of the Prediger Road–Platte Clove Road intersection. Trailhead parking is on the north side of Platte Clove Road 0.2 mile farther east. *DeLorme: New York Atlas & Gazetteer:* Page 52 C1.

The Long Path dips to cross Plattekill Clove on a Kingpost footbridge and then ascends on or beside the historic Overlook Mountain House Road, passing through mixed woods and crossing upper drainages. Interpretive panels introduce features along the way, including old bluestone quarry sites. The path is marked by aqua blazes and preserve disks. At 0.9 mile the Long Path intersects the red-blazed Devils Path at the 1.8-mile junction. Straight ahead leads to Indian Head Mountain, the Devils Kitchen lean-to, Echo Lake, and Overlook Mountain. The right leads to Jimmy Dolan Notch Trail and the Prediger Road trailhead. When starting from the preserve, you shave 0.9 mile off the hike's distance each way, but you increase the overall elevation gain. Be sure to observe all preserve rules and etiquette.

Hike Information

Local Information

Greene County Tourism Promotion Office (Catskills), P.O. Box 527, Catskill 12414; (518) 943-3223 or (800) 355-CATS (2287); www.greenetourism.com

Local Events/Attractions

Mountain Top Arboretum, a nonprofit garden preserve in the northern Catskills, is a living museum with native and introduced trees, plants, and shrubs. Reach it off Highway 23C, 2 miles north of Tannersville on Maude Adams Road. Donation requested. Mountain Top Arboretum P.O. Box 379, Highway 23C, Tannersville 12485; (518) 589-3903; www.mtarbor.org

Accommodations

North–South Lake (DEC) Campground, east of Tannersville via Highway 23A and County Road 18, is open early May through late October and has 219 sites. DEC office: (518) 357-2234; campground phone: (518) 589-5058

Organizations

New York–New Jersey Trail Conference helps maintain, mark, and map trails. NY–NJ Trail Conference, 156 Ramapo Valley Road (U.S. Highway 202), Mahwah, NJ 07430; (201) 512-9348; fax: (201) 512-9012; info@nynjtc.org; www.nynjtc.org

38 Overlook Mountain Hike

While the southern approach to Overlook Mountain is perhaps the most popular peak climb in the entire Catskills, this hike offers an alternative approach, arriving from the north. The route is indeed longer, but it offers a comfortable grade, pleasant backdrop, points of interest, and fewer travelers. A detour en route finds charming Echo Lake, another endorsement. But however you choose to reach the mountaintop, the lookout tower, now in its second life thanks to dedicated volunteers, caps the journey with grand overlooks of the Catskill neighborhood.

Start: At the Prediger Road trailhead

Distance: 13.8 miles out-and-back, including spur to Echo Lake

Approximate hiking time: 8 to 9.5 hours

Difficulty: Moderate

Elevation change: The trail has a 1,250-foot elevation change, with the high point at Overlook Mountain, elevation 3,140 feet.

Trail surface: Earthen path, woods road

Seasons: Best for hiking, spring through fall

Other trail users: Hunters, snowshoers, cross-country skiers

Canine compatibility: Dogs permitted but must be controlled at owner's side by leash or voice command (Keep your animal leashed when crossing private land.)

Land status: Department of Environmental Conservation (DEC) land, private land at start

Nearest town: Tannersville

Fees and permits: No fees or permits required

Schedule: No time restrictions

Maps: New York–New Jersey Trail Conference Trail Map 41, Northeastern Catskill Trails (available at traditional and online bookstores or from the Conference: www.nynjtc.org)

Trail contacts: New York State DEC, Region 3, 21 South Putt Corners Road, New Paltz 12561; (845) 256-3000; www.dec.ny.gov or New York State DEC, Region 4, Stamford Office, 65561 Highway 10, Suite 1, Stamford 12167; (607) 652-7365; www.dec.ny.gov

Special considerations: Because both the parking and the start of the trail occur on private land, respect all posted notices to preserve the access privilege. Heed the posted camping closure at the fire tower.

Finding the trailhead: From the junction of Highway 23A and County Road 16 in Tannersville, head south on CR 16 (Depot Street) for 5.5 miles; the road name changes several times. Turn right on Prediger Road. Go 0.5 mile, finding trail parking along the right shoulder only. Do not clog the road or block the private residence either by parking on the left or too close to the trailhead. Leave enough space between parked vehicles for returning hikers to pull out safely. *DeLorme: New York Atlas & Gazetteer:* Page 52 C1.

The Hike

This hike shares its first 1.9 miles with Indian Head Mountain Loop (the preceding hike). You begin by following the red Devils Path markers away from the old cabin, passing through a stile and crossing a footbridge to enter a hemlock-deciduous woodland, traveling on woods road. Proceed straight ahead, past the blue Jimmy Dolan Notch Trail. The old road tapers.

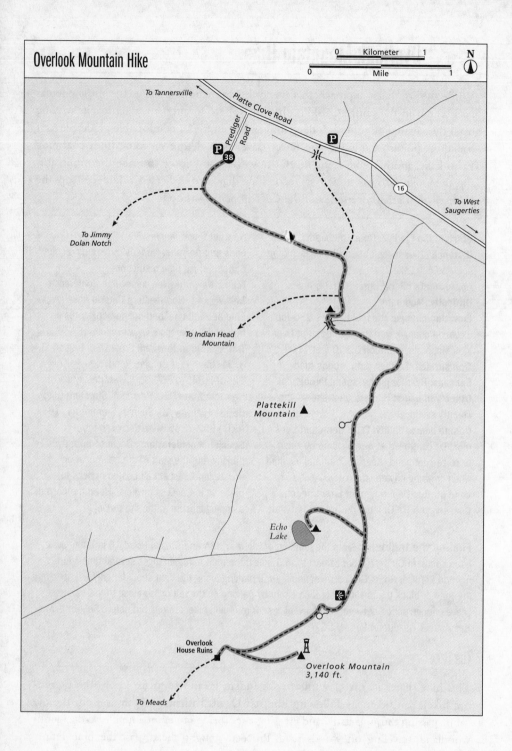

Overlook Mountain Hike

Kilometer
0   1

Mile
0   1

N

To Tannersville

Platte Clove Road

Prediger Road

P 38

P

16

To West Saugerties

To Jimmy Dolan Notch

To Indian Head Mountain

Plattekill Mountain ▲

Echo Lake ▲

Overlook House Ruins

Overlook Mountain 3,140 ft.

To Meads

Big maples and birch weave the canopy above a boulder-studded forest floor. Wildlife can add surprise. You cross a thin creek and turn right on a woods road. Then at the signed junction, you begin following blue markers toward Overlook Mountain.

Next up is the Devils Kitchen lean-to, with its privy and reliable creek source. One weekday in June, the lone occupant was a porcupine. Pass through the lean-to camp and cross the creek footbridge for a steady ascent. Nettles, trillium, clintonia, starflower, and mayflower announce springtime.

Rounding the slope of Plattekill Mountain, you hike past a low stone bench and travel the semishaded brink of an excavation with stone foundations. Here a thin footpath divides the vegetation of the old road, azalea brings its fragrant pink signature, and oaks join the mix.

At the Echo Lake Trail junction, detour right, descending sharply along the former carriage road to the lake and its lean-to, which looks out on a grassy shore. A path rings the lake; above it looms the ridge of Overlook Mountain. In spring thousands of polliwogs can blacken the shallows, while small toads seemingly cause the roadbed to percolate. Summer and fall bring their own nuances to the lake setting. The destination ideally suits novice backpackers.

Resume the southbound trek to Overlook Mountain, ascending along an escarpment edge for the next while. Mountain laurel, azalea, and pockets of beech trees adorn the way. A fuller forest follows. You pass an unusual balanced rock on the right where rock ledges and overhangs characterize the forest. Filtered views stretch to Indian Head and Twin Mountains. Beyond, you may find piped water for wetting the brow.

Young full woods funnel this lightly traveled trail out to the carriage road, just uphill from the two huge concrete shells and other ruins that hauntingly echo to the bygone elegance of Overlook House, a classic nineteenth-century mountain hotel. Built in 1878, the hotel fell to fire in the 1920s. The date 1928 above the doorway of one shell hints at the last effort to rebuild. For a closer look at the mountain hotel, turn right. To proceed to the summit, turn left.

A comfortable ascent on woods road leads to the fire tower. Spurs to the right deliver ledge views stretched south-southeast to the Hudson River, peering down and out Lewis Hollow. The creased rocks shaping the road's left shoulder likewise may beckon a closer look. The nine-story steel-framed lookout tower can be climbed, just heed the posted number allowed up at any one time, which is presently six. The tower cab, though, is only open weekends Memorial Day weekend through Columbus Day, when volunteers are present.

Southern views sweep Ashokan Reservoir, the Slide Mountain area, Cooper Lake, and Mount Tobias. The western vantage rounds up the Saw Kill drainage to Plateau, Sugarloaf, and Twin Mountains, with Hunter Mountain rising beyond Stony Clove Notch. The forest sweep above the 3,000-foot elevation reveals the tattered legacy of the top-lopping so-called Tax Day Storm of 2007, which hit the forest preserve conifers hard. But the event plays a role in nature's cycles, opening the forest for warblers.

A picnic table welcomes a stay for lunch, but camping is prohibited. When ready, backtrack to the trailhead.

Miles and Directions

0.0 Start from the Prediger Road (northern) trailhead; follow the red Devils Path.

0.5 Reach a trail junction; continue straight on the red trail. **Note:** Right is the blue Jimmy Dolan Notch Trail.

1.2 Cross over a thin creek.

1.8 Turn right on a woods road (the Long Path).

1.9 At the marked Indian Head Mountain junction, follow the blue markers straight ahead toward Overlook Mountain.

2.1 Reach the Devils Kitchen lean-to.

4.2 Reach the Echo Lake Trail junction; descend right, following the yellow trail along a former carriage road to the lake.

4.9 Reach Echo Lake; return uphill. **Option:** A 0.5-mile trail rings the lake for additional discovery.

5.6 Reach the Overlook Mountain Trail; turn right.

6.2 Pass an unusual balanced rock on the right.

7.0 Reach a signed junction near a signal tower and the Overlook House ruins. Follow red markers left to the Overlook Mountain summit. **FYI:** From the ruins, the carriage road continues south downhill 2 miles to Meads, suggesting either an alternative start or a spotting site for a shuttle vehicle.

7.6 Reach the Overlook Mountain fire tower; return north to the trailhead, forgoing side trips.

13.8 End at the Prediger Road trailhead.

Options

If time is limited, the summit hike from the Overlook Mountain trailhead in Meads (north of Woodstock) ascends steadily on road grade, reaching the Overlook House ruins in 2 miles and the summit fire tower in 2.6 miles (a 1,500-foot elevation gain). From the common on Highway 212 in Woodstock, turn north toward Meads on County Road 33/Rock City Road. In 0.6 mile continue straight on twisting, paved Meads Mountain Road to reach the trailhead parking in another 2 miles. The lot quickly fills on weekends and in summer. *DeLorme: New York Atlas & Gazetteer.* Page 52 D1.

Hike Information

Local Information

Greene County Tourism Promotion Office (Catskills), P.O. Box 527, Catskill

Echo Lake, Catskill Park

12414; (518) 943-3223 or (800) 355-CATS (2287); www.greenetourism.com or **Woodstock Chamber of Commerce and Arts,** Woodstock 12498; (845) 679-6234; www.woodstockchamber.com

Local Events/Attractions

Woodstock's appeal to artistic senses has attracted a thriving and eclectic artist colony to its midst, and each fall the community hosts an Artist Studio Tour. Various galleries welcome you year-round, and art classes are offered. Contact the Woodstock Chamber of Commerce and Arts.

Accommodations

North–South Lake (DEC) Campground, east of Tannersville via Highway 23A and County Road 18, is open early May through late October and has 219 sites. DEC office: (518) 357-2234; campground phone: (518) 589-5058

Organizations

New York–New Jersey Trail Conference helps maintain, mark, and map trails. NY–NJ Trail Conference, 156 Ramapo Valley Road (U.S. Highway 202), Mahwah, NJ 07430; (201) 512-9348; fax: (201) 512-9012; info@nynjtc.org; www.nynjtc.org

NEW YORK'S HISTORIC FIRE LOOKOUTS

In 1912, New York State authorized the erection of lookout towers across this forested state for the purpose of spotting forest fires. More than one hundred fire towers were erected and staffed atop the state's tallest peaks. Nearly one-fourth watched over the Catskills region; nine of these were in Catskill Park. The building, staffing, and supplying of these steely "watchmen" prompted the blazing of trails into the state's isolated reaches. These trails serve recreational users today.

Fire lookouts served the state for nearly a century. The last fire spotter in the Catskills descended the ladder in 1990, surrendering watch at Red Hill Fire Tower in Claryville. Modern surveillance supplanted the usefulness of human spotters, and a wholesale abandonment of the fire towers followed, often accompanied by the dismantling or razing of the towers for safety. With the abandonment of the towers, a romantic hero, the dutiful and individualistic fire observer, was lost to future generations as well.

The 1990s, though, marked a reversal in trend. Preservation raised a call to arms, and dedicated volunteers and state personnel answered. Now, fire towers lift the public into the clouds for great views and a taste of history. Interpretation and education keep this noble chapter in state and forest history alive.

The Overlook Mountain fire tower is one of five fire towers still standing in Catskill Park. The other four are the Red Hill, Balsam Lake Mountain, Tremper Mountain, and Hunter Mountain towers. The fire tower atop Slide Mountain, the tallest peak in the Catskills, sadly was dismantled before this restoration movement took wings.

The tower at Overlook Mountain (elevation 3,140 feet) has been in place since 1950, although the tower itself boasts an earlier history, dating to 1927. It was originally built on Gallis Hill, west of Kingston, before finding its way to Overlook Mountain. This tower's working life came to an end in 1988. In the late 1990s, committed volunteers began the task of restoring it, replacing its landings and rebuilding stairs.

The tower, on the National Historic Lookout Register, reopened on National Trails Day, June 5, 1999, to once again extend Catskill Park–Hudson River Valley views from 60 feet into the sky. The tower's cab is open to the public when volunteer interpreters staff the tower and the summit cabin information station on weekends, Memorial Day weekend through Columbus Day. Otherwise, the upper landings alone provide the views.

Overlook Mountain, a subject for the Hudson River School of painters in the nineteenth century, has long been a calling card for the Woodstock area. It looms above the 590-acre

Overlook Mountain Wild Forest and offers rewarding views. Two unusual woodland occurrences lend to the mountain's singularity. Red oaks, a lowland species uncommon at 3,100 feet of elevation, strangely find a niche on the Overlook Mountain summit. Not only that, these oaks stand shoulder-to-shoulder with red spruce and balsam fir, trees that typically withhold their presence until the 3,300-foot elevation.

On a plateau below the tower sit the ruins of Overlook Mountain House. This mountain luxury hotel opened for business in the early 1870s, offering a pleasant retreat from the dirt and noise of New York City. Although one of several mountain hotels tucked in the Catskill Mountains, it held the distinction of being the highest mountain hotel, at an elevation of 2,920 feet. The original hotel could accommodate 300 guests but had a tragic history.

Twice burning down, it twice rose from the ashes but never achieved its visioned glory. When the owner's son, a known practical joker, reported the first fire on April 1, 1875, no one took him seriously. The stock market crash during its third building was a hurdle the hotel could not conquer. It never again opened to guests, and looting and time stole its grandeur. Trees now grow in the hotel lobby and halls, and the ruins only whisper to a time now past.

▶ **Dehydration**

Have you ever hiked in hot weather and had a roaring headache and felt fatigued after only a few miles? More than likely you were dehydrated. Symptoms of dehydration include fatigue, headache, and decreased coordination and judgment. When you are hiking, your body's rate of fluid loss depends on the outside temperature, humidity, altitude, and your activity level. On average, a hiker walking in warm weather will lose four liters of fluid a day. That fluid loss is easily replaced by normal consumption of liquids and food. However, if a hiker is walking briskly in hot, dry weather and hauling a heavy pack, he or she can lose one to three liters of water an hour. It's important to always carry plenty of water and to stop often and drink fluids regularly, even if you aren't thirsty.

39 Slide Mountain Loop

Southwest of Woodstock, this hike strings together the yellow Phoenicia–East Branch Trail, the red Wittenberg–Cornell–Slide Trail, and the blue Curtis–Ormsbee Trail for a rolling exploration at the western extent of the Burroughs Range. Traversing hemlock-deciduous woodland and lofty conifer-birch forest, this popular trail tops the highest point in the Catskills and visits the Burroughs Plaque and Curtis–Ormsbee Monument. The loop dishes up vistas and strings past rock features.

Start: At the Slide Mountain trailhead

Distance: 7.2 miles out-and-back, with a midway loop

Approximate hiking time: 4 to 5 hours

Difficulty: Moderate (but with some difficult rocky and wet stretches)

Elevation change: The elevation change is about 1,800 feet, with the summit high point at 4,180 feet.

Trail surface: Earthen or rocky path and woods road

Seasons: Best for hiking, spring through fall

Other trail users: Hunters, snowshoers

Canine compatibility: Dogs permitted but must be controlled at owner's side by leash or voice command

Land status: Department of Environmental Conservation (DEC)

Nearest town: Pine Hill

Fees and permits: No fees or permits required

Schedule: No time restrictions

Maps: DEC Slide Mountain Wilderness map (overview map, but not sufficiently detailed for a hiking aid, available at DEC office); New York–New Jersey Trail Conference Trail Map 43, Southern Catskill Trails (available at traditional and online bookstores or from the Conference: www.nynjtc.org)

Trail contacts: New York State DEC, Region 3, 21 South Putt Corners Road, New Paltz 12561; (845) 256-3000; www.dec.ny.gov

Special considerations: The sensitive nature of this popular peak requires respect. Because the site cannot sustain heavy foot traffic, do not make this an annual trek and keep your hiking party small. Avoid travel during and immediately following a rainstorm. If trails are wet, you should keep to the red Wittenberg-Cornell-Slide Trail, a carriage road that can better handle foot traffic and avoid the delicate Curtis-Ormsbee Trail. Plan a day hike versus an overnight stay. But if you do choose to camp, remember to protect this area's sensitive fir complex. There is no camping and no fires above the 3,500-foot elevation.

Finding the trailhead: From the junction of Highway 214 and Highway 28 in Phoenicia, go west on Highway 28 for 7.9 miles, reaching Big Indian. There turn south on County Road 47, go 9 miles, and turn left to enter the off-road parking area for the Slide Mountain trailhead. *DeLorme: New York Atlas & Gazetteer:* Page 51 D5.

The Hike

You rock-hop across the brook-size West Branch Neversink River and follow the yellow markers for a rocky ascent. An open forest of maple, birch, and beech clads the slope. Where the trail reaches a woods road, follow it right for contouring travel. Past

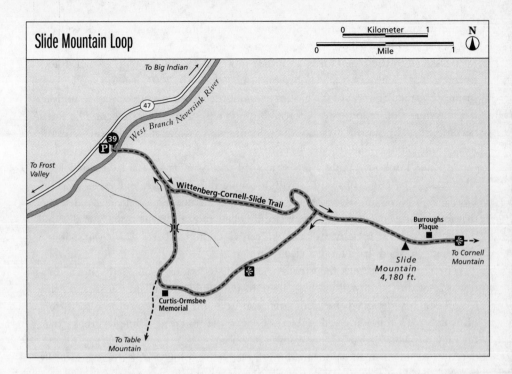

Slide Mountain Loop

To Big Indian

47

West Branch Neversink River

To Frost Valley

P 39

Wittenberg-Cornell-Slide Trail

Burroughs Plaque

Slide Mountain 4,180 ft.

To Cornell Mountain

Curtis-Ormsbee Memorial

To Table Mountain

a pipe providing water (treat trail sources), you reach the initial loop junction. Turn left on the red trail, a rocky woods road; be careful not to turn an ankle.

Leafy branches lace over the ascending trail, offering a fragile shade, while seasonal runoffs race across the route. The trail narrows and steepens, soon pulling above the 3,500-foot elevation. Fir, birch, and snags compose the skyline. Where the trail next contours the slope, tightly spaced firs squeeze the passage. Winds assail the ridge, and weather-watchers can delight in the rapid cloud changes. At the second loop junction, proceed on the red trail to Slide Mountain. The blue Curtis–Ormsbee Trail to the right puts the loop on the hike's return.

En route to Slide Mountain, you climb steadily along the north edge of the ridge, remaining in tightly clustered firs. Mayflower, clintonia, and moss touch green to the forest floor. A ledge to the left offers a view toward Giant Ledge–Panther Mountain. Just ahead, the trail tops the open ledge of Slide Mountain.

Here red markers point downhill to the right. Following this trail, you round the foot of the cliff to view the John Burroughs plaque. This early-day environmental essayist introduced Slide Mountain to the world. He camped where the plaque now rests. From Slide Mountain, views span the spire-topped firs to an all-star lineup of Catskill peaks, including Wittenberg, Plateau, Twin, Indian Head, and Overlook Mountains. Cornell and Friday Mountains form bookends to Ashokan Reservoir. By continuing along Slide Mountain past the summit, you will come to another viewpoint located at a spring and the so-called Ladders, where the trail descends steeply off the mountain via telephone pole–braced steps. From atop the ladder, you can survey the Woodland Valley bowl for grand viewing.

Backtrack to the blue Curtis–Ormsbee foot trail to add the loop. It leads into a fir forest laced with birch and hobblebush. The April 16, 2007, ice and snow event snapped the tops off most of the balsam fir and spruce trees, leaving behind an unusual forest skyline. Before long, steep downhill spurts replace the mild descent. The forest becomes shrubby, with a meadow floor. Stones aid crossing at marshy sites, and the soft ground often records the tracks of deer.

At Paul's Lookout, taking a few strides off trail, you arrive at a ledge for a Table Mountain vista. The trail resumes with a couple more plunges, and views span the East Branch Neversink River. A use of hands may be needed for the sharp descents that follow. After overlooking a rock island pulled away from the slope, you descend to skirt the massive rock. At its base, you can view the road-size gap at the split and see where crossbeds have eroded clean through.

The trail now flattens for a comfortable shady-woods stroll to the next junction, site of the 3-foot-tall marble tribute to trail builders William Curtis and Allen Ormsbee. They designed the scenic trail you have just traveled. You now turn right on woods road, following yellow blazes back to the trailhead. While less rocky than the previous woods roads, springs can muddy boots.

After passing a small woods road on the left, cross a log bridge over a seasonally babbling headwater of the West Branch Neversink. Rocks can prove invaluable for hopscotch travel ahead on the soggy road. Close the loop, turn left, and then take the rocky descent to the trailhead.

Miles and Directions

0.0 Start from the Slide Mountain trailhead; cross the brook-size river on stones or wade.

0.4 Reach a woods road; follow it right. (**Aside:** Take a moment to note the junction here for your return trek.)

0.7 Reach the initial loop junction; turn left on the rocky woods road of the red trail.

2.0 Reach the second loop junction; remain on the red trail to Slide Mountain. **Note:** The blue trail on the right adds the return's loop.

2.5 A ledge to your left offers a northern view.

2.7 Top the open ledge of Slide Mountain; spur right to view the Burroughs plaque and then continue your hike east past the summit to the "Ladders."

2.9 Reach the Ladders, a spring, and a final view; backtrack to the 2-mile junction.

3.8 At the 2-mile junction, follow the blue trail left, adding the loop.

4.6 Reach Paul's Lookout for a view out to Table Mountain.

5.5 Reach the junction at the trail builder monument; turn right on the woods road, following yellow blazes.

6.2 Pass a small woods road to your left and then cross a log bridge over a babbling headwater of the West Branch Neversink River.

6.5 Close the loop at the 0.7-mile junction; turn left on woods road.

6.8 Descend left on footpath, backtracking to the trailhead.

7.2 End at the trailhead.

Hike Information

Local Information

Belleayre Region Lodging and Tourism Association, P.O. Box 18, Fleischmanns 12430; (800) 431-4555; www.catskillhighpeaks.com

Local Events/Attractions

The Delaware and Ulster Railroad, on Highway 28 in Arkville, serves up yesteryear relaxation and nostalgia aboard its historic excursion train. It travels through pastoral and Catskill Mountain settings, traveling along the East Branch of the Delaware between Arkville and Roxbury. Trains run weekends late May through October, with additional runs on Thursday and Friday in July and August. Delaware and Ulster Railroad, 43510 Highway 28, Arkville 12406; (845) 586-DURR; www.durr.org

Accommodations

Woodland Valley (DEC) Campground, south of Woodland (reached south off Highway 28 west of Phoenicia), is open mid-April through Columbus Day and has seventy-two campsites. Reservations: (800) 456-2267; www.reserveamerica.com

Organizations

New York–New Jersey Trail Conference helps maintain, mark, and map trails. NY–NJ Trail Conference, 156 Ramapo Valley Road (U.S. Highway 202), Mahwah, NJ 07430; (201) 512-9348; fax: (201) 512-9012; info@nynjtc.org; www.nynjtc.org

LIVING IN SYMPATHY WITH NATURE

John Burroughs (1837–1921), the Roxbury, New York-born environmentalist and writer, introduced Slide Mountain to the world through his nature essays. He grew up in the Catskills and, in the reflective veins of Emerson, Thoreau, and Whitman, wrote more than thirty books. According to biographer Edward J. Renehan Jr., Burroughs "urged simple living in sympathy with nature." Today the dramatic range arcing from Slide Mountain to Wittenberg Mountain wears the Burroughs name. On his celebrated trek to Slide Mountain, he traveled cross-country from Woodland Valley, coming out just north of the summit. On reaching the mountain, he ascended the 1820s rock slide that gave the peak its name. Forest has since reclaimed the scar. On his mountain sojourns he slept beneath the overhang next to which the Burroughs memorial plaque now hangs. During his lifetime, he traveled with the likes of Theodore Roosevelt and John Muir.

40 Minnewaska State Park Preserve

A former resort and the one-time battleground between developers and environmentalists, this state park preserve unfurls a welcoming and tranquil natural realm. The site boasts white–cliff escarpments, indigo waters, and soothing forests—images to delight poet and photographer. Comfortable carriageways and foot trails travel the preserve. The selected carriageway circuit travels from Lake Minnewaska, around Lake Awosting, and across a Shawangunk escarpment rim for a visually rich trail experience.

Start: At the picnic area trailhead
Distance: 11.8-mile out-and-back lasso-shaped hike that includes spur to Rainbow Falls
Approximate hiking time: 6.5 to 8 hours
Difficulty: Moderate due to distance
Elevation change: The trail has about a 500-foot elevation change.
Trail surface: Slate or earthen carriageways and foot trails
Seasons: Best for hiking, spring through fall
Other trail users: Cyclists, horse riders (permit required), cross-country skiers
Canine compatibility: Leashed dogs permitted (Dogs, however, are not allowed in buildings, on walkways, or in picnic or bathing areas.)
Land status: State park

Nearest town: New Paltz
Fees and permits: Fee site
Schedule: 9:00 a.m. to dusk
Maps: State park flier (obtain at the park); New York–New Jersey Trail Conference Trail Map 104, Shawangunk Trails–South (available at traditional and online bookstores or from the Conference store online: www.nynjtc.org)
Trail contacts: Minnewaska State Park Preserve, P.O. Box 893, New Paltz 12561; (845) 256-0579; http://nysparks.state.ny.us/parks
Special considerations: Deer hunting (season runs October into December) is allowed in sections of the park, but it is generally away from the carriageways. Be cautious along the cliffs and know that rattlesnakes and copperheads find habitat in the park.

Finding the trailhead: From New York State Thruway Interstate 87, take exit 18 for New Paltz and go west on Highway 299 for 7.2 miles. At the junction with U.S. Highway 44/Highway 55, go west on US 44/Highway 55 for 4.4 miles and turn left for the park. The trail starts from the picnic area at the end of the park road. *DeLorme: New York Atlas & Gazetteer:* Page 36 C2.

The Hike

Descend following the red trail to the Minnewaska lakeshore. At the northwest corner of the lake (opposite the swimming area), you take the green Upper Awosting Carriageway west. Its fine-grade slate offers a smooth walking surface. Hemlock, maple, oak, beautiful white birch, and mountain laurel make up the woods. The mild uphill grade is more apparent to the eye than the body. The carefree stroll allows eyes and thoughts to roam; a deer crossing your path may shake you from your reverie.

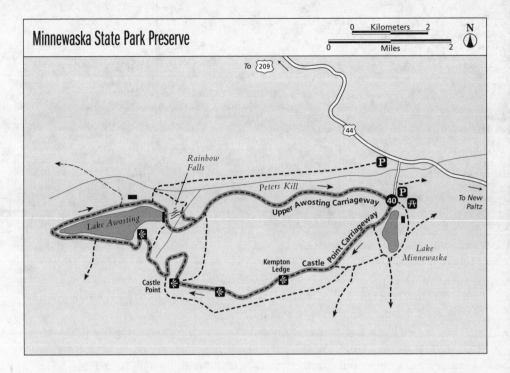

0   Kilometers   2

0   Miles   2

N

To 209

44

To New Paltz

Rainbow Falls

Peters Kill

Upper Awosting Carriageway

Lake Awosting

Castle Point Carriageway

Kempton Ledge

Castle Point Carriageway

Castle Point

Lake Minnewaska

40

At an old orchard, the snarled trees still flower in spring, and rusted pieces of farm equipment blend into the meadow. Side brooks sheet over the outcrops draining to Peters Kill below, and color-coded foot trails branch away. Pass beneath a power line, traveling among scenic rock ledges with vegetated shelves. The aqua-blazed Long Path emerges from a break in Litchfield Ledge and crosses the carriageway.

You'll detour right on the Long Path to visit Rainbow Falls. Descend through a deep woods of mature hemlock and beech, crossing a side drainage and then Huntington Ravine. Rainbow Falls graces a side stream, plunging into the latter. The waterfall's rivulets pour from an overhang, embellishing a color-streaked cliff and a growing streamer of algae.

Continuing west on the Upper Awosting Carriageway, the terrain gradually flattens. At the junction approaching Lake Awosting, turn right onto a black-blazed earthen carriageway for a counterclockwise tour of the lake. The dam presents an open lake view, often busy with ducks, geese, and shorebirds. Pinched at its middle, this huge lake shows scalloped coves, evergreen and deciduous shores, and slopes and ledges of white quartzite. Sweet pepperbush, azalea, and mountain and sheep laurel braid a showy understory display.

You pass a rangers cabin, staying above shore for overlooks and cross-lake views but no lake access. At an open flat, an old foundation, broken bricks, and glass hint at a bygone time. At junctions, keep to the black carriageway. Closer to shore, you pass monstrous hemlocks, scenic pines, and lakeside outcrops; side paths visit small penin-

Lake Minnewaska, Minnewaska State Park

sulas. Past the foot trail to Spruce Glen and Murray Hill, you find the swimming area, its lakeward white outcrop bumpy with quartz.

Stay on the black carriageway, drifting into woods before reaching one final lakeside spur for farewell lake viewing. At the upcoming junction, you head right for the Hamilton and Castle Point Carriageways. The trail alternately tours mixed woods and stands of small, bizarre-shaped pines. Glimpses of the white-gray cliff of Castle Point precede the next junction. Here, you go left on the shale-surfaced Castle Point Carriageway, following blue markers.

Pass beneath jutting overhangs and ledges for views toward Battlement Terrace. Ahead you top Castle Point Terrace, reaching Castle Point for a spectacular 180-degree vista sweeping west and south to Hamilton Point, Gertrude's Nose, Lake Awosting, the wooded rims and swells of the park, and the distant Hudson Valley. On descent, perspectives shift east, adding views of Sky Tower in the nearby Mohonks.

You pass under a power line. From Kempton Ledge, you overlook Palmaghatt Kill, the Hudson Valley, and an isolated outcrop of fluted cliffs. Pale green lichens blotch the smooth white stone, and deep fissures invade the terrace. Stick with the descending blue carriageway. Upon reaching Lakeshore Drive (the red carriageway rounding Lake Minnewaska), turn left to close the loop at the swimming area and return uphill to the picnic area.

Half the size of Lake Awosting, stunning blue-green Lake Minnewaska reflects a partial shoreline of abrupt white cliffs with talus skirts. Atop the terrace sits the attractive stone park office building. Hemlocks and pines interweave the leafy trees of shore. Autumn's paintbrush amplifies the beauty of this closing image.

Miles and Directions

0.0 Start from the picnic area trailhead; descend via the red trail.

0.1 Reach Lake Minnewaska. From the lake's northwest corner, hike west on the green Upper Awosting Carriageway.

2.6 Meet the aqua-blazed Long Path; detour right on the Long Path to Rainbow Falls.

2.9 Reach Rainbow Falls; return to the carriageway tour.

3.2 Continue right (west) on Upper Awosting Carriageway.

3.7 Reach the Lake Awosting junction; turn right, following a black-blazed earthen carriageway for counterclockwise lake travel.

4.1 Pass a rangers cabin.

6.4 The carriageway drifts into woods.

6.7 A spur leads to a ledge overlook of Lake Awosting; follow the carriageway as it turns away from the lake for good.

6.8 Reach a junction; go right for Hamilton and Castle Point Carriageways.

7.5 Reach a junction; go left on the shale-surfaced Castle Point Carriageway, following blue markers.

8.2 Reach Castle Point.

10.5 Reach Kempton Ledge. Follow the blue carriageway downhill, avoiding a spur turning right to Hamilton Carriageway.

11.4 Reach red-blazed Lakeshore Drive (the Lake Minnewaska Carriageway); turn left on it.

11.7 Close the loop; ascend to the picnic area.

11.8 End at the picnic area trailhead.

Hike Information

Local Information
New Paltz Regional Chamber of Commerce, 124 Main Street, New Paltz 12561; (845) 255-0243; www.newpaltzchamber.org

Local Events/Attractions
The **Wallkill River** flowing past the town of New Paltz is popular for canoeing and kayaking. The 12.2-mile cinder- or gravel-surfaced **Wallkill Valley Rail-Trail** travels parallel to but away from the river, offering hiking and mountain biking opportunities. The rail trail extends river views in town and again where it crosses the Wallkill. If you need still greater adventure, **rock climbing and ice climbing** in the Shawangunks are world-renown, with popular routes in Mohonk Preserve west of New Paltz. Climbing guides and clinics operate in the New Paltz area. Contact the New Paltz Regional Chamber of Commerce.

Organizations
New York–New Jersey Trail Conference helps maintain 30 miles of hiking trail in the park. NY–NJ Trail Conference, 156 Ramapo Valley Road (U.S. Highway 202), Mahwah, NJ 07430; (201) 512-9348; fax: (201) 512-9012; info@nynjtc.org; www.nynjtc.org

41 Bashakill Wildlife Management Area

At this 2,200-acre wildlife management and bird conservation area—more than half of it freshwater wetland—a former railroad grade rolls out an avenue to relaxation and nature discovery. Part of the greater Long Path, this rail-to-trail travels at the eastern edge of Bashakill Marsh, which is the largest freshwater marsh in southeastern New York. At this premier bird-watching site, birders delight in spring-nesting warblers and waterfowl, brooding summer birds, and fall migrants. Here both daylight and evening watches are possible. Six trailheads access the rail trail, readily allowing hopscotch or car-shuttle travel.

Start: At the southern trailhead
Distance: 13 miles out-and-back, including side trails
Approximate hiking time: 6.5 to 8.5 hours
Difficulty: Easy
Elevation change: The trail is virtually flat.
Trail surface: Earthen or grassy railroad grade or path
Seasons: Best for hiking, spring through fall
Other trail users: Birders, hunters, mountain bikers, snowshoers, cross-country skiers
Canine compatibility: Dogs permitted but must be controlled at owner's side by leash or voice command
Land status: Department of Environmental Conservation (DEC)
Nearest town: Wurtsboro

Fees and permits: No fees or permits required
Schedule: Year-round, twenty-four hours (In winter, snow and unplowed lots can limit access.)
Maps: Bashakill Wildlife Management Area DEC brochure (obtain at DEC office)
Trail contacts: New York State DEC, Region 3, 21 South Putt Corners Road, New Paltz 12561; (845) 256-3000; www.dec.ny.gov
Special considerations: You will find no amenities here other than parking; bring water. Expect some soggy stretches, and avoid this trail during hunting season. Although the WMA prohibits camping and campfires, night fishing, owl watching, and stargazing are acceptable nighttime activities here.

Finding the trailhead: From Highway 17/Interstate 86, take exit 113 and go south on U.S. Highway 209 for 5.2 miles, turning left onto County Road 163/County Road 61 for Otisville. Go 0.4 mile and turn left to round the WMA's east shore on South Road. In 0.1 mile find a fishing access; in 0.2 mile find the southern trailhead for the WMA's rail trail. You'll find the trail's northern terminus at the southeast outskirts of Wurtsboro. *DeLorme: New York Atlas & Gazetteer.* Page 35 D6.

The Hike

Northbound, you follow the rail trail at the edge of the marsh. Woody vines sag between the trees, shaping a thin border between the trail and the wetland flat. Soggy reaches can claim both sides of the levee. Cross-beams and footbridges ease drainage crossings. In places the old rail ties ripple the trailbed or lie discarded to its side.

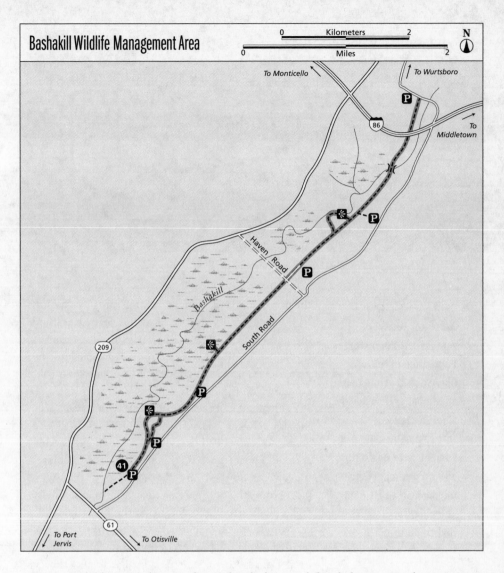

Duckweed, lily pads, clumps of arrowhead, algae, and flooded stumps and snags vary viewing. Morning songbirds regale you.

Columbine, wild geranium, and violet sprinkle color at the trail's sides. Open sites offer fine marsh vantages and fishing access. Oriole, warbler, scarlet tanager, bluebird, green heron, grouse, rail, osprey, vulture, and a wide variety of waterfowl can quickly add checks to your birder's list. Woodchuck, muskrat, beaver, and white-tailed deer are among the mammal sightings.

At the junction near the second trailhead parking lot, you'll veer left off the railroad grade to follow a nature trail before continuing forward. The nature trail takes you closer to the wetland as it swings a loop. Short, dead-end side spurs branch from

Bashakill Marsh, Bashakill Wildlife Management Area

▶ **On the west side of Bashakill Marsh, snatches of the historic Delaware and Hudson Canal (1828–1898) offer additional exploration. A blockade halting soft-coal shipments from England gave rise to this 108-mile canal linking the domestic coal fields of Pennsylvania with the Hudson River ports.**

the nature loop to fishing or viewing spots. Viewpoints take in the open water, treed islands, arrowhead, and lily pads. Canada geese may navigate faint channels through the aquatic vegetation or disappear into the marsh upon a riotous landing. White pines and oaks contrast with marsh views.

Northbound, back on the grade, you travel a scenic aisle of white birch. After crossing a boardwalk and an area of embedded ties, you reach the next parking area and a boat launch. At times red-winged blackbirds fiercely defend their nests, bombing geese that swim past. Nonnative loosestrife chokes the marsh to the right, while arrowhead dominates the main marsh.

Woods travel then follows, with the occasional gnarled maple and pockets of poison ivy tucked in the deeper grass. Where you cross a bridge, skunk cabbage and false hellebore line the brook and riddle the wetland woods as the trail alternates between woods and marsh.

After crossing Haven Road, you'll walk the gravel access road through the parking lot and round the gate to the north, returning to rail trail passage. This is the most popular WMA access and often overflows with birders' vehicles. Past a scenic multitrunked pine, keep an eye out for a side trail ascending the steep incline on the left. In the past a rustic sign here indicated SIDE TRAIL TO LOOKOUT. Tags may identify tree species. The viewing tower overlooks the meandering course of Bashakill and the wetland mosaic. You then continue on the side spur as it hooks past the tower to return to the rail trail. Back on the grade, you pass the next parking area.

Swampy passages ahead can interrupt woods travel. Footbridges over the split flow of Bashakill mark off distance. Sounds of Highway 17/I-86 precede the highway underpass, where Virginia creeper scales the tunnel's concrete walls. The rail corridor opens overhead, and alert turtles plop from the banks as you pass. The hike ends opposite Walker Lane in southeast Wurtsboro; return south. The Long Path continues north.

Miles and Directions

0.0 Start from the southern trailhead; hike the rail trail north. **Note:** The rail trail heading south from here dead-ends in 0.2 mile.

0.5 Reach a junction; turn left and add a clockwise tour of the nature trail loop before resuming northbound. **Note:** The footbridge to the right leads to a trailhead parking lot.

1.2 Return to the rail trail; turn left (north).

1.6 Reach the third parking area and a boat launch.

3.7 Cross Haven Road to the fourth trail parking area; hike the gravel access road through the parking lot and round the gate to the north.

4.4 Head left up the bank to add the viewing tower side loop.

4.6 Turn left (north) upon returning to the rail trail.

4.7 Pass the fifth parking area. **Bailout:** This site makes a good turnaround point or spotting location for a shuttle vehicle because the rail trail ahead encounters more human intrusions.

6.0 Reach the Highway 17/I-86 underpass.

6.5 Reach Walker Lane in southeast Wurtsboro (the sixth access); backtrack south.

13.0 End at the southern trailhead.

Hike Information

Local Information
Sullivan County Visitors Association, 100 North Street, P.O. Box 5012, Monticello 12701; (845) 794-3000, ext. 5010; www.scva.net

Local Events/Attractions
Upper Delaware Scenic Byway (Highway 97) parallels the Delaware River from Port Jervis to Hancock, traversing an area of southern New York rich in natural beauty and history. The river has national park status, designated the Upper Delaware Scenic and Recreational River. Cross-river views find Pennsylvania. Superintendent, 274 River Road, Beach Lake, PA 18405; (570) 729-7134; River Hotline Information: (845) 252-7100; www.nps.gov/upde

Organizations
The **Basha Kill Area Association** leads hikes, conducts volunteer bird watches, and performs cleanups and other projects at Bashakill WMA and publishes and markets a field guide to the wetlands. The Basha Kill Area Association, P.O. Box 1121, Wurtsboro 12790; info@thebashakill.org; www.thebashakill.org

Honorable Mentions

The Catskills

⊤ Little Pond Loop

This moderately difficult hike travels 5.3 miles, exploring the gentle western relief of the Catskill Mountains, swinging between Little Pond and Touchmenot Mountain, with a spur to Cabot Mountain. You will travel mixed forest, conifer plantation, beaver-modified waters, and meadow habitats. Little Pond, a long lake with a small dam at its developed end, sits in between low wooded ridges and holds stocks of pan-size fish. Because this site bustles in summer, you will likely find the pond area more enjoyable before or after the summer vacation season.

On Cabot Mountain, expect to use your hands when climbing among the ledges and overhangs. Below the summit, the open ledge of Beaver Kill Vista offers a leaf-edited view of Touchmenot Mountain, the Catskill ridges beyond Beaver Kill, and the glare of Little Pond. Columbine dresses the rock, drawing hummingbirds to your feet. The summit is wooded but pretty with a lush fern floor.

From Highway 30 on the south shore of Pepacton Reservoir, 13.5 miles equidistant from Margaretville and Downsville, turn southeast onto Beech Hill Road; go 6.3 miles and turn left onto Beaver Kill Road (County Road 54). In 2 miles turn left on Barkaboom Road for 0.2 mile. Now turn left to find the Little Pond entrance station in 0.8 mile. The loop starts near the bathhouse and shower facility above the pond. This is a fee area. *DeLorme: New York Atlas & Gazetteer:* Page 50 D2. Contact New York State Department of Environmental Conservation, Region 4, Stamford Office, 65561 Highway 10, Suite 1, Stamford 12167; (607) 652-7365; www.dec.ny.gov.

∪ Mohonk Mountain House–Mohonk Preserve

In the northern Shawangunks, west of New Paltz, these adjoining private properties introduce the Mohonk Area splendor—one of inspiring cliffs, grand views, and fragile habitats. Mohonk Mountain House, a National Historic Landmark and commercial resort, has served outdoor recreationists since 1869. Although access to the castlelike house (hotel) is restricted to paying guests, its regal exterior complements the trail-webbed Lake Mohonk setting. Linked by an extensive trail network, Mohonk Preserve extends the realm of hiker possibility with its attractive woods and rock features. It is the largest visitor/membership-supported nature preserve in New York State. Although parking and per-person entry fees are charged, payment for a day's hiking at one site buys same-day hiking privileges at the other. Three trails represent the duo.

The 1-mile out-and-back Sky Top Hike (closed in winter) starts at the Mountain

House and ascends from a bygone era and a mystical lake crossing ledges to Hayes Lookout and the Albert K. Smiley Memorial Tower. Views consist of Lake Mohonk, the Mountain House, the Hudson Valley, and Catskill ridges and peaks.

The 4.2-mile out-and-back Bonticou Crag Hike ascends through the preserve's mixed forest. It passes a clearing dubbed "the million-dollar view," skirts historic farm structures, and travels shared-use carriageways and the Northeast Trail, to top and traverse the white rock crag. Mountain laurel, low-stature trees, azalea bushes, and humped outcrops decorate the summit. Views encompass the overhang, wooded Guyot Hill, the Wallkill and Hudson River Valleys, and the Catskills.

The Trapps Loop travels 5.25 miles on the preserve's Overcliff and Undercliff Carriageways. It traverses picturesque woods with old-growth trees, mountain laurel and rhododendron blooms, cliffs, and breakaway boulders. Along Undercliff Carriageway, climbers scale the 200-foot white quartzite cliffs. Early-day climbers first popularized the area.

From New York State Thruway Interstate 87, take exit 18 and go west on Highway 299, passing through New Paltz and crossing over the Wallkill River bridge. Take the first right, turning onto Springtown Road; bear left at the fork in 0.5 mile. This is Mountain Rest Road. Follow it 3.4 miles to enter the Mohonk Mountain House gateway. (Hike the Huguenot Trail or take the fee shuttle bus to Mohonk Mountain House and Lake Mohonk and the hike to Sky Top.) *DeLorme: New York Atlas & Gazetteer:* Page 36 B2.

For the Bonticou Crag Hike, remain on Mountain Rest Road, proceeding another 0.9 mile. Turn right onto Upper Knoll Road and drive 0.2 mile to the preserve's Spring Farm trailhead. *DeLorme: New York Atlas & Gazetteer:* Page 36 B2.

For Mohonk Preserve Trapps Gateway Visitor Center and the Trapps Loop, from I-87 go 7.2 miles west on Highway 299, reaching the junction with U.S. Highway 44/Highway 55. Go west on US 44/Highway 55 for 0.4 mile to locate the center and its parking on the right. The Trapps Loop can be accessed either from the center or from the West Trapps Entry trailhead. Find its parking on the right 1.3 miles west of the center off US 44/Highway 55. *DeLorme: New York Atlas & Gazetteer:* Page 36 C2.

Contact Mohonk Mountain House, 1000 Mountain Rest Road, New Paltz 12561; (845) 255-1000; www.mohonk.com and Mohonk Preserve, P.O. Box 715, New Paltz 12561; (845) 255-0919; www.mohonkpreserve.org.

Hudson Valley

This New York region celebrates the Hudson River—a vital transportation and recreation corridor, past and present. The promise of a northwest passage to China first attracted interest to this continent and this river. In 1609, while sailing for the Dutch East India trading company, Henry Hudson entered the New York harbor and sailed the *Half Moon* up what is now known as the Hudson River, covering about 150 miles before realizing this river was not the anticipated passage. Nonetheless, the Hudson River has played a key role in the development of the nation, westward expansion, and the commerce and growth of New York State. The Revolutionary War, the Erie Canal, and the Hudson River School of painters all have stories tied to this region.

The Hudson Valley is a federal National Heritage Area, and the river is one of only fourteen federally recognized Great American Rivers. By the 1850s an estimated 150 steamboats plied the river. The Hudson River Maritime Museum in Kingston records this era. A recent festival added to the Hudson Valley calendar, the annual Hudson Ferry-go-Round, allows you to revisit the bygone age of ferry transport, traveling from port to port. Participating river towns offer trolley services from the ferry landings to museums, shops, and eateries.

The Hudson Valley landscape is one of ridges, peaks, and valleys. At the northeastern extent of the Hudson Valley, the attractive Taconic skyline separates New York from Massachusetts and Connecticut. In the southern river valley, the striking bookends, East and West Hudson Highlands, overlook the broad-backed river. They stretch 1,000 feet high and 15 miles long. The Palisades, home to the acclaimed Bear Mountain/Harriman state park complex, adds to wilderness bounty, and the Appalachian Trail (AT) spends much of its 95-mile New York sojourn in the land of the Hudson. The AT crosses the Hudson River at Bear Mountain Bridge.

The region rewards with multistate vistas. Mountain laurel, dogwood, and azalea endorse springtime hiking. Tucked away at the Connecticut border is the nation's first registered National Natural Landmark, Mianus River Gorge.

◀ *Appalachian Trail bridge, Sterling Forest State Park*

42 Taconic State Park

In the southern Taconic Mountain Range, abutting 11 miles of the Massachusetts and Connecticut border, this New York state park blurs state lines. Bash Bish Falls, which annually brings 100,000 visitors to Taconic State Park, actually lies in Massachusetts but is best reached by this park's trail. The park's skyline South Taconic Trail meanders in and out of New York and Massachusetts with an equal disregard of borders. The southbound trek to Brace Mountain, featured here, offers tri-state views. The park's waterfall trail can put a refreshing exclamation mark on the featured hike; a north-bound mountain trek can extend exploration.

Start: At the Bash Bish trailhead
Distance: 16.2 miles out-and-back to Brace Mountain
Approximate hiking time: 9 to 11 hours
Difficulty: Strenuous
Elevation change: Southbound, the South Taconic Trail starts at an elevation of 800 feet, tops Alander Mountain at 2,250 feet, and then rolls between 1,500 and 2,300 feet, tagging Brace Mountain at 2,311 feet.
Trail surface: Earthen foot trail and woods road
Seasons: Best for hiking, spring through fall
Other trail users: Hunters, snowmobilers
Canine compatibility: Leashed dogs permitted (Be sure to clean up after your dogs on the waterfall trail.)
Land status: All state lands: New York state park and Massachusetts state land
Nearest town: Copake Falls
Fees and permits: Entrance fee
Schedule: Sunrise to sunset in New York
Maps: State park trail flier (obtain at the park); New York–New Jersey Trail Conference Trail Map, South Taconic Trail (available at traditional and online bookstores or from the Conference: www.nynjtc.org)
Trail contacts: Taconic State Park, Route 344, P.O. Box 100, Copake Falls 12517; (518) 329-3993; http://nysparks.state.ny.us/parks
Special considerations: Although this New York state park prohibits trailside camping within reach of the South Taconic Trail, Massachusetts has a first come, first served cabin and fifteen backcountry campsites (fee and permit required; contact Mount Washington State Forest, RD 3, East Street, Mount Washington, MA 01258; (413) 528-0330; www.mass.gov/dcr/parks/western/mwas.htm). It is best to avoid the trails during deer season (November through December) in both New York State and Massachusetts. But if you do hike, wear orange or bright-colored clothing. Bear and bobcat sightings have been reported, so store food safely and be watchful of your children and pets.

Finding the trailhead: From Copake Falls go 0.7 mile east on Highway 344 to reach the park's Bash Bish trailhead on the right. *DeLorme: New York Atlas & Gazetteer:* Page 53 D5.

The Hike

For the featured hike on the South Taconic Trail, you'll follow the signature white markings south along the limited-access road that angles downhill to the cabins, west

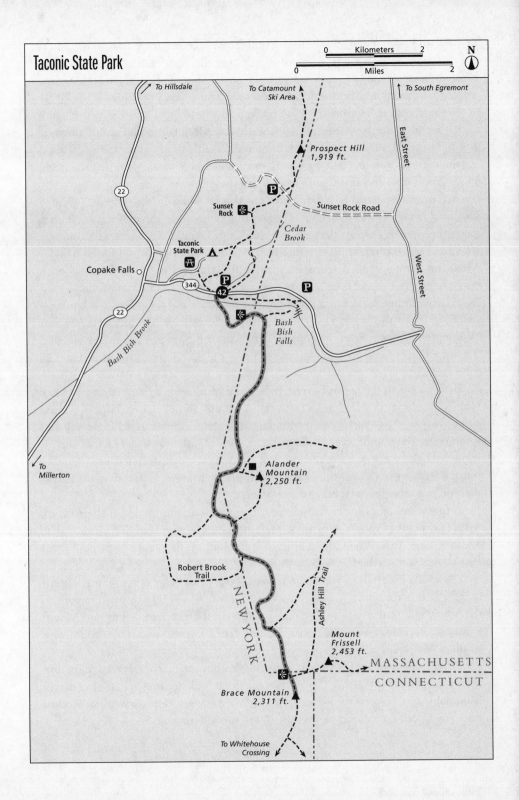

Taconic State Park

Kilometers 0   2

Miles 0   2

N

To Hillsdale

To Catamount Ski Area

To South Egremont

Prospect Hill
1,919 ft.

East Street

22

P

Sunset Rock Road

Sunset Rock

Cedar Brook

West Street

Taconic State Park

Copake Falls

344

42

P

P

Bash Bish Brook

Bash Bish Falls

To Millerton

Alander Mountain
2,250 ft.

Robert Brook Trail

Ashley Hill Trail

NEW YORK

Mount Frissell
2,453 ft.

MASSACHUSETTS

CONNECTICUT

Brace Mountain
2,311 ft.

To Whitehouse Crossing

of the Bash Bish trailhead. You cross the bridge and hike past the cabins before entering the wilds on a foot trail. A contouring ascent through mountain laurel, a sharp climb through a stand of 1- to 3-foot-diameter hemlocks, and passages in high-canopy maple forest and pine-oak woods carry you to the ridge and a junction.

A short detour here on the blue-marked spur leads to a vantage that extends a 180-degree western perspective, with Washburn Mountain prominent. The white South Taconic Trail continues its southbound ascent in oak woodland and later a hemlock grove, soon bypassing a second blue trail and generally hugging the ridge. Pines appear now and again, and views flip to the east.

Before reaching an old lookout site on Alander Ridge, you come to a painted blue marker on a flat, exposed outcrop. Depending on when the trail was last blazed, it may be faint, so keep an alert eye. For the South Taconic Trail alone, you continue straight ahead, staying with the white blazes. Should you opt instead for an Alander Mountain detour, you'd descend left on the blue trail, coming to a saddle where a rustic cabin sits. The cabin offers a dry overnight wayside on a first come, first served basis. Early summer azalea and laurel fancy it up. From the cabin area, the blue trail descending past the structure is the one that leads through Massachusetts's Mount Washington State Forest to the designated backpacker campsites, a considerable hike. The blue-marked route climbing eastward tags the Alander summit in about 0.25 mile for a view.

Before long on the South Taconic Trail, you'll come upon a fine 270-degree view with Massachusetts's Alander Mountain and Mount Frissell, Connecticut's Round Mountain, and New York's Brace Mountain and the westward stretching valley and foothills. An outcrop of wavy-patterned schist provides the vantage. The trail, shaded by mixed oaks, maple, and beech, now drops away, sometimes steeply. Where it comes out at a former woods road, follow the woods road left. As you ascend from a drainage dip, you pass an overgrown blue trail on the left.

A few white pines tower trailside near the junction with the red Robert Brook Trail. Fragments of rock wall or waist-high ostrich ferns next lend decoration to the South Taconic Trail. Where the mountain laurel bushes close ranks, a splendid floral aisle escorts you skyward in early summer.

Look for a foot trail to veer right. It leads you across a ridge outcrop to a western vantage before returning you once more to the woods road. Hike past the path to the Ashley Hill Trail. After the grade has eased, a red trail descends left toward Mount Frissell and Tristate Point. The South Taconic Trail continues on an old woods road to Brace Mountain.

Where the road trail forks, go right. A shrubby, open complex contains this moderate-grade route. Ahead you take the foot trail heading left to top Brace Mountain at an impressive 5-foot-tall cairn. Views sweep the tristate area. Return now as you came, or continue south to Whitehouse Crossing.

Miles and Directions

0.0   Start west of the Bash Bish trailhead; descend the limited-access road that angles downhill to the cabins.

1.1   Reach a ridge junction; follow the 0.1-mile blue spur to a vantage point before continuing on the white-blazed ascent.

3.0   Reach a notch.

3.5   Reach the junction on the Alander Mountain ridge near the former lookout site; continue south. **Option:** For an Alander Mountain detour, descend left on the blue trail, coming to a saddle and a cabin. The blue fork descending past the cabin traverses Massachusetts's Mount Washington State Forest, eventually reaching backpacker campsites. The blue fork ascending east tags Alander summit in 0.3 mile for views.

5.2   Pass the red-blazed Robert Brook Trail.

6.7   Follow the foot trail that veers right for a crescent spur to a western vantage, returning to the woods road.

6.8   Hike past the Ashley Hill Trail (blue).

7.6   Pass the Mount Frissell Trail (the red trail descending left). **Option:** You can detour along this trail, finding first Tristate Point (just a simple border cairn, which happens to be the highest point in Connecticut) and then the oak-crowned summit of Massachusetts's Mount Frissell, but no views.

7.8   At the road fork, go right, continuing on the South Taconic Trail.

8.2   Spur left, topping Brace Mountain; backtrack on the South Taconic Trail to the trailhead. **Option:** You can continue hiking south on the South Taconic Trail to Whitehouse Crossing.

16.2   End west of the Bash Bish trailhead.

Options

For the 1.5-mile out-and-back hike to **Bash Bish Falls,** follow the closed service road east upstream from the falls trailhead. You overlook Bash Bish Brook, a sparkling stream coursing over bedrock. Although the deep pools invite, swimming is not allowed. Hemlock and maple lace over the trail. Stairs then descend to the boot-polished schist outcrop that serves up unobstructed falls viewing. Bash Bish Falls spills in an energetic rush around a skyward-pointing rock wedge. The right half shows a tiered veil broadening at the base; the left, a showery drop ending in a water slide. An emerald pool cupped in a crescent cliff captures the water.

The **South Taconic Trail** (North) offers a moderate 7.4-mile out-and-back to Prospect Hill or a 4.2-mile shuttle. To spot the shuttle vehicle, you'd take Cemetery Road north from Copake Falls to North Mountain Road. Continue north on North Mountain Road for 1.4 miles and turn right onto unmarked Sunset Rock Road, a seasonally maintained single-lane gravel road. Drive 1.1 miles more to trail parking on the right. *DeLorme: New York Atlas & Gazetteer.* Page 53 D5.

Northbound from the falls trailhead, you'd angle west across Highway 344, following white blazes up a wooded slope to the left of the Cedar Brook drainage. The

Brace Mountain summit on South Taconic Trail, Taconic State Park

marked route travels woods roads through changing forests; colored trails arrive and depart. Tall pines and maples offer shade, but with each burst of ascent, the trail opens up. At 2.5 miles you exit a shrub corridor to find an unmarked 0.1-mile spur leading left to Sunset Rock; the continuation of the South Taconic Trail follows the faint jeep track straight ahead. The bump of westward-facing Sunset Rock (elevation 1,788 feet) overlooks the immediate valley farmland, with the Catskills and Hudson Valley some 50 miles distant.

The South Taconic Trail ahead flattens as it follows the grassy jeep track through an arbor of oak, pine, and mountain laurel. It then dips and angles downhill across Sunset Rock Road (the shuttle parking) at 3.2 miles, setting up the final climb to Prospect Hill. Outcrops on the summit ridge extend western views of farmland, eastern views of Mounts Everett and Darby, and southern views of Bash Bish and Alander Mountains. Before a New York–Massachusetts boundary marker, you turn left, topping Prospect Hill (elevation 1,919 feet) at 3.7 miles, bettering the view from Sunset Rock. Backtrack to the trailhead or to your shuttle vehicle.

Hike Information

Local Information
Columbia County Tourism Department, Hudson 12534; (518) 828-3375; www .travelhudsonvalley.org

Local Events/Attractions

Harlem Valley Rail Trail, built on the old railroad bed that connected New York City, the Harlem Valley, and Chatham, extends a paved discovery route to hikers and cyclists. You'll find accesses in Ancram, Copake, and Copake Falls/Taconic State Park. HVRT Association, (518) 789-9591; www.hvrt.org

Accommodations

Taconic State Park Campground, open early May through October, has more than one hundred sites (serving both tent and trailer campers) and three cabin areas. Reservations: (800) 456-2267; www.reserveamerica.com

---

▶ Lightning

Thunderstorms build over the mountains almost every day during the summer. Lightning is generated by thunderheads and can strike without warning, even several miles away from the nearest overhead cloud. The best rule of thumb is to start leaving exposed peaks, ridges, and canyon rims by about noon. This time can vary a little depending on storm buildup. Keep an eye on cloud formation and don't underestimate how fast a storm can build. The bigger they get, the more likely a thunderstorm will happen. Lightning takes the path of least resistance, so if you're the high point, it might choose you. Ducking under a rock overhang is dangerous as you form the shortest path between the rock and ground. If you dash below treeline, avoid standing under the only or the tallest tree. If you are caught above treeline, stay away from anything metal you might be carrying, Move down off the ridge slightly to a low, treeless point and squat until the storm passes. If you have an insulating pad, squat on it. Avoid having both your hands and feet touching the ground at once and never lay flat. If you hear a buzzing sound or feel your hair standing on end, move quickly as an electrical charge is building up.

---

43 Appalachian Trail

This 2,175-mile national scenic trail from Maine to Georgia cuts across the southeast corner of New York State, rolling along ridges and dipping to roads. The New York leg spans 95 miles between the Connecticut and New Jersey state lines. It travels in low-elevation mixed forest, gathers views, passes historic stone walls, and applauds the changing of the seasons.

Start: At the Connecticut border (northern) trailhead

Distance: 95.2 miles from the Connecticut border to the New Jersey border, with the northern 7.2 miles of trail slipping in and out of Connecticut

Approximate hiking time: An average of 7 to 10 days

Difficulty: Strenuous

Elevation change: In New York, the rolling trail travels between a low point of 125 feet along the Hudson River to a high point of 1,433 feet at Prospect Rock on Bellvale Mountain.

Trail surface: Earthen and rocky path, woods road, developed roads

Seasons: Best for hiking, spring through fall

Other trail users: Snowshoers, cross-country skiers, hunters (on lands where allowed)

Canine compatibility: Leashed dogs permitted (When through-hiking with your dog, you need to carry adequate food and water for your animal as well. You and your dog must hike around the zoo area at Bear Mountain, and you may be rerouted elsewhere on the route where pets are not allowed, so do some research.)

Land status: National park linear trail, crossing multiple public lands with a few private sections; heed postings

Nearest town: Pawling (north) and Greenwood Lake or Warwick (south)

Fees and permits: No fees or permits required

Schedule: No time restrictions, except at the zoo area of Bear Mountain (If your arrival doesn't coincide with the zoo area hours, you will have to skirt around the site.)

Maps: Appalachian Trail Conservancy (ATC), Appalachian Trail maps (available at traditional and online bookstores or from the ATC online store: www.atctrailstore.org)

Trail contacts: ATC, P.O. Box 807, 799 Washington Street, Harpers Ferry, WV 25425-0807; (304) 535-6331; www.appalachiantrail.org

Special considerations: You need to work out the logistics of carrying and obtaining adequate food and supplies, plan what to do in case of an emergency, and arrange for transportation at the end of the trail. You should expect rocky, difficult conditions. Having strong map and compass skills will ease travel.

Stay alert for the white blazes; they occur at regular intervals. If you have hiked 0.25 mile without spying one or some other clue to the trail, backtrack to the last-spied blaze and reassess. If the trail still does not reveal itself, you may have to backtrack. Just as with any long-distance trail, keep your senses and exercise judgment about the safety of proceeding. Be alert for temporary changes and/or reroutes. As a heads-up, talks are in the works about a reroute in the Bear Mountain area, so watch for it.

Only eight lean-tos sit along or just off the trail in New York, so a tent is standard equipment. Because lean-tos are offered first come, first served, chancing that you will be the first to arrive and claim one for the night is both unwise and an unnecessary wilderness risk. When pitching a tent, camp in an established site.

The AT is for foot-propelled use only; no bikes, no vehicles, and no horses, llamas, goats, or other pack animals. During fall

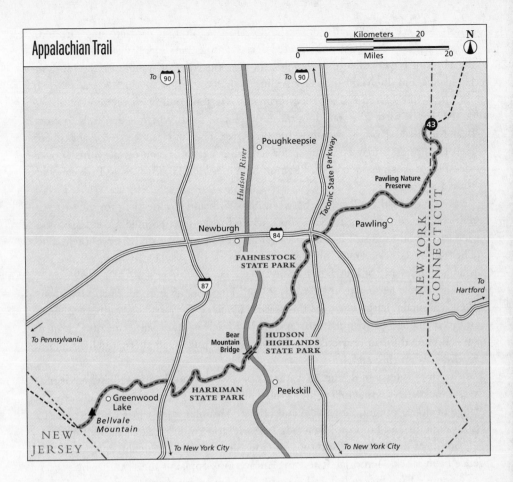

Appalachian Trail

hunting season, orange-colored clothing is a wise precaution. Keep to the narrow protected greenway to avoid straying onto private land. Beware of rattlesnakes.

Finding the trailhead: The Appalachian Trail crosses many New York state and county routes and traverses Fahnestock, Hudson Highlands, and Bear Mountain–Harriman State Parks. If hiking through New York State, you will find the northernmost road access to the Appalachian Trail at the intersection of Highway 55/Connecticut Highway 55 and Hoyt Road. *DeLorme: New York Atlas & Gazetteer:* Page 37 C7. The southernmost road access is along Highway 17A near Greenwood Lake. *DeLorme: New York Atlas & Gazetteer:* Page 32 C1.

The Hike

Striking a diagonal across southeastern New York, the AT rolls across low, rugged ridges and hilltops, passing through low-elevation deciduous woods and hemlock forests. The AT dips to cross brooks and drainages (often at road crossings), rounds lakes and ponds but gains only limited access, and gathers grand views that include the Hudson River Valley, the Taconics, the Catskills, the Shawangunks, the Hudson Highlands, and the Manhattan city skyline.

The white-blazed AT advances primarily via foot trail, with sections of abandoned woods road. The trail does travel developed roads where it descends to cross Bear Mountain Bridge over the Hudson River. The trail can be rocky and steep; use of your hands may be required for steadying, climbing, and easing yourself over rocks. Tight passages such as the "Lemon Squeezer" in Harriman State Park can add comedy to travel.

Southbound, the AT sashays between New York and Connecticut for the first 7.2 miles before committing to New York's watch for the next 88 miles. As it travels the rich hardwood forests of Hammersley Ridge in Pawling Nature Reserve (owned by The Nature Conservancy), marshy sites can mark the way. Early views feature the rolling countryside of Dutchess County.

The 7-mile leg between Highway 22 and Highway 55 finds an open view from West Mountain. Large oaks and fields claim much of the way. The southern 2 miles of this segment pass within a quarter mile of a nuclear-fuel testing site, now cleaned up and cleared for unrestricted use. But if you feel uneasy, an alternate blue trail on roadway avoids this stretch.

South of Interstate 84 the AT gathers open views from Depot Hill, where it traverses rock ledges while rolling along the wooded ridge. The undulating trail keeps to ridge or slope, topping Stormville and Hosner Mountains for views of the Catskills, Shawangunks, and Hudson Highlands. Historic stone walls recall an earlier time.

South of the Taconic Parkway, you cross Shenandoah Mountain, entering Clarence Fahnestock Memorial State Park. An overlook applauds the shimmering platter of Canopus Lake before the trail descends to round the wooded slope and ridge of the west shore. The AT only reaches the Canopus Lake level where the trail crosses Highway 301. Ahead you briefly follow the bed of an 1862 narrow-gauge railroad once used to transport iron ore. Hemlock groves, swamps, and ridgetop views advance and vary the AT. Blueberry patches and mountain laurel bring seasonal flourish.

At Denning Hill, the New York City skyline assumes its place in the panorama. While traversing the Hudson Highlands, enjoy spectacular Hudson River views. The tour is rugged but the rewards great. A steep, grueling descent leads to Bear Mountain Bridge for the Hudson River crossing.

The popular Bear Mountain–Harriman State Park recreation complex next hosts the AT. State park trails meeting the AT allow for day-hike loops.

After you pass through the developed area of Bear Mountain State Park, a hearty ascent follows. You top Bear Mountain at Perkins Memorial Tower (1,305 feet). You'll secure vistas from Bear, West, and Black Mountains before skirting Island Pond. The terrain remains steep and rugged as the trail continues to collect peaks and vistas.

Fitzgerald Falls, a hemlock-shaded 25-foot waterfall spilling down a rocky cleft, wins admirers about 10 miles north of the New Jersey state line. New York's send-off to the AT comes at Bellvale Mountain, where ledges reward with views of Greenwood Lake and Ramapo Hills.

Because spatial constraints necessarily limit this description, if you are through-trail hiking, or even just day hiking the AT, you should contact the ATC for official maps and point-to-point guides. Entire books have been devoted to this premier trail and to the New York–New Jersey trail component alone; look for them.

Miles and Directions

0.0 Start from the northernmost crossing from Connecticut into New York; hike south.

7.2 Reach Hoyt Road (AT now remains in New York).

14.2 Reach Highway 22.

21.2 Reach Highway 55.

27.0 Reach the I-84 overpass.

33.0 Reach Taconic Parkway.

36.1 Reach Shenandoah Mountain.

40.3 Reach Highway 301/Canopus Lake in Fahnestock State Park.

52.8 Reach U.S. Highway 9.

58.6 Cross Bear Mountain Bridge.

61.2 Reach Bear Mountain.

65.6 Reach Palisades Parkway.

77.4 Reach Highway 17/I-86.

83.5 Reach Mombasha High Point.

85.5 Reach Fitzgerald Falls.

89.4 Reach Highway 17A.

95.2 Reach the New York–New Jersey state line.

Hike Information

Local Information

Travel Hudson Valley, (800) 232-4782; www.travelhudsonvalley.org, or Dutchess County Tourism, 3 Neptune Road, Poughkeepsie 12601; (845) 463-4000 or (800) 445-3131; www.dutchesstourism.com, or **Putnam Visitors Bureau,** 110 Old Route 6, Building 3, Carmel 10512; (845) 225-0381 or (800) 470-4854; www.visit putnam.org, or **Rockland County Office of Tourism,** 18 Hempstead Road, New City 10956; (845) 708-7300 or (800) 295-5723; www.rockland.org, or **Orange County Tourism,** 124 Main Street, Goshen 10924; (845) 291-2136 or (800) 762-8687; www.orangetourism.org

Local Events/Attractions

Besides superb trailed woods and mountaintop views, **Bear Mountain State Park** holds the historic and still operating 1915-built Bear Mountain Inn, above Hessian Lake. Other park attractions are the Trailside Museums and Zoo, a winter outdoor skating rink, and a prized merry-go-round. First proposed in 1915 and again in the 1930s, it wasn't until 2000 that a merry-go-round graced Bear Mountain.

Constructed of wood, the carousel features hand-painted scenes of the park and forty-two hand-carved animals: bear, deer, otter, raccoon, and jumping horses. The carousel is open weekends and holidays, with daily hours in summer. The thirty-two-acre Bear Mountain Trailside Museums and Zoo consists of four natural and cultural museums and a zoo of native New York animals that cannot be released safely into the wild. The site is open daily (weather permitting); a modest fee is charged. Bear Mountain State Park, Bear Mountain 10911; (845) 786-2701; www.bearmountainzoo.org

Organizations

New York–New Jersey Trail Conference maintains the AT in New York. NY–NJ Trail Conference, 156 Ramapo Valley Road (U.S. Highway 202), Mahwah, NJ 07430; (201) 512-9348; fax: (201) 512-9012; info@nynjtc.org; www.nynjtc.org

HISTORY OF THE APPALACHIAN TRAIL

President Lyndon B. Johnson's "Natural Beauty" message, delivered February 8, 1965, called for development of a system of trails throughout the land for citizen recreation. He saw the Appalachian Trail as the nation's blueprint. Study, debate, and legislation by Congress followed, and in 1968 President Johnson signed into law the National Trails Act. It designated three national trail categories: scenic, historic, and recreation, with national scenic trails symbolizing the standard of excellence.

Not surprisingly, one of the first trails in the nation to win federal scenic trail distinction was the 2,175-mile Appalachian Trail (AT). Conceived in the early 1920s, this hiker filament rolls atop the ancient Appalachian Mountains, dipping to cross the important eastern river valleys. It salutes the mountain wilds of fourteen eastern states. Although most of the AT greenway has permanent public protection, a few private easements still exist. The push continues to make this entire treasured hiking route completely public. An army of 5,500 volunteers, along with some 200 public agencies, maintain and oversee the trail.

The Appalachian Trail represents the vision of Benton MacKaye (1879-1975), a free thinker with revolutionary ideas about wilderness. As a regional planner in 1921, he first gave voice to the idea of a long-distance mountain trail. He proposed the development of a network of mountain camps and communities stitched together by a single trail, what he called the "Appalachian Trail." MacKaye felt civilized beings needed such wilderness resources to escape the pressures of city and society. (Imagine what he'd think today!) Although fellow planners and politicians scoffed, the simple yet exquisite idea caught fire in the imaginations of like-minded outdoorspeople, and a trail was born.

The Appalachian Trail got its start on the ground in New York State. On October 7, 1923, the first section of the AT between Bear Mountain and Delaware Water Gap was christened and officially opened to walking during a ceremony at the state's popular Bear Mountain–Harriman State Park complex. It became the model for all other sections of the AT yet to be blazed. Throughout the eastern mountain states, local and regional trail groups independently planned and built the remaining sections that eventually linked up to form this one exciting trail. The trail thrived, except for a brief period during World War II, when sections fell to neglect. A strong renewal effort in 1952 corrected the lapse.

This premier trail of the land is joined by the 2,650-mile Pacific Crest National Scenic Trail (also named in the Act of 1968) and the more-than-3,000-mile Continental Divide National Scenic Trail, as well as others that meet the high criteria. Together, the Appalachian, Pacific Crest, and Continental Divide Trails make up the triple crown of hiking. The AT, being the forerunner and sitting within an hour's drive of two-thirds of the nation's population, draws three to four million section hikers annually and documents the most trail completions. Since 1936, more than 9,000 hikers have completed the entire AT, either in sections or all at once, thus becoming members of the elite "2,000-milers" club. Lee Barry, trail moniker "Easy One," became the oldest through-trail hiker at the age of eighty-one.

It is estimated that each year about 3,000 hikers will attempt to through-hike the Appalachian Trail and 300 the Pacific Crest Trail. But only about thirty hikers will take on the through-trail challenge of the brutal Continental Divide Trail. As of this writing, fewer than one hundred have completed the triple crown. Two men, "Flyin'" Brian Robinson in 2001 and Matt "Squeaky" Hazley of Britain in 2005, accomplished this superhuman endeavor in a single calendar year. Matt did it in a madcap 240 days!

44 Breakneck Ridge Trail

On the east side of the Hudson River in Hudson Highlands State Park, this trail makes a rugged ascent from near river-level to roll along a knobby ridge to an old fire lookout tower. From the ridgetop and the tower's location, you take in views of the Hudson River, the Shawangunks, and the Catskill Mountains. A mixed forest with embellishments of mountain laurel and spring and summer wildflowers characterizes much of the hike.

Start: At the tunnel trailhead

Distance: 9.6 miles out-and-back with a loop return

Approximate hiking time: 5.5 to 7 hours

Difficulty: Strenuous due to the initial hand-over-hand rock scramble

Elevation change: The trail has a 1,500-foot elevation change, with the high point atop South Beacon Mountain.

Trail surface: Rocks, earthen path, woods road

Seasons: Best for hiking, spring through fall

Other trail users: Hunters (during the bow deer hunt and spring shotgun turkey hunt)

Canine compatibility: Leashed dogs permitted (When hiking with your dog, start at the Breakneck Bypass/Wilkinson trailhead, avoiding the initial rock scramble, a danger for your pet.)

Land status: State park or private easements

Nearest town: Beacon

Fees and permits: No fees or permits required

Schedule: Sunrise to sunset

Maps: State park flier (available at the Clarence Fahnestock park office); New York–New Jersey Trail Conference Trail Map 102, East Hudson Trails (available at traditional and online bookstores or from the Conference: www.nynjtc.org)

Trail contacts: Hudson Highlands State Park, c/o Clarence Fahnestock State Park, 1498 Highway 301, Carmel 10512; (845) 225-7207; http://nysparks.state.ny.us/parks

Special considerations: Expect some hand-over-hand rock scrambles, and wear boots that protect ankles. High winds and rain increase the risk on the rocky ascent. Avoid the trail's rock ascent during snow and ice. There is no camping and no building fires. The turkey hunt is managed to minimize conflict, with no hunting after 10:00 a.m. and none on weekends.

Finding the trailhead: From the Highway 301–Highway 9D junction in Cold Spring (8.5 miles north of Bear Mountain Bridge), go north on Highway 9D for 2 miles to find the trailhead and parking for two vehicles just north of the tunnel, on the west side of the highway. Find additional parking 0.1 mile north on the left and the Breakneck Bypass trailhead 0.2 mile north on the right. *DeLorme: New York Atlas & Gazetteer:* Page 32 A4.

The Hike

Follow the trail marked by white blazes and Taconic State Park disks south from the trailhead. It passes through a narrow tree corridor at the north end of the Highway 9D tunnel. You'll collect a couple of early Hudson River views before the trail slips into its "go for it" character with a rigorous rocky ascent of the tunnel embankment and the steep west flank of Breakneck Ridge. Sumac, birch, viburnum, and grasses intersperse the rock, although they may go unnoticed because the climb demands full attention. Graffiti can mar the lower rocks, one of the drawbacks of the trail's easy road access.

With a few directional changes (arrows point the way), you attain the rocky shoulder of the ridge for more views of the river, Pollepel Island, Storm King Mountain across the way, and Palisades Interstate Park to the south. The ascent now follows the ridgeline, adding looks at the steep drainage shaped by Breakneck Ridge and Mount Taurus.

At a mile you reach the first vista knoll as the trail rolls from bump to bump, traversing the ridge north. Oaks, maple, ash, and birch weave a woods passage between the knobs. Where fuller woods claim the dips, grouse and deer can surprise you.

South Beacon Fire Tower, Hudson Highlands State Park

Before long, the red Breakneck Bypass trail descends left. It offers a saner return to the trailhead, but first continue the trek north. The next rise holds a 360-degree view of the Hudson River, the valley communities, the Interstate 84 bridge, and South and North Beacon Mountains. On your descent from the rise, a blue trail arrives on the right to share the ridge route. Patches of mountain laurel spot the forest.

The blue trail departs to the left where the white trail enters a brief forested ascent to tag Sunset Point—a rock outcrop ringed by low oaks. A flatter tour follows before the sharp descent to Squirrel Hollow Brook, which generally carries enough water to dampen a bandanna. Cross the brook and briefly merge with the yellow Wilkinson Trail, a woods road. Follow it right for a short distance and then break away left for a demanding ascent via Devils Ladder. White arrows point the way up this steep, rocky slope. A past fire swept this site. Young birch and big-toothed aspen top the list of

Breakneck Ridge Trail

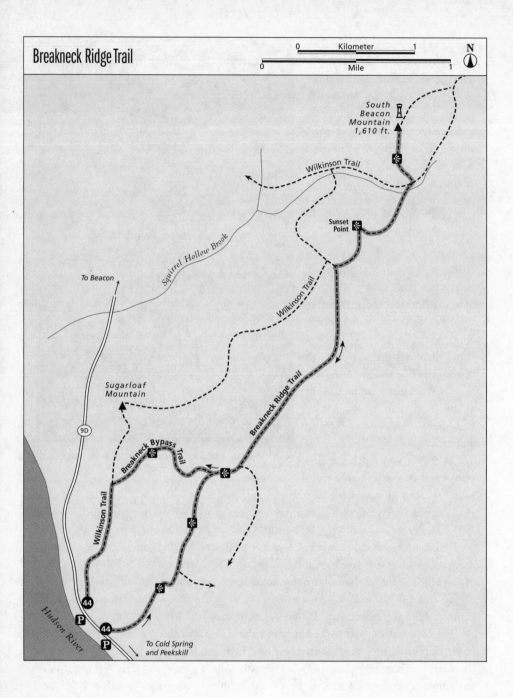

0   Kilometer   1

0   Mile   1

N

South Beacon Mountain 1,610 ft.

Wilkinson Trail

Sunset Point

Squirrel Hollow Brook

To Beacon

Wilkinson Trail

Sugarloaf Mountain

9D

Breakneck Ridge Trail

Breakneck Bypass Trail

Wilkinson Trail

Hudson River

44

P

44

P

To Cold Spring and Peekskill

▶ **The South Beacon summit did not support a fire tower until 1931. Before that, spotters sighting a fire had to hike 0.25 mile down off the mountain to a tree where the telephone line ended, scale that tree to get to a temporary phone, and then call in the report.**

succession species reclaiming the slope. The trail then grades into woods before emerging into the open at South Beacon Tower.

Currently, the 1931 steel tower is unusable, but a friends group is looking to adopt and rehabilitate it. Even without the tower's loft, the view from atop the breezy ridge trumps all previous ones. Take in the river, the ridge, and nearby peaks as well as the distant flat skyline of the Shawangunks and more ragged outline of the Catskills. Although the white trail continues north, for this hike retrace your steps to the Breakneck Bypass for the return to your vehicle.

You will follow the red-blazed Breakneck Bypass foot trail down the deciduous-wooded west flank. Mountain laurel gains a stronghold, while viburnum and huckleberry weave a complement. At times the descent is markedly steep. After following a thin seasonal drainage, you will reach an outcrop with limited river views and a good look at Sugarloaf Mountain. Where you meet the woods road of the yellow-marked Wilkinson Trail, bear left on it, descending to Highway 9D. Big tulip trees and dogwoods decorate the lower slope. The trail comes out on the east side of the highway. Turn left (south) to reach your vehicle back at the tunnel.

Miles and Directions

0.0 Start from the tunnel trailhead; climb the tunnel embankment to the west slope.

1.0 Reach the first vista knob on the ridge.

1.5 Reach Breakneck Bypass (the return); continue north on the white-blazed ridge trail.
Bailout: If time is limited, you can shorten the hike, descending left now on the bypass trail and left again where you meet the Wilkinson Trail for a 3.2-mile loop.

2.0 The ridge trail briefly merges with the blue Notch Trail.

4.1 Cross Squirrel Hollow Brook, coming to the woods road of the yellow Wilkinson Trail; follow it right for a short distance and then break away left.

4.2 Ascend Devils Ladder (white arrows point the way up this steep, rocky slope).

4.7 Reach South Beacon Tower; backtrack to the Breakneck Bypass trail.

7.9 Reach the red-blazed Breakneck Bypass; turn right for the descent to Highway 9D.

8.9 Meet the Wilkinson Trail; head left on it.

9.4 Emerge on the east side of Highway 9D; turn left (south) to return to your vehicle.

9.6 End at the tunnel trailhead.

Hike Information

Local Information

Putnam Visitors Bureau, 110 Old Route 6, Building 3, Carmel 10512; (845) 225-0381 or (800) 470-4854; www.visitputnam.org, or **Travel Hudson Valley,** (800) 232-4782; www.travelhudsonvalley.org, or **Dutchess County Tourism,** 3 Neptune Road, Poughkeepsie 12601; (845) 463-4000 or (800) 445-3131; www.dutchesstourism.com

Local Events/Attractions

The Hudson Valley is home to **Mount Gulian Historic Site,** the colonial homestead of the Verplanck family that served as General von Steuben's headquarters in the Revolutionary War. A Verplanck descendent who trained, led, and fought alongside the U.S. Colored Troops in the Civil War recorded his experiences in fifty-nine letters. An escaped slave served as the property's gardener. These are just some of the stories that permeate this home, shown by guided tour. Mount Gulian Historic Site, 145 Sterling Street, Beacon 12508; (845) 831-8172; www.mountgulian.org

Accommodations

Clarence Fahnestock State Park, off Highway 301 east of the trailhead, is open late April through early December and has eighty-one campsites. Reservations: (800) 456-2267; www.reserveamerica.com

Organizations

New York–New Jersey Trail Conference helps maintain, mark, and map trails. NY–NJ Trail Conference, 156 Ramapo Valley Road (U.S. Highway 202), Mahwah, NJ 07430; (201) 512-9348; fax: (201) 512-9012; info@nynjtc.org; www.nynjtc.org

45 Pine Meadow Lake Loop

Pine Meadow Lake is the anchor to this rolling, circuitous meander through the milder reaches of Harriman State Park. The loop takes you through woodland, atop hills and rock features, and past brook, lake, and swamp. History, birds, and the seasonal embellishments applied by nature complement the physical exertion. The counterclockwise loop unites the area's Pine Meadow, Suffern–Bear Mountain, Tuxedo–Mount Ivy, and Seven Hills Trails.

Start: At the Reeves Meadow trailhead
Distance: 13.2-mile loop
Approximate hiking time: 7 to 9 hours
Difficulty: Moderate
Elevation change: The trail travels between 500 and 1,200 feet above sea level, with the high point atop Diamond Mountain.
Trail surface: Rocky and earthen trail, woods road
Seasons: Best for hiking, spring through fall
Other trail users: None
Canine compatibility: Dogs permitted if both leashed and muzzled and only on trails
Land status: State park
Nearest town: Suffern
Fees and permits: No fees or permits required
Schedule: Daylight hours; Reeves Meadow Visitor Center (and restroom), Memorial Day through Labor Day
Maps: New York-New Jersey Trail Conference

Trail Map 3, Southern Harriman-Bear Mountain Trails (available at traditional and online bookstores or from the Conference: www.nynjtc.org)
Trail contacts: Harriman State Park, Administration Building, Palisades Interstate Park Commission, Bear Mountain 10911; (845) 786-2701; http://nysparks.state.ny.us/parks
Special considerations: Expect muddy passages, especially in early spring and following rains. A precarious rocky descent off Diamond Mountain requires caution and the use of hands. There is no camping and no fires along the trail. Rangers caution hikers to wear a watch and carry emergency flashlights, especially when getting a late start, and to be alert to which trails they have followed. Cell phones often don't work in this dead zone, so don't trust your safety to them. Obtain and use a reliable map to ensure a good and safe time. Bring drinking water.

Finding the trailhead: From New York State Thruway Interstate 87, take exit 15 and go north on Highway 17/Interstate 86 for 2.1 miles, passing through Sloatsburg. Turn right onto Seven Lakes Drive and go 1.5 miles to find Reeves Meadow Visitor Center on the right and additional parking 500 feet past it on the left. *DeLorme: New York Atlas & Gazetteer:* Page 32 C2.

The Hike

From the east side of the visitor center, hike north to locate an old woods road entering the woods on the right. This is the Pine Meadow Trail, marked with red or red-on-white blazing. You follow it upstream along Stony Brook, an attractive bouldery stream, accented by cascades and pools. Hemlock, oak, maple, birch, and beech fashion this shady woods, a shelter for deer.

Pine Meadow Lake Loop

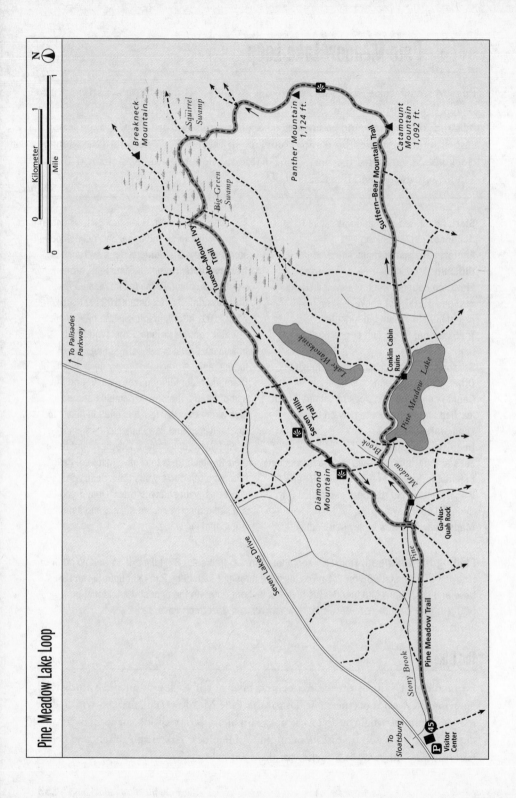

Stony Brook, Harriman State Park

Bear right uphill, still following red markers on a wide rocky trail threaded by small drainages. On the slope, mountain laurel contributes to the full midstory. After the Hillburn–Torne–Sebago Trail briefly shares the route, bear left at the fork. Tulip trees and box elder appear helter-skelter as you continue upstream along quiet-spilling Pine Meadow Brook, a headwater of Stony Brook. Where the trail grows soggy, rocks become allies instead of obstacles. A small fireplace sits where the blue Seven Hills Trail merges from the right.

Across the Pine Meadow Brook footbridge, the red and blue trails divide. This is the loop junction. Follow the red Pine Meadow Trail upstream (right) to Pine Meadow Lake for counterclockwise travel. You pass a scenic moss-and-fern-dressed boulder before reaching trailside Ga-Nus-Quah (Giant Stones) Rock, a room-size boulder overlooking Pine Meadow Brook. A side loop heads left, passing a stone foundation. Ahead, a remnant pipeline and old holding pond echo to the days of the Civilian Conservation Corps camps. At Pine Meadow Lake, detour right to the dam for an open lake vista. Elsewhere, shrubs deny such open views. You pass the ruins of Conklin Cabin, which dates to 1778. Before reaching the inlet, the trail swings left away from Pine Meadow Lake.

With a brook crossing, swampy stretches again suggest hopscotch travel from rock to rock. Azaleas favor the moist reaches. Upon meeting the yellow Suffern–Bear Mountain Trail; follow it left. A steep descent precedes the ascent of Panther Mountain, a scooped hilltop with twin peaks. Outcrops at the first summit provide the lone views east and south. The quiet terrain rolling away offers no clue that New York City lies within 30 miles.

Descend from the second summit into a full, rich forest. Oriole, grouse, turkey, towhee, and tanager add to bird sightings. The trail rolls from rise to brook, arriving at another fireplace ruin and an overgrown woods road, the red-blazed Tuxedo–Mount Ivy Trail; go left on it.

The trail now skirts Squirrel and Big Green Swamps, with filtered looks at the shrub-filled bottomlands. Where the trail meets a woods road between the two, bear right. Cross a footbridge and continue left through a mountain laurel showcase in June. At the white Breakneck Mountain Trail, stay on the red trail as it curves left. After you cross a gravel road and view the lower end of Big Green Swamp, the trail climbs, traveling the flat outcrops of a small rise. Because there is less foot traffic here, watch for markers.

Beyond a woods road, you follow the blue Seven Hills Trail left; it is again better defined. With a brief woods road passage, the rolling foot trail traverses woods, overlooks the watery arm of Lake Sebago, and resumes straight ahead at a junction with the yellow trail. Stay on the blue trail, crossing Diamond Mountain with its striated granites.

Brief, complicated descents lead to and from an open outcrop ledge, offering a grand view across the treetops and out the Pine Meadow Brook drainage. Think through each descent, being watchful of thin ledges. Use your hands as needed, but look before you reach because snakes live here. Where the blue trail comes out at Pine Meadow Brook, turn left (upstream) to close the loop. Cross the footbridge and turn right, retracing your steps to Reeves Meadow Visitor Center.

Miles and Directions

0.0   Start from the Reeves Meadow trailhead; hike north to pick up the Pine Meadow Trail, here a woods road heading right (red or red-on-white blazing).

1.2   The Hillburn-Torne-Sebago Trail briefly shares the route; 500 feet ahead, bear left at the fork.

1.5   The blue Seven Hills Trail merges from the right.

1.6   Cross the Pine Meadow Brook footbridge, reaching the loop junction; head right (upstream) following red markers.

2.2   A side loop to the left passes a stone foundation.

2.4   Reach the dam and a Pine Meadow Lake vista.

3.0   Pass the ruins of Conklin Cabin.

4.7   Meet the yellow Suffern-Bear Mountain Trail; follow it left for the loop.

5.4   Reach Panther Mountain.

6.5   Meet the overgrown woods road of the red-blazed Tuxedo-Mount Ivy Trail; go left on it.

8.0   Reach the white Breakneck Mountain Trail; stay on the red trail as it curves left.

9.9   Reach the blue Seven Hills Trail; follow it left.

10.5 Reach a yellow trail; continue straight ahead on the blue Seven Hills Trail.

10.6 Reach Diamond Mountain; continue following blue blazes.

11.6 Close the loop; cross the footbridge and turn right to backtrack the red Pine Meadow Trail to the trailhead.

13.2 End back at the Reeves Meadow Visitor Center.

Hike Information

Local Information

Rockland County Office of Tourism, 18 New Hempstead Road, New City 10956; (845) 708-7300 or (800) 295-5723; www.rockland.org, or **Travel Hudson Valley,** (800) 232-4782; www.travelhudsonvalley.org

Local Events/Attractions

Stony Point Battlefield State Historic Site, a fee site, brings to life a page of early Hudson River history. During the Revolutionary War, Brigadier General "Mad Anthony" Wayne captured the British fortification here in a midnight bayonet strike, giving the Americans control over the river. The park offers museum military exhibits, a slide program, a grounds interpretive trail, a military encampment, the restored 1826 lighthouse (the oldest remaining light on the Hudson), and weekend camp cooking and musket demonstrations. The park has daily hours mid-April through October and a reduced schedule in winter (call for details). Stony Point Battlefield State Historic Site, 44 Battlefield Road, Stony Point 10980; (845) 786-2521; http://nysparks.state.ny.us/sites.

Accommodations

Harriman State Park's Beaver Pond Campground (open early April through Columbus Day weekend) has 314 campsites. Reservations: (800) 456-2267; www.reserveamerica.com

Organizations

New York–New Jersey Trail Conference helps maintain, mark, and map trails. NY–NJ Trail Conference, 156 Ramapo Valley Road (U.S. Highway 202), Mahwah, NJ 07430; (201) 512-9348; fax: (201) 512-9012; info@nynjtc.org; www.nynjtc.org

Honorable Mentions

Hudson Valley

V Bear Mountain Loop

This demanding 9.7-mile loop rolls through the steep wooded terrain of Bear Mountain State Park, topping Bear and West Mountains and offering views of the Lower Hudson River area. Counterclockwise, you travel the Major Welch (red), the Appalachian and 1777 (both white), the Timp–Torne (blue), and the Suffern–Bear Mountain (yellow) Trails.

From the south side of Bear Mountain Inn, hike west to follow the Major Welch Trail north along the west shore of developed Hessian Lake. You then ascend the treed north flank of Bear Mountain. Steep spurts and contouring passages give way to the granitic outcrop leading to Perkins Tower (2.2 miles)—an attractive five-story 1930s stone tower.

Still following red, you descend the outcrop ledges to the southeast below the tower, rolling between granite ledge terraces and tilted outcrops, adding views south and west. At 3 miles you cross a road and follow left the white-blazed Appalachian Trail (AT), staying along the road shoulder for 0.5 mile before turning right into open woods. The AT descends steeply to cross Seven Lakes Drive (4.2 miles), where you follow the historic 1777 Trail for 0.1 mile. The 1777 Trail retraces the path taken by the British when they stunned the colonists by overtaking two crucial forts along the Hudson River in the Revolutionary War.

Turn right at a pine plantation to ascend briefly on woods road before following foot trail. Atop West Mountain, outcrops extend views. The trail then merges with the blue Timp–Torne Trail for rolling travel, tagging the high point at 5.1 miles. An old fire zone claims the upper reaches of West Mountain. The fire-opened views here may one day close because of plant succession. Remain on the blue trail, soon merging with the yellow Suffern–Bear Mountain Trail for rolling ridge and forest travel. Keep to the yellow trail, generally descending to cross and parallel Doodletown Brook downstream. You again meet and follow the 1777 Trail through mature woods. After crossing Seven Lakes Drive, meet once more with the AT. Continue forward, following the yellow and white blazes to end at the southwest corner of Hessian Lake.

From the Bear Mountain toll bridge over the Hudson River, go south on U.S. Highway 9W for 0.4 mile; turn right to reach the fee parking lot at Bear Mountain Inn. *DeLorme: New York Atlas & Gazetteer.* Page 32 B4. Contact Bear Mountain State Park, Palisades Interstate Park Commission, Bear Mountain 10911; (845) 786-2701; http://nysparks.state.ny.us/parks.

W Mianus River Gorge Preserve

Not the awesome sandstone-shale gorges of the Finger Lakes Region, the steep ravine of Mianus River Gorge southeast of Mount Kisco captivates with a dark-woods enchantment. Spared the ax because of its steep character, the preserve boasts one of the few intact stands of old-growth eastern forest. This 750-acre preserve, a pioneer land project of The Nature Conservancy (TNC) managed by Mianus River Gorge Preserve, bears the distinction of being the nation's first Registered Natural History Landmark with the U.S. Department of Interior. The 2.5 miles of inter-locking colored trails lead you along gorge and rim, past 350-year-old hemlocks, charming cascades, quiet-spilling 20-foot-wide Mianus River, and a historic quartz-feldspar quarry excavated by Native Americans 4,000 years ago. The preserve is open early April through November, 8:30 a.m. to 5:00 p.m.; donations welcomed (no pets, smoking, picnicking, or wheeled vehicles).

From the Bedford Village green, go 0.8 mile east on Highway 172 (Pound Ridge Road) and turn right onto Stamford/Long Ridge Road. In 0.5 mile turn right onto Miller's Mill Road, cross the bridge in 300 feet, and turn left onto Mianus River Road. Find the trailhead on the left in 0.6 mile. Or, from the Merritt Parkway (Connecticut Highway 15) in Connecticut, take exit 34; go north on Connecticut Highway 104 (Long Ridge/Stamford Road) for 7.2 miles, and turn left onto Miller's Mill Road, crossing the bridge and turning left for the preserve. *DeLorme: New York Atlas & Gazetteer:* Page 33 C6. Contact Mianus River Gorge Preserve, 167 Mianus River Road, Bedford 10506; (914) 234-3455; http://mianus.org.

X Clarence Fahnestock Memorial State Park

The blue 3.7-mile Three Lakes Trail offers a linear sampling of the lake-woods offering of this 14,000-acre state park in Putnam and Dutchess Counties. The four-season park is noted for its Taconic Outdoor Education Center and great family recreation, including groomed ski trails. Three Lakes Trail strings together Canopus Lake, Hidden Pond, and John Allen Pond. It follows along Canopus Creek, tours tranquil woods and outcrop rises, skirts meadow and marsh, and runs through aisles of mountain laurel. Songbirds, frogs, dragonflies, and deer contribute to the trail's sounds and sights. The diverse canopy is a leaf-peeper's joy, and delicate lilies can adorn ponds. Stone walls hint at long-ago farms, and old iron mines harken to the nineteenth century, when the iron industry flourished here.

From Interstate 84 east of Beacon, take exit 16S, heading south on the Taconic State Parkway toward New York City. Go 5.8 miles on the parkway and take the Cold Spring–Carmel exit, heading west on Highway 301 toward Cold Spring and Clarence Fahnestock Memorial State Park. Go 1.2 miles, passing the park campground and Pelton Lake Picnic Area, to find trail parking on the right (north) side of Highway 301 at Canopus Lake. Three Lakes Trail heads south on the opposite side of the road, just east of the Appalachian Trail (AT). Use care in crossing the road. *DeLorme: New York Atlas & Gazetteer.* Page 33 A5. Contact Clarence Fahnestock State Park, 1498 Highway 301, Carmel 10512; (845) 225-7207; http://nysparks.state.ny.us/parks.

Y Sterling Forest

Sterling Forest encompasses nearly 20,000 acres in New York State and stretches across another 2,000 acres in New Jersey. This natural area in the most densely populated pocket of the nation extends great hiking in a historic forest. It has routes of varying length and challenge, including a stretch of the iconic Appalachian Trail. Sterling Forest traces its name to Scotland's Fifth Earl of Stirling, who purchased this land from the Iroquois Indians. The forest's mineral-rich outcrops supported a thriving iron industry for 175 years, ending in 1920. More recently, the forest became a battle line and race between preservationists and developers. Preservation prevailed, with New Jersey's 2,000 acres fully protected and 18,000 acres now under the auspices of the New York State park system. A push to save the rest continues.

Trails in New York can be accessed off Highway 17A and County Roads 5, 19, 84, and 91, among others. *DeLorme: New York Atlas & Gazetteer.* Page 32 B2–C2. Contact Sterling Forest State Park, 116 Old Forge Road, Tuxedo 10987; (845) 351-5907; http://nysparks.state.ny.us/parks.

Long Island

Completing the New York State puzzle is this island domain at the state's southeastern extreme, the 118-mile-long sandy footprint of this boot-shaped state. The tidal strait of the East River isolates Long Island from the New York mainland. Over eons this land mass evolved, with the recognizable island appearing as the seas rose at the end of the last ice age. Features such as the remnant moraines running along the North Shore and the island spine, kettle lakes, and sandy plains of glacial silt ideal for farming speak to the island's ice age start.

The island's earliest inhabitants were peaceful native peoples, unlike their neighbors. Extortion soon resulted, with the bullying neighbors forcing the tribe to pay tribute to continue their tranquil existence. Paumanok, the Algonquin name for Long Island, has been translated to mean "a place where tribute is brought." Other translations include "fish-shaped" or "land where there is traveling by water." Each has its fit and proponents.

After World War II and the soldiers' return home, Long Island assumed its modern persona: the suburban reply to New York City. Much of the residential island is indeed classic suburbia: individual family homes, backyard swings, and PTA meetings—the American Dream. The Hamptons, world-known through film and novel, painted a second layer on the island—that of an upscale beach getaway. But there is much more to Long Island. It has offerings that appeal to a broad spectrum of people: a prized fly-fishing river, produce stands, vineyards, wineries, Colonial homes, lighthouses, maritime museums, aquariums, campgrounds, and hiking trails.

Despite its proximity to Manhattan, the island boasts a surprising wealth of natural discovery and even spots for solitary reverie. Between Gateway National Recreation Area and Montauk Point, Long Island brings together rare pine barrens; seaward, bay, and Long Island Sound shores and beaches; ghost forests; dune habitats; and spring-fed rivers—all ripe for discovery. At-risk piping plovers and least terns choose to nest on the island's barrier and bay beaches. Terrapin, fox, deer, owl, and osprey are other wild inhabitants. This region is even home to the state's lone federally designated wilderness, the Otis Pike High Dune Wilderness at Fire Island National Seashore.

46 West Pond Trail

At Gateway National Recreation Area, southwest of John F. Kennedy International Airport, this simple interpretive loop within the Jamaica Bay Wildlife Refuge introduces the wildlife and natural habitat of West Pond, Jamaica Bay, and the island's outwash plain. The site boasts 330 bird species, with a full calendar of seasonal arrivals: warblers (April/May), shorebirds (July/August), raptors (September through November), and winter waterfowl (March through early April). Terrapins nest here June and July. What's unexpected is this natural bounty sits within sight of the New York City skyline.

Start: At the visitor contact station trailhead

Distance: 2-mile loop (Seasonally, you may add the Terrapin Trail for a 2.5-mile total distance.)

Approximate hiking time: 1 to 2 hours

Difficulty: Easy

Elevation change: The hike is flat.

Trail surface: Gravel walking path

Seasons: Year-round

Other trail users: Birders

Canine compatibility: Dogs not permitted

Land status: National park

Nearest town: Howard Beach

Fees and permits: No fees, but permit required (Regardless of the hour of your visit, you are required to carry a free visitor pass while touring the refuge trails. Acquire your pass at the visitor contact station. If you are planning an early-morning visit, obtain your pass the preceding day.)

Schedule: Year-round, sunrise to sunset; visitor contact station, 8:30 a.m. to 5:00 p.m. daily, except major holidays

Maps: Trail Guide to West Pond (online: www.nps.gov/archive/gate/jbu/jbu_nature.htm or available at the site)

Trail contacts: Gateway National Recreation Area, Jamaica Bay Unit, Building 69, Floyd Bennett Field, Brooklyn 11234; (718) 318-4340; www.nps.gov/gate

Special considerations: Stay on the trails, be alert for poison ivy, and respect closures for wildlife. Come prepared for mosquitos and ticks. There is no food, no smoking, no pets, and no jogging allowed on the trails.

Finding the trailhead: From the Belt Parkway in New York City (Brooklyn), take exit 17S and go south on Cross Bay Boulevard for Gateway National Recreation Area. In 3.5 miles turn right (west) for the visitor center and trailhead. *DeLorme: New York Atlas & Gazetteer.* Page 25 D5.

The Hike

Protected by Rockaway Peninsula, the islands of Jamaica Bay Wildlife Refuge make up a vital habitat and sanctuary for native and migratory wildlife. West Pond Trail encircles one of the impoundment ponds protected originally as a New York City park, now as part of the national park system.

At the back door of the visitor contact station, near a registry for bird sightings, hike the wide gravel path heading left; the path to the right is the Upland nature trail. A flowering shrub and vine thicket borders the pond trail. Interpretive signs, bird and

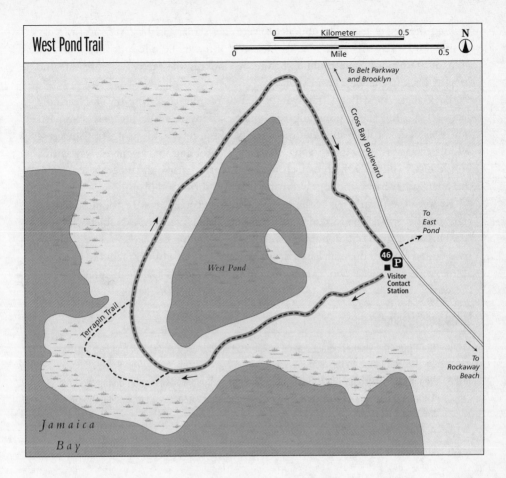

West Pond Trail

0 — Kilometer — 0.5
0 — Mile — 0.5

N

To Belt Parkway
and Brooklyn

Cross Bay Boulevard

To East Pond

46 P
Visitor Contact Station

West Pond

Terrapin Trail

To Rockaway Beach

Jamaica Bay

bat nesting boxes, osprey nesting platforms, and frequent benches can slow your pace. The circuit gradually dishes up views of Jamaica Bay with its mudflats, saltwater marsh, and open water. West Pond viewing features the dense pond rim and a crooked-arm peninsula of phragmites (tall marsh grass). Cross-bay views find the Manhattan skyline. The refuge is an enigma—a natural island in an oh-so-urban wild.

With the change of seasons comes a change in residents: warblers in spring, snowy egrets followed by the shorebirds in summer, and snow geese and raptors in fall. Throughout the year a vibrant harmony of melodic and raucous notes rides the coastal breeze, with trills, honks, squawks, pipings, and plaintive screeches. Kestrel, ibis, red-winged blackbird, tern, gull, goose, duck, heron, cormorant, vireo, and thrush suggest repeat visits.

The shrub corridors grow more broken as an outwash plain hosts travel. Its desert soils give rise to cactus and yucca, which bloom in June. Ahead you may add the side spur along the Terrapin Trail, if it is not nesting season (June 1 through September 1). This trail's sandy path passes between a shrub border and the outwash plain overlooking the riprap bank of a mudflat toward low estuary islands. At times, a frenzy of shorebirds crisscrosses the mudflat in search of food. The side spur then collects a view of the Empire State Building before overlooking the pretty bay curvature and looping back to the West Pond Trail.

Back at the West Pond Trail, you go left to resume clockwise travel. Nearshore snags overlay the water, providing cormorants a convenient drying post. The periodic roar of an airplane amplifies the serenity of the refuge. In spring, Canada geese waddle the paths with their young, sometimes enforcing their right-of-way with a hostile hiss. Eventually the broad, channeled estuarine marsh distances the trail from the open-water bay as the tour alternates between shrub and plain.

Keep to the main track of the loop. As you approach Cross Bay Boulevard, turn right on the gravel lane to return to the visitor contact station; a doubletrack heads left. This last section of trail holds the first shade of the hike. In the past, tree swallows have nested close to the trail. Pass a drinking fountain and a birder's blind to end back at the visitor contact station. Evening primrose, bouncing Bet, and salt-spray rose line the way.

Miles and Directions

0.0 Start from the visitor contact station trailhead; hike the wide gravel trail heading left. **Note:** The Upland Trail is to the right.

0.5 Reach the seasonally open Terrapin Trail; remain on the West Pond Loop during the June 1 through September 1 closure. **Option:** Hike the spur when it is open, adding 0.5 mile to the total distance.

1.5 Approach Cross Bay Boulevard; turn right on the gravel lane.

2.0 End back at the contact station.

Options

▶ **Jamaica Bay is the largest natural open space in New York City, covering a whopping 32 square miles.**

The Upland Trail, an hour-long interpretive trail with numbered posts and a companion brochure (available at the visitor contact station), introduces more of the area habitat. It identifies the trees and shrubs, their characteristics, and roles. Also, the native plant garden surrounding the newly renovated and "green" contact station attracts butterflies for butterfly watching.

Hike Information

Local Information

Brooklyn Tourism and Visitors Center, at Historic Brooklyn Borough Hall, 209 Joralemon Street, Brooklyn 11201; (718) 802-3846; www.visitbrooklyn.org

Local Events/Attractions

The **Jamaica Bay Unit of Gateway National Recreation Area** has beaches, other natural areas, and historic sites to visit. Dunes, upland, lawn areas, and Atlantic and bay shores engage visitors. Jacob Riis Park, Fort Tilden (a coastal defense site established in 1917), and Breezy Point are all on Rockaway Peninsula. Canarsie Pier, Plumb Beach, and Frank Charles Park sit off Shore Parkway. Many are popular with birders. Gateway National Recreation Area, www.nps.gov/gate

▶ Hiking with Children

Hiking with children is all about seeing and experiencing nature through their eyes. Kids like to explore and have fun. They like to stop and point out bugs and plants, look under rocks, jump in puddles, and throw sticks. If you're taking a toddler or young child on a hike, start with a trail that you're familiar with. Trails that have interesting things for kids, like piles of leaves to play in or a small stream to wade through during the summer, will make the hike much more enjoyable for them and will keep them from getting bored.

You can keep your child's attention if you have a strategy before starting on the trail. Using games is not only an effective way to keep a child's attention, it's also a great way to teach him or her about nature. Play hide and seek, where your child is the mouse and you are the hawk. Quiz children on the names of plants and animals. If your children are old enough, let them carry their own daypacks filled with snacks and water. So that you are sure to go at their pace and not yours, let them lead the way. Playing follow the leader works particularly well when you have a group of children. Have each child take a turn at being the leader.

47 Rocky Point Natural Resources Management Area

For $1, New York State purchased this 5,100-acre pine barrens and oak-wooded parcel formerly used by Radio Corporation of America (RCA) for transatlantic broadcasting. Now only the concrete footings of the transmission towers remain. The northern reaches of this natural resources management area (NRMA) mildly roll, while the southern extent stretches out flat. Rocky Point Road slices the area into east-west halves. Color-coded hiking trails crisscross sandy woods roads and firebreaks, some of which double as mountain bike or horse trails. Here, independent trail systems serve each user.

Start: At the Whiskey Road trailhead
Distance: 10.9-mile lasso-shaped hike
Approximate hiking time: 5.5 to 7.5 hours
Difficulty: Easy
Elevation change: The trail has a 100-foot elevation change.
Trail surface: Sandy path, woods road, and firebreaks
Seasons: Best for hiking, spring through fall
Other trail users: Mountain bikers and horseback riders (on separate intersecting or parallel trails), hunters
Canine compatibility: Leashed dogs permitted (Carry water for your animal and clean up after your pet.)
Land status: Department of Environmental Conservation (DEC)
Nearest town: Rocky Point
Fees and permits: No fees but permit required

(Contact the access permit desk, 631-444-0273, with questions or to obtain a permit application.)
Schedule: Daylight hours, February through December and weekends in January
Maps: Rocky Point Natural Resources Management Area trail map (available from DEC office)
Trail contacts: New York State DEC, Region 1, SUNY at Stony Brook, 50 Circle Road, Stony Brook 11790; (631) 444-0285; www.dec.ny .gov
Special considerations: Rangers recommend all users wear blaze orange, November through January. Because ticks are present and numerous in some areas, take all precautions, keeping to trails, wearing light-colored clothing, and making frequent tick checks while at the management area and immediately after you return home.

Finding the trailhead: From the junction of Rocky Point Road (County Road 21) and Highway 25A in Rocky Point, go south on Rocky Point Road for 2.5 miles, then turn left (east) onto Whiskey Road. In 1.1 miles turn left (north) to enter the trail parking lot. *DeLorme: New York Atlas & Gazetteer.* Page 27 A5.

The Hike

Cross the stair stile into the NRMA and follow the footpath north into a pine stand that later fills out with oak and huckleberry. Red trail markers and Paumanok Path symbols mark the way. At the loop junction, you bear right for a counterclockwise

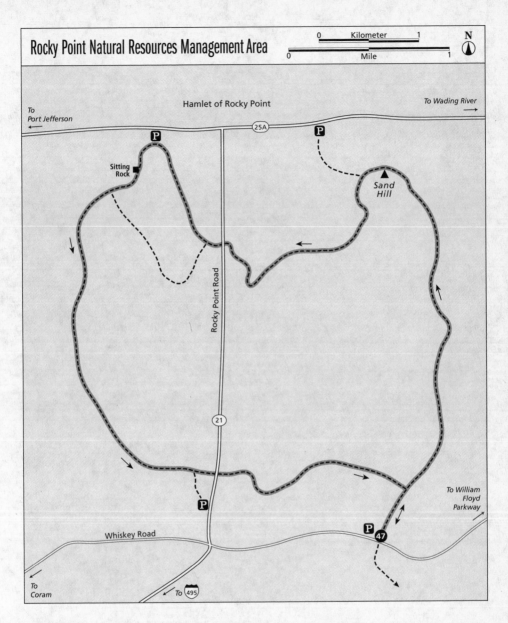

Rocky Point Natural Resources Management Area

0 — Kilometer — 1

0 — Mile — 1

N

Hamlet of Rocky Point

To Wading River →

← To Port Jefferson

25A

P

P

Sitting Rock

Sand Hill

Rocky Point Road

21

P

P

47

To William Floyd Parkway

Whiskey Road

← To Coram

To 495

tour, staying on the red trail. The blue trail concludes the loop. You now part company with the Paumanok Path (a burgeoning 100-mile-long trail traversing Long Island's pine barrens from Rocky Point to Montauk Point). The flatness of the hike and the sameness of the forest can lull you into relaxation.

Crossing over woods roads and passing firebreak clearings, the trail ascends and tops Sand Hill. The hill likely owes its start to a stream that flowed over a glacier, depositing silt over time. When the glacier receded at the end of the last ice age, this

modest hill remained. You trace a curve left over the sandy summit, which extends no views, to again find the red trail. It leads you on a brief, sharp descent before it turns left. The yellow trail straight ahead rolls over the next rise to reach a trailhead on Highway 25A.

The well-marked loop continues through oak woodland, crossing fire grades and woods roads, with pines once more winning a place in the forest. Throughout the tract, bountiful ferns announce recently burned areas. Fire regenerates the pine forest. Because an ever-encroaching society objects to such burns, the survival of this habitat depends on setting aside large intact tracts. Pine barrens once covered 250,000 acres of Long Island; now only one-third of the barrens remains. The island's primordial forest most likely comprised oak, chestnut, and hickory.

A narrow footpath leads to the crossing of Rocky Point Road and the western half of the preserve, clad in oaks and huckleberry bushes. At the upcoming junction, continue straight on the red trail. The gently rolling route passes through firebreak field and pine-oak woods.

You near the NRMA boundary before emerging at an open flat with concrete walks and roads, an old foundation, and an untamed border of maple, chokecherry, dogwood, and poison ivy. Skirt the site, following the broken paved route to the right. Where the abandoned avenue forks, go left for the loop, once again finding the white blazes of the Paumanok Path. To the right lies Highway 25A with its fast-food eateries, should you want to grab a burger or soft drink. As you round the foundation flat, keep an eye out for the blue-blazed path on the right, which continues the loop.

The trail now passes through varied woods of red cedar, ash, cherry, oak, and pine, with an understory of grass, Virginia creeper, fern, and poison ivy. Pass a pair of rocks, identified as Sitting Rock on the NRMA map. As the lone rocks on the circuit, they do indeed suggest a seat.

At the junction with a yellow trail, continue following the blue-marked route, encountering more road and trail crossings. Ant mounds riddle the forest. Where the trail bottoms out, it again travels a pine stand with an open cathedral and only patchy shade. Long straightaways characterize travel. Scarlet tanagers can capture attention with their color, while cinquefoil and violet touch springtime to the porous sand. After taller oaks fill out the forest, you eventually reach the next junction, where you follow the blue trail back across Rocky Point Road.

The trail continues much as it has through pine barrens to close the loop. Turn right on the red trail, retracing the hike's start to Whiskey Road.

◀ *Ferns and huckleberry in oak forest, Rocky Point Natural Resources Management Area*

Miles and Directions

0.0 Start from the Whiskey Road trailhead; hike north.

0.5 Reach the loop junction; bear right, following red markers.

2.9 Top Sand Hill; begin a descent.

3.0 Reach a junction; follow the red trail as it turns left. **Note:** The yellow trail straight ahead crosses the next rise to reach Highway 25A.

4.5 Cross Rocky Point Road to the western half of the preserve.

4.6 Reach a junction; continue straight on the red trail.

5.4 Where the abandoned avenue forks, go left, round the foundation flat, and seek out and follow the blue-blazed path on the right.

5.6 Pass Sitting Rock.

5.9 Reach a junction; continue following the blue markers. **Note:** The yellow trail journeys left 0.5 mile to Lookout Point for an uninspired woods view overlooking a firebreak corridor.

8.7 Cross back over Rocky Point Road.

10.4 Complete the loop; turn right to return to the trailhead.

10.9 End back at the Whiskey Road trailhead.

Hike Information

Local Information

Port Jefferson Chamber of Commerce, 118 West Broadway, Port Jefferson 11777; (631) 473-1414; www.portjeffchamber.com, or **Long Island Convention and Visitors Bureau and Sports Commission,** 330 Motor Parkway, Suite 203, Hauppauge 11788; (877) FUN-ON-LI; www.discoverlongisland.com

Local Events/Attractions

You can tour Long Island Sound aboard the *Martha Jefferson,* an 85-foot Mississippi River paddleboat that departs from Port Jefferson Harbor. (631) 331-3333; www .marthajefferson.com

Accommodations

Wildwood State Park, east of the NRMA, is open mid–April through late October and has 138 campsites. Reservations: (800) 456-2267; www.reserveamerica.com

Organizations

The **Long Island Greenbelt Trail Conference** promotes Long Island trails. Long Island Greenbelt Trail Conference, P.O. Box 5636, Hauppauge 11788; (631) 360-0753; www.ligreenbelt.org

48 Fire Island National Seashore

Fire Island, a barrier island, stretches 32 miles long and protects Long Island's south shore from the punishing Atlantic. This circuit travels the beach and back bay between Smith Point and Watch Hill. The back bay and dune swales compose Otis Pike High Dune Wilderness, the only federally designated wilderness in New York State. Flowering beach plum and heather and wild rose accent the dunes in spring. The toe of the seaward dune attracts nesting piping plovers and least terns April through August. A rich coastal landscape, wildlife, and Atlantic Ocean and Great South Bay views jam-pack this compelling journey.

Start: At the Smith Point Ranger Station trailhead

Distance: 14.2-mile loop, with opportunities to shorten the hike

Approximate hiking time: 7.5 to 9.5 hours

Difficulty: Moderate

Elevation change: Beach portion is flat; back-bay return has less than a 100-foot elevation change.

Trail surface: Sandy beach and dunes track, boardwalk crossings

Seasons: Year-round

Other trail users: Beachgoers

Canine compatibility: Although leashed dogs are allowed at the park, it is better to leave them at home. Dogs are not allowed in the wilderness, in public areas, or along the beach during bird nesting season (March through Labor Day). If you do plan to have your dog along, phone ahead to find out where it is appropriate. Know that deer ticks are a concern for animals, as well as you, and carry drinking water for your pet.

Land status: National park with public inholdings

Nearest town: Shirley

Fees and permits: No fees, but because the national seashore only has handicapped parking, you must park next door at Smith Point County Park, a fee area. For hikes entering the wilderness, rangers recommend you register at Smith Point Ranger Station to alert them to your presence in this little-used area. If you plan to wilderness camp, a permit is required (obtain one from the Watch Hill Visitor Center or from the Wilderness Visitor Center when open).

Schedule: National seashore and Smith Point Ranger Station, year-round; Watch Hill Visitor Center, daily July and August and weekends, May, June, September, and October

Maps: Fire Island National Seashore Official Map and Guide (available online, obtain at the park, or call to request a copy)

Trail contacts: Fire Island National Seashore, 120 Laurel Street, Patchogue 11772; (631) 687-4750; www.nps.gov/fiis

Special considerations: Heed closures for nesting piping plovers and terns, and be sensitive of the primary dunes, crossing only at designated stairways and boardwalks. Because mosquitos are common, carry repellent. In vegetation, be alert for poison ivy and, most especially, deer ticks (Lyme disease carriers). These ticks exist year-round, so take the necessary precautions. You will find drinking water at Smith Point and Watch Hill, but carry an ample quantity. Toilets can be found at the visitor centers (when open) and seasonally at Old Inlet. Pack in, pack out.

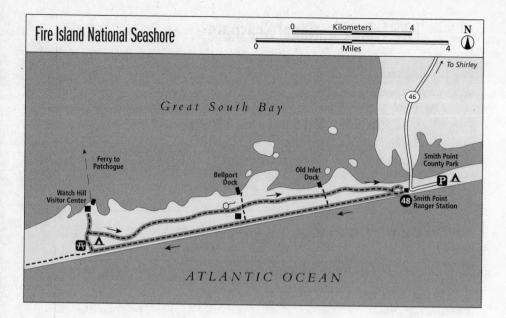

Kilometers

Miles

N

To Shirley

46

Great South Bay

Ferry to
Patchogue

Bellport
Dock

Old Inlet
Dock

Smith Point
County Park

P

Watch Hill
Visitor Center

48 Smith Point
Ranger Station

ATLANTIC OCEAN

Finding the trailhead: On Long Island at Shirley, take exit 58S from Highway 27 (Sunrise Highway) and go south on Highway 46 (William Floyd Parkway) for 5 miles, crossing over the bridge to reach Fire Island National Seashore and Smith Point Suffolk County Park. Park at Smith Point County Park, a fee area. *DeLorme: New York Atlas & Gazetteer:* Page 27 C6. A ferry operating out of Patchogue, New York, accesses the Watch Hill area for an alternative approach to the national seashore.

The Hike

Descend the seaward-stretching boardwalk at Smith Point Ranger Station and turn right onto the 150-foot-wide strand. The fine, light-colored crystalline sand tosses back the sun. Energy spreads along the wave crests, and churned foam slides up the beach.

Along the beach, staggered posts mark off the seasonal nesting sites, and protective covers safeguard the nests from foxes. Grant the birds a wide berth so as not to interfere with their nesting. The lower beach typically offers easier walking anyway, with tide-compressed sand. After about a mile, a gap in the primary dune offers a glimpse north toward Great South Bay. Later, the stairway to Old Inlet offers an opportunity to shorten the loop and view the bay from an attractive T-shaped dock. Seasonally, toilets are open at this crossing.

Horseshoe crab, Fire Island National Seashore ▶

Clam shells, skate egg cases, sea-polished pebbles, and horseshoe crabs being toyed with by gulls seasonally amuse beachcombers. Calf muscles tire where the cant to the ocean grows more pronounced. The dunes now fluctuate from a few feet high to 20 feet high.

The next landmark is a slat-roofed deck overlooking the beach. Owned by the village of Bellport, this site offers you a shady resting stop and another turnaround point. For this hike continue west along the beach; terns swoop the waves. At 7.1 miles find the boardwalk that crosses the primary dunes to the Watch Hill area and campground, both hidden by the rise. A slat-roof lean-to for shade, a restroom/changing facility, showers, phone, drinking fountain, and snack bar shape this oasis. In July and August lifeguards oversee the beach.

From the campground boardwalk, you will find sandy Burma Road at the base of the seaward dune. Follow it eastward away from camp to close the loop. The trail alternately tours loose sand or overgrown track, passing through a shrub swale with beach plum, beach grass, sweet pepperbush, salt-spray rose, and poison ivy.

Where Burma Road forks, bear left and continue east across the dune-protected

Beach sunrise, Fire Island National Seashore

area. Caches of tall, feathery-headed phragmites, springtime puddles pulsing with toads, and a lush, green estuary vary viewing. The route dips into a sandy bowl and tops its rim for a bay overlook and the merest peek at the ocean. The trail then levels, traversing areas of beach grass and beach heather, sandy plains, and pockets of pitch pine. Beware of poison ivy and brier, common beneath the pines, and make frequent inspections for ticks.

Where the trail curves toward the beach, it travels the loose sand of a secondary dune, skirting blown-out depressions. Wooden debris, an old cable route, and seashells are possible sightings, but the shifting sand frequently rewrites the discovery. You continue past the site where an old well feeds a circle of green before crossing over the boardwalk to the picnic shelter owned by Bellport Village. The sandy track now rolls up rims and through bowls, soon traversing a broad coastal plain. Views of the small bay island and cottage off Old Inlet precede your crossing of the Old Inlet boardwalk.

The track becomes grassier, and shrubs reappear as the trail draws a straight, shadeless line back to Smith Point Ranger Station. It arrives at the boardwalk interpretive trail near the midpoint; head either way to end back at the ranger station.

Miles and Directions

0.0 Start from Smith Point Ranger Station; descend to the beach and turn right to hike it west.

2.0 Pass the stairway to Old Inlet. **Bailout:** The stairway to Old Inlet offers the first opportunity to shorten the loop to about 4 miles. Hike north on the Old Inlet boardwalk. Partway the faint track of Burma Road (a nature-reclaimed jeep road that predates the wilderness) intersects the boardwalk; hike east on Burma Road to return to Smith Point Ranger Station.

3.6 Pass a viewing deck atop the dunes. **Bailout:** Here, too, you'd follow the boardwalk toward the bay, reach the dune trail where it bisects the boardwalk, and turn right onto the dune trail to return to Smith Point for about a 7.2-mile loop.

7.1 Reach Watch Hill and Burma Road; follow Burma Road east for the loop's return.

7.8 Burma Road forks; bear left, continuing east across the dunes.

11.0 Pass the boardwalk to the viewing deck/picnic shelter (first seen at 3.6 miles).

12.6 Pass the Old Inlet boardwalk.

13.9 Reach the boardwalk interpretive trail; go either way.

14.2 End at the ranger station.

Hike Information

Local Information

Long Island Convention and Visitors Bureau and Sports Commission, 330 Motor Parkway, Suite 203, Hauppauge 11788; (877) FUN-ON-LI; www.discover longisland.com

Local Events/Attractions

The **William Floyd Estate,** donated to Fire Island National Seashore in 1965, records three centuries of American life and consists of the ancestral home (the twenty-five-room "Old Mastic House"), attractive grounds, and the Floyd family cemetery. William Floyd, a general in the Revolutionary War and signer of the Declaration of Independence, was born in this house in 1743. Guided tours introduce the home and cemetery. William Floyd Estate, 245 Park Drive, Mastic Beach 11951; (631) 399-2030; www.nps.gov/fiis

Accommodations

Watch Hill Campground offers twenty-six sites mid-May through mid-October and is concession operated. You must reserve sites by mail, two-night limit. Any unreserved sites are available first come, first served, but there's no guarantee you'll get a site. Contact Fire Island Concessions, P.O. Box 4, Sayville 11742; (631) 567-6664 or (631) 597-3109; www.watchhillfi.com

Smith Point Suffolk County Park campground is open year-round and has 279 campsites. Reservations: (631) 244-7275; www.co.suffolk.ny.us

49 Mashomack Preserve

Covering the southeastern third of Shelter Island, this 2,000-acre preserve of The Nature Conservancy (TNC) encompasses a maritime environment of tidal creeks, woodlands, fields, swamps, freshwater ponds, and 10 miles of stirring but inaccessible coastline. Four interlocking color-coded trails, a short barrier-free Braille trail, and the wheelchair-and-stroller-friendly 1-mile Joan Coles Trail introduce the preserve. A nature garden displays common vegetation. A natural osprey nesting colony and a rare pine swamp are two of the site's sterling characteristics.

Start: At the Trail House (preserve visitor center) trailhead

Distance: 12 miles out-and-back (Hike travels each of the four interlocking loops in its entirety, backtracking on itself only once between junctions 3 and 4.)

Approximate hiking time: 6 to 8 hours

Difficulty: Easy

Elevation change: Despite only a modest elevation change, this rolling hike accumulates elevation 10 to 20 feet at a time.

Trail surface: Earthen path, woods road, boardwalk, and management (service) road

Seasons: Year-round

Other trail users: Birders and, when sufficient snow, cross-country skiers and snowshoers

Canine compatibility: Dogs not permitted

Land status: Private preserve

Nearest town: Greenport or North Haven

Fees and permits: Fees for the ferry service to the island; suggested donation to TNC

Schedule: Preserve, year-round, daily except Tuesday (exceptions: seven days a week in July and August; weekends only in January), 9:00 a.m. to 5:00 p.m. (9:00 a.m. to 4:00 p.m. November through February)

Maps: Preserve trail map (available at visitor center or online: www.nature.org/wherewework; navigate to Mashomack Preserve, "Take a Hike" to get to the map download)

Trail contacts: Mashomack Preserve, P.O. Box 850, 79 South Ferry Road, Shelter Island 11964; (631) 749-1001 or The Nature Conservancy, South Fork–Shelter Island Chapter, P.O. Box 5125, East Hampton 11937; (631) 329-7689; www.nature.org

Special considerations: Keep to the trail and obey posted rules, which include no pets, no bikes, and no horses. There is no beach access for humans; beaches are for wildlife only. As TNC has marked the trails for just one direction of travel, follow the flow pattern indicated on the preserve map to avoid losing your way. Take the necessary precautions for ticks; they are prevalent here. There is no hiking access to the preserve on January weekdays because of hunting.

Finding the trailhead: From North Haven take the South Ferry to Shelter Island and go 1 mile north on Highway 114, turning right (east) to enter the preserve. Arriving from the North Ferry out of Greenport, follow Highway 114 south 3 miles to the entrance. *DeLorme: New York Atlas & Gazetteer:* Page 28 B3.

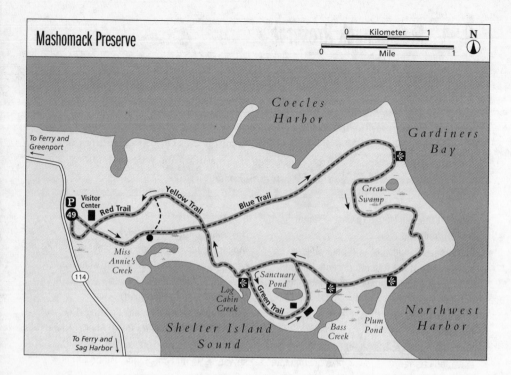

Coecles
Harbor

Gardiners
Bay

To Ferry and
Greenport

Visitor
Center

Yellow Trail

Red Trail

Blue Trail

Great
Swamp

Miss
Annie's
Creek

Sanctuary
Pond

Green Trail

Log
Cabin
Creek

Bass
Creek

Plum
Pond

Northwest
Harbor

Shelter Island
Sound

To Ferry and
Sag Harbor

The Hike

Near the Trail House, the color-coded trails head east off the entry road into a rich woodland of mixed oak, red maple, hickory, beech, dogwood, and black locust. Approaching a service road, bear right per the red arrow. The trail merges with a wide woods lane, rounding to a gazebo overlooking Miss Annie's Creek—a tidal-marsh bay with sandy strands and a treed island. Views stretch south, overlooking Shelter Island Sound and the South Ferry crossing.

At junction 1 bear right for the yellow, green, and blue trails. A boardwalk continues the hike, crossing a salt meadow extension of the marsh. Here keep an eye out for the osprey nesting platform. After crossing a management road, twisted oaks and an open field precede the descent to junction 2. Here the yellow trail heads left to close its loop, the blue trail heads straight, and the green trail bears right.

Follow the blue-marked trail through a field to explore the largest of the preserve loops. Before long, you enter the shade of a beech-climax woods. The trail changes direction a couple of times before following a semishaded woods road as it curves east toward the bluff rim for sunnier travel. You pass a bench overlooking Gardiners Bay and Island. As the blue trail travels the outskirts of Great Swamp, a foot trail takes the baton; keep to the rim. Bullbrier entangles the woods as the open trail rolls south, trading looks at Gardiners Bay for looks at Northwest Harbor. Dogwoods lend their signature beauty.

> ▶ A rare pine swamp, recognized for its uniqueness by the New York State Department of Environmental Quality, occupies the western edge of this preserve. Rimmed by swamp azalea, water willow, and highbush blueberry, the pines spring from a floating mat of sphagnum moss.

Plum Pond Overlook extends a fine Northwest Harbor view, although Plum Pond itself may be masked by a leafy shroud. The trail then rounds above a kettle depression, bearing right and coming to a birding blind. Set back in the woods and camouflaged by phragmites, the blind overlooks the upper estuary of Bass Creek. At the blind you might spy a sapsucker-drilled trunk, its circumference ringed by holes every few inches.

Where the blue trail tags the green loop at junction 4, bear right to stay on the marked trail and follow the flow pattern indicated on the preserve map. The trail passes through mixed woods and crosses a service road to reach junction 3 (the head of the green trail loop). Here you bear left to add the green loop. The green loop passes through diverse woodland, overlooks the blue waters of Smith Cove, and reaches a blind looking out at Log Cabin Creek.

Ahead you turn right on the management road, passing through the staff residence area, with its wood-shingled buildings, groomed lawns, shade trees, tidal ponds, and freshwater Sanctuary Pond. The buildings are off-limits to the public, but an attractive addition to travel. The road becomes a doubletrack as it reenters woods, skirting the Bass Creek estuary. An upland woods ascent leads back to junction 4. Go left, retracing the stretch between junctions 4 and 3.

Once again at junction 3, follow the green trail, ascending the steps to the right, now heading toward the visitor center. Scenic oaks lend shade as the trail traverses a coastal bluff. Below the trail sits a pristine, thin pebble beach reserved for wildlife (off-limits to the public). Upon crossing the management road, pass through woods and fields to junction 2. Take the right fork of the yellow trail, tracking the yellow and red arrows back to Trail House. After again crossing the management road, bear right on the wood-shavings path of the red trail. You then turn left onto a closed roadway for the return to the visitor center. Plaques identify the vegetation.

Miles and Directions

0.0 Start from the Trail House trailhead; head east off the entry road for the red trail.

0.3 Approaching a service road, bear right per the red arrow.

0.8 Reach junction 1; bear right for the yellow, green, and blue trails. **Note:** The red trail hooks left, returning to the visitor center.

1.2 Reach junction 2; hike the blue trail straight ahead. **Note:** The yellow trail heads left to close its loop; the green trail bears right.

3.1 Reach Gardiners Bay Overlook.

5.6 Reach Plum Pond Overlook.

6.0 Reach the wildlife blind at Bass Creek.

6.6 Reach junction 4 and the green trail. Bear right, following the mapped flow pattern.

7.3 Cross a service road to junction 3 (the head of the green trail loop); bear left. **Note:** Going right here returns you to the visitor center.

7.5 Reach the wildlife blind at Log Cabin Creek.

8.8 Return to junction 4; go left, retracing the trail between junctions 4 and 3.

9.5 At junction 3, follow the green trail up the steps to the right toward the visitor center.

10.3 Reach junction 2; take the right fork of the yellow trail.

11.0 Cross the management road and in 0.1 mile bear right on the wood-shavings path of the red trail.

11.2 Turn left onto a closed roadway indicated as the return to the Trail House visitor center.

12.0 End at Trail House.

Hike Information

Local Information

Long Island Convention and Visitors Bureau and Sports Commission, 330 Motor Parkway, Suite 203, Hauppauge 11788; (877) FUN-ON-LI; www.discover longisland.com

Local Events/Attractions

Shelter Island Kayak Tours offers guided trips on the pretty creeks and harbors of Shelter Island. Shelter Island Kayak Tours, P.O. Box 360, Shelter Island 11964; (631) 749-1990; www.kayaksi.com.

Greenport's East End Seaport Museum and Marine Foundation together with the town's annual Maritime Festival in September keep the area's nautical roots intact. The museum offers you the chance to ride aboard a 1906 sailing schooner and has a wind exhibit demonstrating the physics of sailing, models of local sailing ships, sail-making artifacts, fishing and oystering memorabilia, and more. The museum is open mid-May through September, varying days and times. East End Seaport Museum and Marine Foundation, Third Street at the ferry dock, Greenport 11944; (631) 477-2100; www.eastendseaport.org

Accommodations

Cedar Point Suffolk County Park campground in East Hampton is open mid-May to mid-October and has 189 campsites. Reservations: (631) 244-7275; www.co .suffolk.ny.us

50 Hither Hills State Park

On Long Island's east end, this 1,755-acre state park brings together a superb lineup: walking dunes, "phantom forests," a pristine mile of Atlantic beach, the cobbled shore of Napeague Bay, and Goff Point, where piping plovers, terns, and oyster-catchers nest. An interior region of pine barrens, dune heath, and maritime grassland completes the offering. The selected hiking loop travels the Napeague shoreline and makes an interior return via the Paumanok Path, Long Island's premier long-distance trail linking the island barrens between Montauk Point and the Rocky Point Natural Resources Management Area.

Start: At the Napeague Harbor Road harbor/dunes trailhead

Distance: 14.5-mile loop (13.5 miles when nesting season closes off Goff Point)

Approximate hiking time: 8 to 9 hours

Difficulty: Moderate

Elevation change: The hike has about a 50-foot elevation change.

Trail surface: Sand and cobbled beach, sandy path, jeep grade

Seasons: Best for hiking, fall through spring (summers hot and humid, carry extra water)

Other trail users: Mountain bikers (on interior trails), horse riders, hunters

Canine compatibility: Leashed dogs permitted (Keep dogs tightly restrained and away from nesting sites or, better yet, leave them at home during nesting season. Carry water for your pet.)

Land status: State park

Nearest town: Montauk

Fees and permits: None for selected hike; park entrance fee at developed area of park and for Atlantic shoreline access

Schedule: Year-round, daylight hours

Maps: State park map (request at campground)

Trail contacts: Hither Hills State Park, 50 South Fairview Avenue, Montauk 11954; (631) 668-2554; http://nysparks.state.ny.us/parks

Special considerations: Obey all posted closures. It is best to avoid Goff Point during nesting season (late May through June) and to give seals ample space when they haul out on the Atlantic beach in winter. On the Walking Dunes, the shifting canvas of sand can alter course. Because hunting occurs weekdays in December and January, confine hiking to weekends during those months. But, should you choose to hike weekdays, wear orange. Carry ample drinking water.

A jeep trail between the Napeague Bay shore and the Paumanok Path offers a way to vary the featured loop. During nesting season, high tides, or strong winds, it can replace bay travel.

Finding the trailhead: From Amagansett go 6 miles east on Highway 27 (Montauk Highway) and turn right (north) on Napeague Harbor Road to find the Paumanok Path on the right in 0.4 mile (no parking). The shared trailhead for Walking Dunes and Napeague Shoreline is at road's end, in another 0.3 mile. Although sand drifts reduce parking here to a few spaces, do not block the limited-use vehicle access to the beach. *DeLorme: New York Atlas & Gazetteer.* Page 29 B5. For Atlantic beach access, from Amagansett drive 7.2 miles east on Highway 27 and Old Montauk Highway, turning south to enter the park, a fee area. *DeLorme: New York Atlas & Gazetteer.* Page 29 B5.

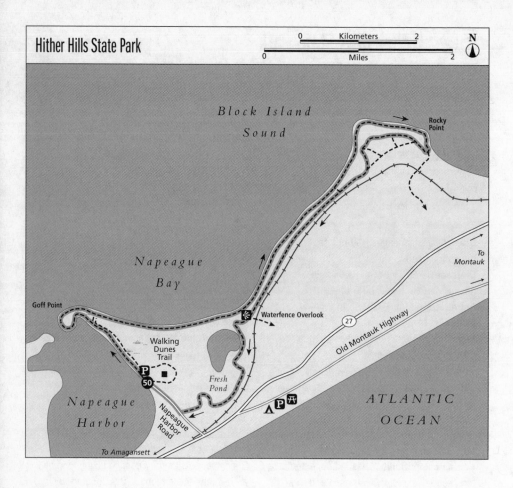

Hither Hills State Park

Block Island Sound

Rocky Point

To Montauk

Napeague Bay

Goff Point

Waterfence Overlook

27

Old Montauk Highway

Walking Dunes Trail

P 50

Fresh Pond

Napeague Harbor Road

Napeague Harbor

Δ P ⛺

ATLANTIC OCEAN

To Amagansett

The Hike

From the end of Napeague Harbor Road, hike the harbor shoreline north, traveling an avenue of pinkish-orange sand and cobbles. A scattering of open-hinged scallops may record the recent passing of a turnstone.

At the neck of Goff Point, the season will determine your course of travel. Because oyster-catchers, piping plovers, and terns each have nesting territories on Goff Point, you should bypass the point altogether during nesting, late May through June, and instead cross at the neck to follow the bayshore east. When point travel is appropriate, its broad flat still attracts feeding piping plovers and resting terns. Sit quietly and watch their antics. Waterspouts can betray the presence of clams. Continue north around the spit, but keep below the high-tide line. At the head of Goff Point, gulls congregate, cormorants string offshore, and slipper and orange jingle shells collect in stringy deposits. You'll leave Goff Point opposite Skonk Hole, a wet depression, to continue east along the bayshore.

Dune breaches offer looks south at a maritime grassland of beard and switch grass, with beach plum adorning the dunetop in showy spring finery. Rounded cobbles and shells create a crunchy thoroughfare. Before long, looks east find the pilings of a shellfish bed and distant Rocky Point. The beach eventually shows more sand, and the dune gives way to a 25-foot bluff with an abrupt slip face. Colonies of swallows nest in the solid seams. Boulders on the beach offer dry seating.

You again have cobbles underfoot as you round Rocky Point and a cliff rises above the beach. After you tag the point, your bayshore travel ends at Dyer's Landing, which affords eastern views of Fort Pond Bay and Culloden Point. Now seek out and follow the foot trail heading uphill to the right. You quickly meet a road and follow the blazed Paumanok Path right. Regularly marked with white blazes or Paumanok Path markers, the route passes among tangled oaks.

At the upcoming Y junction; head right. Openings and spurs to the right present views of Block Island Sound; spurs left lead to Old North Road. Watch for blazes to point you through a series of T junctions. After a stretch in the brushy coastal thicket of the marine terrace, oak woodland again offers shade. Forest changes bring the additions of maple, hickory, and basswood. Soon you meet Old North Road and follow it right.

Comfortable and tree-draped, Old North Road pleasantly pieces together the segments of the Paumanok Path. At the road junction ahead, a right leads to Quince-tree Landing. Keep to the Paumanok Path, which later turns right off Old North Road to pass closer to shore atop cliffs or the coastal slope. Although the path dips to shore level, you never actually reach shore.

Eventually the hike is back in oaks and passing parallel to a railroad track, usually hidden from view by the dense forest. At the next crossroads, a detour to the right finds Waterfence Overlook, with its fine vantage and spur trails to the beach. For the Paumanok Path alone, proceed forward, drifting farther from shore. Keep an eye out for guiding blazes at junctions and for box turtles.

At the four-way junction in 0.5 mile, the Paumanok Path heads left to round Fresh Pond. A short detour right here leads to shore. Fresh Pond is a large, open bass pond rimmed by sweet pepperbush and high-canopy forest. The next crossroads offers another chance for pond access.

On the last leg, pitch pines make an appearance and eventually gain dominance. Sounds from Highway 27 creep into the hike's peace. Where you emerge at Napeague Harbor Road, turn right to return to the trail's start.

Miles and Directions

0.0 Start from the harbor/dunes trailhead; hike the harbor shore north.

1.2 Reach the neck of Goff Point; round the point when appropriate. Late May through June (nesting), cross at the neck and hike east along the bayshore.

2.2 End the stroll of Goff Point opposite Skonk Hole; hike the bayshore east.

5.9 Begin to round Rocky Point.

7.4 Reach Rocky Point.

7.5 End bayshore travel at Dyer's Landing; turn inland.

7.6 Reach the Paumanok Path; turn right.

7.8 Reach a Y junction; head right.

8.2 Reach a T junction; head right.

8.6 Reach a T junction; head left.

9.0 Meet and follow right Old North Road.

9.5 Reach the Quincetree Landing junction; continue forward on Old North Road, following the Paumanok Path, which later turns right off the road to pass closer to shore.

11.5 Reach a crossroads; proceed forward on the Paumanok, drifting farther from shore.
Option: A 0.5-mile detour to the right finds Waterfence Overlook, with its fine vantage and spur trails to the beach.

11.9 Reach a four-way junction; follow the Paumanok Path left, skirting Fresh Pond.

14.2 Emerge at Napeague Harbor Road; turn right.

14.5 End at the harbor/dunes trailhead.

Options

The 1-mile **Walking Dunes Trail,** with its 40-foot dunes and buried forests, fits naturally with a Napeague Shoreline–Paumanok Path hike, offering a pleasant start or cap. An interpretive brochure (seasonally at the trailhead) corresponds to numbered posts. Head right (east) off the end of Napeague Harbor Road, following a sandy path into a maritime corridor of mixed oak, beach grass, beach plum, pitch pine, and poison ivy. Next enter the rare zone of shifting sand that "walks" over trees 30 feet tall. Only the crowns of the nearby oaks clear the burying sand. With a gust of wind, the sands go walking. The trail contours and gradually ascends the dunes, with first forest and then wetland sweeping away to the right. Minerals can streak the dunes purple or black. As the dune curves noticeably northwest, angle to its top for a grand area overview. The trail then descends to a western bowl and phantom forest. Snags record past forests overtaken and ultimately killed by the sand. Counterclockwise, you then skirt a native cranberry bog. Stay left. After passing through bayberry, aim for the wide sand track ahead and follow it over a rise and into the next bowl to reach the harbor beach (0.8 mile). Turn left to return to the vehicle (1 mile).

 Block Island Sound shore, Hither Hills State Park

Hike Information

Local Information

Long Island Convention and Visitors Bureau and Sports Commission, 330 Motor Parkway, Suite 203, Hauppauge 11788; (877) FUN-ON-LI; www.discover longisland.com

Local Events/Attractions

Montauk Point Lighthouse Museum and Light, a National Maritime Historic Landmark, will entice you to the eastern tip of Long Island. The museum's exhibits, video, and tower climb introduce you to the oldest lighthouse in New York, established in 1796. The light with its 80-foot sandstone tower occupies the spot where the British Royal Navy lit signal bonfires to guide its ships in the Revolutionary War. Montauk Point Lighthouse Museum and Light, 2000 Montauk Highway, Montauk 11954; (631) 668-2544; www.montauklighthouse.com

Accommodations

Hither Hills State Park's oceanside campground, open early April to mid-November, has 168 sites. Reservations: (800) 456-2267 or www.reserveamerica.com

Organizations

The **Long Island Greenbelt Trail Conference** maintains and promotes Long Island trails and leads hikes, including here at Hither Hills. Long Island Greenbelt Trail Conference, P.O. Box 5636, Hauppauge 11788; (631) 360-0753; www.ligreen belt.org

Honorable Mentions

Long Island

Z David A. Sarnoff Pine Barrens Preserve

South of Riverhead, this 2,056-acre preserve features classic pine barrens, wetlands, and kettle depressions. County Road 104 divides the preserve into east-west tracts, with the larger piece sitting west of the highway. A loop trail explores each tract. A round-trip on the Western Loop measures 5.4 miles and passes Frog Pond; the Eastern Loop measures 3.6 miles. Discovery can include the subtle changes in the pine-oak mix, size, canopy, and tightness of forest. Access is by permit only. You may request the free permit and map, either in person or in writing (two weeks in advance), from the New York State Department of Environmental Conservation in Stony Brook. In written requests state your name, address, and intended activity and specify David A. Sarnoff Pine Barrens. The preserve is closed to hiking during the January deer season.

For the Western Loop, from the Highway 24 rotary in South Riverhead, take County Road 63 south for 0.2 mile, finding off-road parking on the east side of CR 63. *DeLorme: New York Atlas & Gazetteer:* Page 27 A7. For the Eastern Loop, from the Highway 24 rotary, go south on CR 104 for 2.2 miles, finding off-road parking on the west side of the highway. *DeLorme: New York Atlas & Gazetteer:* Page 27 A7. Contact New York State Department of Environmental Conservation, Region 1, SUNY at Stony Brook, 50 Circle Road, Stony Brook 11790; (631) 444-0285; www.dec.ny.gov.

AA Connetquot River State Park Preserve

Color-coded primary and unmarked secondary trails explore this 3,500-acre state park preserve west of Oakdale. The site's previous life was as a private trout and hunting reservation for an elite sportsman's club, whose membership included such names as Tiffany, Vanderbilt, Belmont, and Carnegie. Ulysses S. Grant, Daniel Webster, and General Sherman were honored guests. A fish hatchery, a restored gristmill, and the rustic buildings of the historic lodge recall the era. The river springs from an aquifer beneath the pine barrens. Big trout swim in its pools. Deer, swan, fox, osprey, heron, hawk, and box turtle contribute to the wild menagerie.

A lazy 9.8-mile loop follows former carriage roads and trails through this unique natural area. It travels from the historic park and Mill Pond, along the river, past the fish hatchery and Deep Pond, and across the preserve past Collins Junction, before reaching Veterans Highway and turning east. It then follows Cordwood Road southward, again swinging west past Slade Pond to end back at the historic area.

Park access requires a free permit. You may request it in writing two weeks in advance. Indicate your name and address, intended activity (hiking, fishing, horseback riding), number in party, and planned date of visit and include a legal-size self-addressed envelope. You must carry the permit and proper identification while touring the preserve. There is no smoking and no pets.

From Oakdale on Highway 27 (Sunrise Highway), go 1.4 miles west and turn north, entering the park. Eastbound traffic must make a U-turn in Oakdale, as there is only westbound access. *DeLorme: New York Atlas & Gazetteer:* Page 26 C3. Contact Connetquot River State Park Preserve, P.O. Box 505, Oakdale 11769; (631) 581-1005; http://nysparks.state.ny.us/parks.

Appendix: Clubs and Trail Groups

Adirondack Mountain Club (ADK) is a nonprofit membership organization that protects wild lands and waters through a balanced approach of conservation and advocacy, environmental education, and responsible recreation. It carries out its mission in New York State forest preserves, parks, and other wild places. Adirondack Mountain Club, 814 Goggins Road, Lake George, NY 12845; (518) 668-4447 or (800) 395-8080; adkinfo@adk.org; www.adk.org

Appalachian Mountain Club (AMC), the nation's oldest outdoor recreation and conservation organization (active since 1876), promotes the protection, enjoyment, and wise use of mountains, rivers, and trails in the Appalachian region. Appalachian Mountain Club, AMC Main Office, 5 Joy Street, Boston, MA 02108; (617) 523-0655; fax: (617) 523-0722; www.outdoors.org

Appalachian Trail Conservancy (ATC), formerly known as the Appalachian Trail Conference, is a volunteer-based, private nonprofit organization dedicated to the conservation of the 2,175-mile Appalachian National Scenic Trail (AT) and its 250,000-acre greenway extending from Maine to Georgia. The ATC has done so since 1925 and also provides AT information and education. It works in unison with the National Park Service, thirty maintaining clubs, and a host of partners and volunteers. Appalachian Trail Conservancy, P.O. Box 807, 799 Washington Street, Harpers Ferry, WV 25425-0807; (304) 535-6331; www.appalachiantrail.org

Catskill Mountain Club, a community-based volunteer organization, promotes responsible, safe, and sustainable outdoor recreation in the Catskill region through its outdoor recreational programs, educational programs, volunteer stewardship, and environmental and recreational advocacy. Catskill Mountain Club, P.O. Box 558, Pine Hill, NY 12465; info@catskillmountainclub.org; http://catskillmountainclub.org

Finger Lakes Trail Conference (FLTC) has the mission to build, protect, and enhance the Finger Lakes Trail, a continuous footpath across New York State. Volunteers annually log about 15,000 hours of trail work. But more than physical labor, the FLTC supports and promotes the trail and provides services to members, partners, and the general public. The conference also maintains and markets up-to-date maps for the Finger Lakes Trail. FLTC, 6111 Visitor Center Road, Mount Morris, NY 14510-9527; (585) 658-9320; www.fingerlakestrail.org

Long Island Greenbelt Trail Conference is a nonprofit grassroots organization dedicated to preserving open space and developing trails on Long Island. With a dedicated core of volunteers, the group has established more than 200 miles of hiking trails (including two national recreation trails), offers guided hikes, and produces and sells Long Island trail maps. Long Island Greenbelt Trail Conference, P.O. Box 5636, Hauppauge, NY 11788; (631) 360-0753; fax: (631) 360-8127; ligreenbelt@verizon .net; http://www.hike-ligreenbelt.com/

New York–New Jersey Trail Conference is a federation of member clubs and individuals that takes a leadership role in building, maintaining, marking, and promoting trails and advocating for open space in the New York–New Jersey region. The constituent clubs have a combined membership of over 100,000. The network's handiwork touches 1,600 miles of foot trails from the Delaware Water Gap north to beyond the Catskills. New York–New Jersey Trail Conference, 156 Ramapo Valley Road (U.S. Highway 202), Mahwah, NJ 07430; (201) 512-9348; fax: (201) 512-9012; info@nynjtc.org; www.nynjtc.org

Parks & Trails New York, founded in 1985, has grown from a handful of park advocates to a statewide organization of over 5,000 members and supporters. The group helps promote, expand, and protect trails, parks, and open spaces across the state. They advance both traditional and newly conceived parks and trails between villages and natural spaces. Parks & Trails New York, 29 Elk Street, Albany, NY 12207; (518) 434-1583; fax: (518) 427-0067; ptny@ptny.org; www.ptny.org

Sierra Club is a nonprofit membership organization that promotes conservation of the natural environment through grassroots advocacy, public education, outdoor activities, and lobbying. Founded in 1892, the club has 700,000 members nationwide. The Atlantic Chapter applies the principles of the national organization to environmental issues facing New York State. Sierra Club, Atlantic Chapter, P.O. Box 886, Syosset, NY 11791-0886; http://www.sierraclub.org/ny/ or http://newyork.sierraclub.org

Taconic Hiking Club helps maintain trails and the trail register sheets throughout the Capital District. The club welcomes members interested in hiking, cycling, canoeing, kayaking, snowshoeing, and cross-country skiing. Their newsletter lists activities and projects. Taconic Hiking Club, 45 Kakely Street, Albany, NY 12209; http://taconichikingclub.blogspot.com

Index

About the Authors

Writer Rhonda Ostertag and photographer George Ostertag have collaborated on twenty outdoor guides and travel books over the last two decades and, more recently, on coffee-table photography books. Their bylines appear on thousands of articles in national and regional publications, almost always on topics of nature, travel, and outdoor recreation. Their books include *Our Washington, Our Oregon, Backroads of Oregon, California State Parks: A Complete Recreation Guide, Best Short Hikes in Northwest Oregon*, and the FalconGuides *Hiking Southern New England* and *Camping Oregon.*

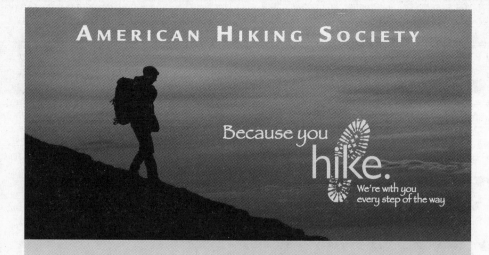